OUTLAWS *of the* LAKES

BOOTLEGGING & SMUGGLING
From Colonial Times to Prohibition

Editor: Barbara Chisholm
Front Cover: The Purple Gang (Detroit News); Schooner (Archives of Ontario) Back Cover (from upper left): Jennie Justo (Frank & Rosalie Potts); Justo in the headlines (Metro Toronto Reference Library); Al Capone (International News Photos); rum-runner's speedboat (Queen's University Archives); Hymie Weiss after being shot (Metro Toronto Reference Library); medicinal alcohol permit (Frank & Rosalie Potts); hiding liquor (Detroit News)

Printed and bound in Canada by Transcontinental Printing Inc.

We acknowledge the support of the Government of Ontario through the OntarioMedia Development Corporation's Ontario Book Initiative

Edward Butts

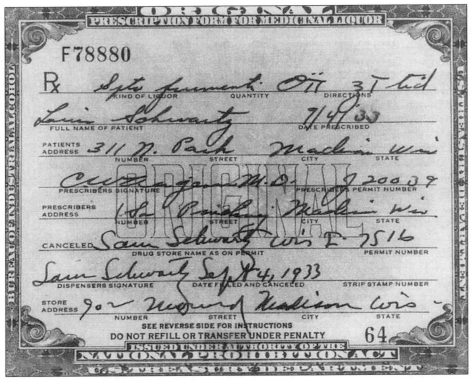

With the passing of the Volstead Act, many Americans suddenly came down with "ailments," so doctors would issue permits like this one for medicinal alcohol.

This book is dedicated to the memory
of my good friend Ray Lobb.

Temperance poster: Death serves up the demon rum in a hellish tavern. Two children, starvation lurking behind them, plead with their father to come home.

TABLE OF CONTENTS

Detroit police show off beer and liquor seized in a raid.
Note distilling apparatus in the foreground.

INTRODUCTION

" A smuggler is a wretch who, in defiance of the laws, imports
or exports goods without payment of the customs."
                                        —Dr. Samuel Johnson

" I like a smuggler; he is the only honest thief."
                                        —Charles Lamb

The vast frontier of the Great Lakes and the St. Lawrence River, along
with the small but strategically located corridor of Lake Champlain,
have presented Canadians and Americans with an almost irresistible invitation to smuggle. From the days of New France, when colonists smuggled
brandy and furs under the noses of the Church and Royal Governors, the
lakes and the great river have been highways for illicit trade. Smuggling on
these waterways has brought prosperity and sparked violence. It has influ-
enced the outcome of war and bred corruption. It has been noble, as in the
case of the Underground Railroad, and it has been shameful, as in the blood-
soaked tale of the Chicago gang wars of the Roaring Twenties.

A smuggler, by definition, is someone who takes something into or
out of a place secretly and illegally. The materials and commodities that
have been smuggled across the lakes have included everything from potash
to timber to books. At times the situation was ludicrous: American farmers
smuggling food to British–Canadian troops about to engage American

(Above) Nothing was sacred to the smugglers or the police. U.S. Customs officers find booze hidden in a hearse. (Below) A bottle of bootleg "whiskey" might contain just about anything. The "good stuff"—unadulterated scotch or Canadian rye—was available, but for a steep price.

troops. Canadian Customs men living in fear of injury or death at the hands of armed men smuggling common goods such as tea.

A bootlegger is a smuggler who specializes in alcoholic beverages. The name originates with old-time English smugglers who concealed bottles of liquor in their high-topped boots. While rum and whiskey were always part of the North American smuggler's stock in trade dating back to colonial times, it was the Prohibition Era which saw the bootlegger rise to the pinnacle of the criminal hierarchy. Prohibition bootlegging was smuggling carried out on a scale the world had never before witnessed, and it had an impact upon North American society that is still evident today. Nowhere was the flow of bootleg liquor greater than it was across the Great Lakes.

The smugglers and bootleggers described in these stories were adventurous and cunning, underhanded and violent. They transported their cargoes in fast boats, falsely labelled crates and even in an undertaker's wagon. Secrecy was their byword, and when that failed they would reach for their guns. The agents of the law who tried to intercept them were like-wise courageous and clever, and sometimes too quick on the trigger. For almost three hundred years, the outlaws and the lawmen engaged in a bat-tle of wits and bullets on and around the waters of the Great Lakes. One side tried to uphold the law, while the other said they were only "giving the people what they want."

Interior of the Walker Distillery near Windsor, Ontario. Canadian distillers were hard pressed to keep up with the demand for liquor in "dry" America.

(Above) Barrels of Canadian whiskey are destroyed in a raid on a blind pig. Enough liquor and beer was successfully smuggled across the border to fill a Great Lake. "Blind pig" was another term for a speakeasy, a place in which bootleg alcohol was served.

THE SMUGGLERS

PART ONE
Defying the Crown and Congress

Concrete evidence! Rum-runners used ingenious methods to conceal their cargoes. Here, an officer displays bottles of liquor hidden in cement building blocks.

Antoine Cadillac strikes a heroic figure in this illustration. His contemporaries considered him a charlatan and a "bare faced liar."

ANTOINE CADILLAC: THE HAWK

Antoine Laumet de la Mothe de Cadillac was a scoundrel. He owed his nickname, Hawk, to his rather prominent nose, but the name suited his predatory nature. He was a charlatan, an embezzler, a con man, and probably the first big-time bootlegger on the Great Lakes. In order to peddle his alcoholic wares to the Indians without interference from French authorities in Canada, Cadillac did the one thing for which he is famous. He founded the city of Detroit.

In the seventeenth century, Canada's economy—indeed, its sole reason for being—was the fur trade. Native trappers brought their pelts, mostly beaver, into the French trading posts to exchange for European trade goods: blankets, iron pots, steel knives and hatchets, various trinkets... and brandy. Brandy, in fact, was the most lucrative trade item of all. It was cheap (especially the stuff made for the Indian trade), easy to transport, and tended to render the customers senseless, thus making them easy to exploit. The Catholic Church, a powerful force in French Canada, frowned upon the use of alcohol in trade with Indians and fought stubbornly to have it outlawed, even threatening to excommunicate French traders who sold or gave it to Indians.

The proponents of the brandy trade pointed out, quite accurately, that if the Natives couldn't get French brandy, they would take their furs south to Albany and get rum from the hated English. They proposed controlling the trade by limiting the amount of liquor a trader could sell to the Indians, and cutting it liberally with water.

Controlling the flow of alcohol, however, was easier said than done. In a society in which cash money was scarce, booze was a form of currency.

Cadillac and his wife, Marie Thérèse. She was the niece of a notorious privateer.

Brandy, wine, cider, a type of home-brewed beer called *bouillon*, and even that demon English rum could be traded for almost anything. Only a few licensed traders were allowed to do business with the Indians, but everybody from otherwise honest *habitants* to the outlawed *coureurs de bois* did it on the sly, in spite of harsh punishments. While the colony's administrators fretted over the illegal Indian trade, they themselves were not above corruption. To maximize their profits from the fur trade, they smuggled every pelt they could past the king's agents in order to avoid taxes. Such knavery was carried out on a large enough scale to cause one honest official to lament, "Poor king! How you are robbed!" It was a tailor-made situation for a man one twentieth-century historian would call "one of the worst scoundrels ever to set foot in New France."

Cadillac was born Antoine Laumet at les Laumets in Gascony, France, in 1658. He was the son of commoners, his father being a lowly provincial magistrate. Little is known about his early life because he told a different story to almost everyone he met. He arrived in Acadia (Nova Scotia) in 1683 bearing a fake aristocratic name, de la Mothe de Cadillac; a fake family coat of arms (which would one day be adopted by an American automobile manufacturer); and a fake background as a man of noble parentage. He was penniless when he stepped off the boat, but boasting experience as a soldier of fortune (which may or may not have been true), he fell in with the privateer François Guion. He cruised with Guion in search of English prey, gaining a knowledge of the New England coast that would prove invaluable to him in creating for himself the image of a dashing man of the world.

Imposter that he was, Cadillac could also be charming and witty, and was evidently well educated. He wooed and married Marie Thérèse, the niece of his privateer boss; lying about his age and his pedigree on the marriage certificate. He was granted a seigneury in Acadia, but was unable to develop it due to his run-ins with the governor of the colony and the local Jesuit priests. They apparently objected to his involvement in some illegal trade. The governor called him "a scatter brain who has been driven out of France for who knows what crimes."

In 1691 Cadillac took his family to Quebec, and there turned on the charm for the governor general, Comte de Frontenac. The governor general liked the boisterous, if somewhat rascally, adventurer, and made him an officer in the colonial army. Then, in 1694, he gave Cadillac command of the important post of Michilimackinac, located at the junction of Lakes Huron and Michigan. It was a position he held for three years. His duties as the military commander of the whole western section of the French Empire in North America were to keep the western tribes in alliance with France, discourage them from fighting each other, and encourage them to harass the Iroquois, who were allied with the English. Cadillac failed on all three counts. What he did do was make money—a small fortune, in fact.

Boatloads of brandy plied the waterways of New France to Michilimackinac, where Cadillac indulged the Indians, selling them as much liquor as they could afford to buy. He also cheated the *coureurs de bois* who went to trade there by not paying them full value for their furs. Those Frenchmen were hardly in a position to complain since Cadillac was known to be a friend of the great Frontenac himself. One officer at Michilimackinac wrote, "Never has a man amassed so much wealth in so short a time, and caused so much talk by the wrongs suffered by the individuals who advance funds to his sort of trading ventures."

In 1697, a glut of low-quality furs on the French market was knocking the bottom out of the industry, and the Crown ordered most of the posts in the West closed. Only a few, including Michilimackinac, were to be kept open for strictly military purposes. For Cadillac, avarice always won out over patriotism. He wasn't going to endure the hardships of life in the howling wilderness for no greater reward than the meagre pay of an army officer. Moreover, his administration at Michilimackinac had come under severe criticism in Quebec, where there were complaints over the "extremely confused" state of affairs in the Great Lakes region. Cadillac was able (and apparently to Frontenac's satisfaction) to pass off the blame for his failures onto others, but it was difficult to sidestep the accusations of the Jesuit priests over his debauching the Indians with liquor. An enmity developed between Cadillac and the Jesuit Order which was to last for the rest of his life. Even after his death, Jesuit writers would denounce Cadillac as a thorough villain.

In 1698, Cadillac had one of those strokes of genius that come to a person only once in a lifetime. It was so brilliant that he travelled to Versailles to present his idea at Court. He gained the ear of Jerome de Pontchartrain, King Louis XIV's Minister of the Marine. Cadillac's proposal was to establish a major settlement at *le detroit*, "the strait"; the narrow waterway connecting Lake St. Clair to Lake Erie. (Technically, it is a strait, not a river.) The advantages, Cadillac explained enthusiastically, would be many. It would be a colony where Frenchmen and Indians could live side by side, and the "savages" could be assimilated into French culture. It would shut the English off from western expansion. It would be a place of employment for the otherwise idle *coureurs de bois*. It would be a bastion from which to keep an eye on the ever-troublesome Iroquois. What's more, Cadillac, as governor of the colony, could ensure that only the very best furs were shipped to France.

All that, of course, was to win over Pontchartrain. As events were to prove, foremost in Cadillac's mind was a colony, separate from Canada, under his sole command, where he could become fabulously rich trading brandy for furs with impunity. Considering the role Detroit would one day play in Prohibition rum-running, it seems almost fitting that the city came into being because of a turn-of-the-eighteenth-century bootlegger.

Pontchartrain liked Cadillac's idea, but others had reservations. It took Cadillac two trips to Versailles and a lot of persuasion, but in 1700 he finally gained royal approval. On June 4, 1701, he left Montreal with one hundred soldiers and settlers and two priests, and on July 24 he founded a new community when he began construction of Fort Pontchartrain du Detroit.

The fort covered one square *arpent* (192.75 sq. feet) and was surrounded by a 12-foot-high wooden palisade. The first building erected was a church, in which a Franciscan priest said Mass. The other priest, a Jesuit, left the colony almost immediately, disgusted with Cadillac's policies of selling liquor to Indians and allowing his men to take Indian "wives." At first Cadillac did not have his own way as far as running the settlement was concerned. Actual ownership of the colony went to a Canadian company, of which Cadillac had to submit to being an employee. However, the slipshod manner in which Company business was being conducted indicated that Cadillac was devoting most of his energy to the brandy trade. Houses for the colonists were small and rudely constructed, with only bark, straw, or animal hides for roofing. Doors were simply propped up in doorways. Only a few buildings had wooden floors; the rest had packed dirt. Quebec was receiving reports of violence and debauchery.

When a Company clerk was sent out to check on him, Cadillac threw the man in jail and then went to Quebec to demand that he be given full command of the post. He was tossed into jail himself, but talked his way out of charges made against him of incompetence and corruption. He was released and sent back to Detroit, where he promptly arrested one of his own officers for illegal trading. Sharing the swag just wasn't in Cadillac's makeup. This officer had connections in high places, and he brought counter-charges against Cadillac. But Cadillac had an even better connection in Pontchartrain. It is a testament to Cadillac's powers of persuasion that he not only had these new charges dismissed, but he also finally got what he wanted—absolute control of Detroit.

For the next few years, Cadillac ran Detroit like a robber baron. The brandy flowed freely, and was, in fact, the only reason for any fort being there at all. But the booze cost ten times what it sold for in Montreal. There was discontent at every level in the colony. The soldiers were fed half rations. Cadillac charged tradesmen exorbitant fees for the right to work. Various tribes who were allied to the French had been encouraged to relo-cate to the vicinity of Detroit, putting them dangerously close to the Iroquois Confederacy. Native groups who were friendly to the French did not necessarily get along well with each other, and alcohol was a deadly substance to mix with tribal rivalries. There were murders, and clashes in which many Indians and a few Frenchmen were killed. As commander of the post, Cadillac had been instructed to settle any problems with the Indians through diplomacy. Instead, he used violence and intimidation. His greed, short-sightedness and tyrannical administration earned him the hatred of Frenchmen and Indians alike.

(Above) Fort Pontchartrain, named for Cadillac's patron, looks much more orderly in this illustration than it ever did under Cadillac's command. His was a ramshackle post, rife with with discontent, violence and debauchery. (Right) Cadillac lands at le detroit, *site of the city of Detroit. He wanted a location where he could peddle alcohol to the Indians, free from the interference of Church or state.*

Cadillac was sending glowing reports to French authorities in Canada about how Detroit was growing and prospering: that it was a self-sufficient colony of happy settlers and Indians which needed no assistance from Canada. But reports from other sources told a different story. Instead of vast fields of crops, as Cadillac had claimed, Detroit had but a few hundred acres under cultivation, growing only some Indian corn (which Cadillac owned). The people were poorly housed, and the fort itself was falling into disrepair. Angry Indians were turning their backs on the French and taking their furs to Albany. There were suspicions that Cadillac himself was doing business with the English. A report, which landed on Pontchartrain's desk, said, "Detroit is a post very burdensome to the colony of Canada and will achieve its complete ruin if it continues to be sustained."

Pontchartrain was in a dilemma. To report Cadillac's misdeeds to the king could bring royal displeasure on his own head, as it had been he who had supported Cadillac in the first place. Instead, he buried the bad report and sang Cadillac's praises to the king. He recommended that this excellent man be sent to govern the French colony at Louisiana. At that time, Louisiana was considered the most dismal corner of the French

Empire in North America. Pontchartrain could pull Cadillac out of Detroit without getting his own fingers burned, and send him to a place where affairs were already in such a mess that even a man as corrupt and incompetent as Cadillac couldn't make them worse. But Cadillac could.

In 1710, with great reluctance, Cadillac left his personal liquor-based gold mine at Detroit. With him gone, the colony would eventually flourish and grow into one of the principal cities of America. Amazingly, the chroniclers of American history would turn a blind eye to the truth, and elevate a cunning, money-grasping booze peddler into one of the great visionaries of the French Regime. Like Cadillac himself, they would blame "lesser men" for his failures.

Cadillac was a disaster as the governor of Louisiana. He didn't even go there until two years after the position had been bestowed upon him. Once he arrived, his corruption and high-handed manner quickly alienated the French population, and his policies toward the Indians resulted in deteriorating relationships between the French and the Natives. He tried, and failed, to establish trade with Mexico. His one accomplishment was the discovery of a copper mine. In 1717 he was removed from office. He sailed to France, where he was imprisoned in the Bastille in Paris, accused of making "improper statements against the government of France" while he was in the colonies. There are, however, times when Fortune smiles upon the wicked. After a few months Cadillac was released, decorated with the Cross of the Order of St. Louis for his years of colonial service, and paid a substantial amount of money. In 1723, he became the governor of the French town of Castelsarrasin, where he died in 1730.

In the documents written by Cadillac's contemporaries, it is difficult to find anything positive said about him. Those who knew him wrote of his dishonesty, his arrogance and his avarice. Perhaps the line that best told the story was penned by a French official who was with Cadillac on the voyage to Louisiana. Cadillac had warned the man never to cross him because he possessed a superior mind. This prompted the official to write that Cadillac was "the most bare faced liar I had ever seen."

Push on York Volunteers!

The heroic example of General Isaac Brock inspired British and Canadian troops in the War of 1812, but supplies smuggled over from the United States kept them fed.

SMUGGLING IN THE WAR OF 1812

The War of 1812 did not have the overwhelming support of the people of the United States. While the war hawks of the South rattled their sabres and demanded the gauntlet be thrown down to arrogant Britain, many Americans living on the shores of the Great Lakes and along the Canadian border were strongly against an Anglo-American conflict. Neither did their Canadian neighbours really want a war. Yet, it wasn't necessarily a chummy case of "hands across the border," even though in many instances people had relatives living on the other side of the line. The Americans, waving their banner of "Life, Liberty, and the Pursuit of Happiness," still spoke disdainfully of British tyranny, while the Canadians looked down their noses at republicanism, and held firm to the British ideal of "Peace, Order, and Good Government."

There *was*, however, a very strong case of dollars (and pounds) across the border. The neighbouring populations were each others' best customers, and war just wouldn't be very good for business. It simply didn't make sense to be shooting at someone with whom one had a good trading relationship. For people living in backwoods communities on the Upper St. Lawrence River or the rim of Lake Ontario, what did it matter if Washington and London couldn't sort out their differences? Business was business.

In the years leading up to the war, the American Embargo Act of 1807, followed by the Nonintercourse Act of 1809, were designed to hurt British commerce by shutting down U.S. trade with Great Britain and Canada. These measures backfired because they strangled American commerce while doing relatively little economic harm to Britain. Moreover, while legitimate American trade withered and cargo ships sat empty at their moorings, new avenues opened up for smugglers. Illicit traders saw nothing wrong with crossing the border by land or water with potash, produce, timber, livestock, and good American "corn likker," and returning with salt, sugar, manufactured goods, money and good English rum. They certainly objected to the efforts of government men to interfere with their business. "My life and the lives of my deputies are threatened daily," wrote one unhappy American customs collector. Technically, the smugglers were criminals, even *traitors*! But they claimed the trade embargoes were unconstitutional, which handily made *right* a comfortable bedfellow with profit. And hadn't heroes of the Revolution like John Hancock been called "traitors" for trading illegally with Britain's enemies before and during the War of Independence?

While some of the smugglers were certainly ruffians and desperadoes, others were just ordinary citizens trying to make a living. A few were even prominent men, such as Jacob Brown of New York. Born to a Pennsylvania Quaker family, Brown was a schoolteacher, land speculator, county court judge and founder of the town of Brownville, New York. This good citizen defied his government's embargo by smuggling potash across Lake Ontario to the British—so much of it that he was known as "Potash Brown," and a New York country road he used was called "Brown's Smuggler's Road." This violator of federal law would become a general in the American army and an unsung hero of the War of 1812.

Even when war was finally declared and hostilities commenced in 1812, smuggling did not stop. A man named Ramon Manzuco simply shipped goods across the lakes under the neutral Spanish flag. Vermonters assured the British and the Canadians that an inconvenient war wasn't going to put a damper on their illicit trade. Some New England states even considered withdrawing from the Union so they could conduct their economic affairs without interference from Washington. In an article on "cross border shopping" in the War of 1812, Canadian historian Graeme Decarie states that if it had not been for American farmers smuggling food up to the British

Canadian and American homesteaders relied on cross-border trade to survive. In turbulent times, smugglers kept the lines of commerce open.

army, the British could not have sustained themselves on the Great Lakes. One British general in Canada claimed that eighty percent of the meat his troops were eating was being shipped up by American farmers. Montreal and Quebec City were keeping their larders stocked with food purchased from Americans. Some American farmers, in fact, preferred selling their produce to the British army rather than to the American army, because the Redcoats paid better. An exasperated American general wrote to the Secretary of War, "Like herds of buffaloes they [the smugglers] pressed through the forests, making paths for themselves... Were it not for the supplies, the British force in Canada soon would be suffering from famine, or their government would be subjected to enormous expenses for their maintenance." Along the Atlantic seaboard, American coastal vessels even supplied British warships with fresh water. Victuals weren't the only contraband goods to cross the border. Vermonters were happy to sell the British war supplies, such as spars for the Royal Navy. When an American military patrol caught some smugglers, the civilian authorities not only released the prisoners, but also arrested the army officer for exceeding his authority.

One man who made a tidy profit during the war was a Mr. John Howe, an aged veteran of the Revolutionary War who had spied for both the British and the Americans. In 1812, in spite of his advanced years, Howe was with General Henry Hull's army at Detroit when the post was captured by General Isaac Brock. The British released the old man, and he turned his hand to smuggling. He purchased five hundred dollars worth of dry goods in Montreal and took them over the border to New York. He was betrayed, however, when an American officer he had bribed informed on him and the goods were seized.

Sackets Harbor, New York. Smugglers here forced a U.S. Customs agent to resign his post.

Determined to get even for what was known as a "Yankee trick," Howe engaged an Irish carpenter identified only as Pat, and had him construct a black coffin with a glass window in the lid. They carved a human head from a block of wood, and using hair, milk, flour and blood, gave it the appearance of a face "in a state of putrefaction." The two men loaded the coffin, as well as secret compartments in their wagon, with brass wire, hardware goods and broadcloth purchased in Canada, and set off to sell it in the United States. Their story was that they were taking a deceased friend to be buried amongst his family in New England. Customs men and soldiers who looked through the coffin-lid window at the ghastly face waved the smugglers on, fearful that the man had died of smallpox.

Howe used this nineteenth-century fear of contagion on another occasion. For this trip he enlisted the aid of Pat's wife and two sons, aged nine and eleven. Pat built a sleigh that was a smuggler's dream. It was made of hollowed-out planks filled with expensive gilt buttons, and its tongue was a bar of contraband steel covered with wood. The seats were boxes stuffed with silks. Howe dressed everybody up like paupers, and, for good measure, took along a bad-tempered dog. He had information that the American customs agent he would have to deal with lived in mortal fear of disease, especially "spotted fever." Two miles from the customs post, Howe gave the young boys large portions of brandy. By the time they got to the checkpoint, the liquor was taking effect. When the agent came out to inspect the sleigh, the boys were puking, and groaning pitifully in their mother's arms. The agent asked what was wrong with them, and Howe said they had come down with the spotted fever and he was looking for a doctor. That, and the growling dog, was enough to send the agent running back to his office, shouting orders for them to drive on.

Howe and Pat made one more trip, this time dressed as women, with contraband silks sewn into their petticoats. Their one problem, he said, was in keeping their faces closely shaven. No one caught on, and they eventually sold their goods at a nice profit in Boston.

The American government and military high command, of course, took a dim view of all this "disloyalty," especially since U.S. soldiers had to spend time chasing after smugglers when they might have been preparing to fight the British and Canadians. It galled them that in Ogdensburg in northern New York, Canadians and even British officers from across the river regularly strolled around town with impunity, buying whatever they needed and sparing the locals the trouble of smuggling it over the border. St. Lawrence County, in which Ogdensburg lay, was solidly behind the Federalist Party, which bitterly opposed the war. Even after Ogdensburg was partially destroyed in a British raid (which was made in retaliation for an American raid on Cornwall) the smuggling continued as heavily as ever. One resident wrote, "it is incredible what quantities of cattle & sheep are driven into Canada. We can hardly get any for love or money; the day before yesterday upwards of 100 oxen went through Prescott; yesterday about 200."

One man sent by Washington to bring a halt to the smuggling was Lieutenant Melancthon T. Woolsey of the United States Navy. In 1808 Woolsey arrived in Oswego, New York, on the southern shore of Lake Ontario, and ordered the construction of the *Oneida*, a well-armed, anti-smuggling vessel. He also stationed militia units at various locations along the lakeshore, including Sackets Harbor at the eastern end of the lake. This port was such a notorious smugglers' lair that the collector of customs, Augustus Sacket, had to resign his post. Woolsey cramped the smugglers' style somewhat, but he could not completely stop their activities.

With war looming on the horizon, Woolsey made a list of schooners that could be pressed into military service. One of the vessels he commandeered was the 76-ton American merchant ship *Diana*, which was fitted out for war and renamed the *Hamilton*. Two weeks before war broke out, Woolsey, on board the *Oneida*, stopped the 45-ton Canadian merchant ship

The Hamilton *(foreground) and* Scourge *go down in a storm on Lake Ontario, causing the largest loss of life on the Lakes in the War of 1812. Formerly the Canadian ship* Lord Nelson, *the* Scourge *had been seized by the Americans as a smuggler.*

the *Lord Nelson*, and confiscated it as a smuggler. He wrote in his account of the seizure, "...she had no papers on board other than a loose Journal and a bill of lading of a part of her Cargo but no Register, licence or clearance… I accordingly took her crew out and sent her with my gunner on board as prize master to this port."

Woolsey took the *Lord Nelson* back to Sackets Harbor, armed the ship with cannon, and renamed it the *Scourge*. James Crooks, the original owner of the *Lord Nelson*, angrily complained that his vessel had been seized before war had been declared, and therefore could not be a legitimate prize. He spent the rest of his life trying in vain to get compensation for it.

(The case would not be settled until 1930, when the American government paid over $23,000 to Crooks' descendants.) Woolsey auctioned off the *Lord Nelson*'s cargo of dry goods, sugar and liquor, but gallantly tried to spare several trunks full of women's clothing belonging to a Mrs. McCormick of Queenston. He thought it would be dishonourable to have a lady's private effects put up for auction. One of the trunks was returned to her in 1815, at the end of the war.

The former smugglers' vessel, *Scourge*, mounting ten guns, and its sister ship *Hamilton*, with nine guns, participated in attacks on York (Toronto) and Fort George near Niagara in 1813, and then became part of Great Lakes lore on August 8 of that year. According to an old maritime superstition, "once christened, a ship's name must never be changed or disaster will befall craft and crew alike." Bad luck in the worst form was about to strike the *Hamilton* and the *Scourge*, formerly the *Diana* and the *Lord Nelson*. As part of the American fleet of Commodore Isaac Chauncey, they were maneuvering against the British fleet of Commodore Sir James Yeo, when a sudden squall blowing across Lake Ontario caught them directly on the beam. The two ships capsized and sank, with a loss of 53 men. It was the largest loss of life on the Great Lakes in the War of 1812. The two vessels lie just off St. Catharines, Ontario, three hundred feet down. The cold waters of the lake have caused them to be among the most well preserved wooden wrecks in North America.

Another officer sent out by Washington to crack down on smuggling was General Zebulon Pike. A man with a rather mediocre career as a soldier and an explorer (he probably never saw the peak that bears his name), Pike arrived in Sackets Harbor in March of 1813. He almost immediately began receiving letters complaining about the activities of smugglers. The customs collector at the town of Oswegatchie, New York, A. Richards, wrote:

> The practice of smugglers has become so general in this district, and the plans of those engaged in it so systemized it is impossible for the customs house officers with all their vigilance to detect them—if a speedy stop is not put to the nefarious traffic, I fear the whole country will become disaffected to the government and engage in it.

Richards went on to recommend certain militiamen who had been effective in suppressing smuggling, and to complain about American citizens crossing over to Canada, and British officers and Indians searching Ogdensburg for deserters. He was especially incensed that one of his inspectors had captured a smuggler and some contraband, and then found himself a captive of Indians. It was only because of the intercession of the rescued smuggler that the Indians hadn't hauled the inspector across the river to Cornwall. Richards ended the letter with an urgent request for horses and men.

General Pike's response was swift and positive: "I have sent two detachments down into your quarter to punish those miscreants who possess so little patriotism as to wish success to an enemy." Pike advised Richards to provide the soldiers with written information on all those involved in "treasonable practices" and to make a list of witnesses. The villains, he assured him, would be apprehended. Pike then sent orders to a Lieutenant Loring Austin, telling him to take his detachment to St. Lawrence County and to be on the lookout for British troops and hostile Indians. Austin was to contact the customs officer Richards, and to arrest any suspected smugglers. Just to give the smugglers something more to worry about, he told Austin to "hold out to the disaffected that it is not improbable but 1,000 men may shortly be established at Ogdensburg," which was actually an exaggeration. He added that if Austin approached Ogsdensburg with stealth, he might capture the British officers who made such free use of the town.

When Lt. Austin reached Ogdensburg he didn't find any British officers, but with Richards' help he did nab eight smugglers whom he sent to jail in Sackets Harbor. Then everything went wrong.

General Pike received a letter from Austin dated April 9, telling him that he and his men had been arrested by civil authorities for interfering with the activities of "free and independent" citizens of the state of New York. The soldiers were charged with trespassing, assault and false imprisonment. Austin and his men were being held prisoner, and the local authorities had set bail at $12,000—which they soon raised to $90,000! The young lieutenant was desperate: "For heavens sake, sir, exert authority to extricate us from these disguised enemies and oblige."

A day later, Austin wrote again. "You may conceive, sir, the unpleasant situation in which I am placed by this legal patronage of absolute treason and I trust those who are vested with the proper authority will speedily rescue me from it."

Pike wrote to the civil authorities holding Austin and his men, diplomatically urging a solution to the "unpleasant situation." Presumably the general's letter was enough to secure young Austin's release, as there seems to have been nothing more said about it. Less than two weeks later, General Zebulon Pike was killed in the American attack on York, Upper Canada, one of the many Americans slain when the retreating British blew up their powder magazine.

The war continued until the end of 1814. As the casualty lists grew and atrocities were committed on both sides of the border, feelings hardened and smuggling decreased somewhat. But it was never completely eradicated. As long as there was money to be made, there was always someone willing to endure the strong odour of treason.

(Above) General Zebulon Pike, explorer for whom Pike's Peak was named, tried to stop the "treasonous practices" of American smugglers in the War of 1812. (Left) Pike is killed by the explosion of the British powder magazine at Fort York in 1813.

Fort York, Upper Canada. After the war, many Americans crossed Lake Ontario to find new opportunities in Canada. Their first stop in the town of York had to be the customs house.

LEONARD WILCOX
HARD TIMES FOR HONEST MEN

S muggling, like many criminal activities, can be a catalyst for corruption and abuse of power. It can also ensnare the innocent, even those who are involved in the fight against it. In the long history of smuggling in the region of the Great Lakes there have certainly been people in customs offices who have allowed greed to overcome conscience. One little known incident took place in the early days in old York (Toronto).

In August 1815, Leonard Wilcox left his native state of New York and sailed across Lake Ontario to the little settlement of York, Upper Canada. The name of his boat has been lost, but we know that it was a sub-stantial craft—about fifty feet long and ten feet in the beam, and equipped with rigging and sail. Its market value, according to a contemporary, would have been more than three hundred dollars, a considerable sum at that time. Wilcox wasn't expecting any trouble. He had visited York in the spring and liked the place. He liked it so much, in fact, that now that the hostilities of the War of 1812 were over, he was bringing his wife and children to make a new home in the British colony.

Wilcox tied up at the York dock, then went to the customs house to declare his boat and goods, and pay whatever duties were required, just as he had done on his earlier visit. The chief customs officer, William Allan—one of the most influential men in the colony—was away. On duty in his place was his deputy, a Mr. Hamilton, who examined Wilcox's boat and goods. The latter included shawls and some muslin (a type of fine cotton material), cooking utensils, dishes, decanters, knives and forks. Wilcox

Toronto in 1824.

intended to open an inn. To his surprise, Hamilton told him that some of the items in his cargo were contraband. He seized the boat and all of its contents (total value over five hundred pounds). Wilcox told Hamilton that if he were not permitted by law to bring his property into Canada, he would just take it back to the United States. Hamilton would not allow that, and Wilcox lost everything. His boat was sold at auction for a mere twenty pounds, but without the rigging and sail, which had been stolen. Some of his kitchenware turned up in a dry-goods store owned by Hamilton. A later investigation could produce no documentation of the seizure or of the auction.

In spite of the setback, Wilcox went ahead and built an inn at a location on Yonge Street, 13 miles north of York. It cost him all of the money he had left. By the summer of 1817 he was ready to open. He applied for a licence, and was refused because he had not yet taken the Oath of Allegiance. Armed with a letter signed by nine Canadians of solid standing in the community and good British subjects attesting to his industrious and honest character, Wilcox went to a magistrate to take the Oath. He was told, however, that his case was a special one, and he would have to get permission from the Lieutenant Governor of Upper Canada to take the Oath. He applied to Lieutenant Governor Samuel Smith and was refused. Nothing was put down in writing, but it seems he was denied because he was reputed to have been "a smuggler."

Meanwhile, Wilcox had imported a carding machine (used for processing wool, cotton, etc.) from the United States. He had been told the

The town of York, Upper Canada, wanted settlers, but American emigrant Leonard Wilcox complained of injustice at the hands of the collector of customs. (Inset) Early image of Yonge Street and toll gate. A licence was required for the operation of a business here. Falsely accused of smuggling, Leonard Wilcox could not obtain one.

import duty on the machine would be ten percent of its cost, but when the machine was unloaded at the York harbour, Wilcox was obliged to pay thirty percent. He paid, but again, years later when the matter was under inquiry, the customs officer could produce no documentation.

Because he could not take the Oath of Allegiance and therefore could not obtain a licence, Wilcox had a friend take out the licence so he could operate his inn and support his family. Six months later, on the complaint of William Allan, under whose authority such licensing fell (among many other things), Wilcox was summoned before a magistrate and fined twenty pounds plus costs for operating an inn and selling liquor without a licence. He also had to close his inn. Wilcox blamed all his "persecutions and hard usage" on "the vindictive conduct of said Collector of Customs and his Colleagues which I always considered contrary to the intentions of His Majesty's Proclamation inviting Settlers to come into the Province, and contrary to humanity and common justice."

Most people would have given up and gone back from whence they came, but Leonard Wilcox was a persistent man. In 1826 he tried again to take the Oath of Allegiance, this time with Lieutenant Governor Peregrine Maitland. Once again he was denied, even though by this time he was the clerk of the Township of Vaughan. By 1830, Wilcox had been temporarily jailed for debt, and was still trying to get justice in the courts, and all because a dishonest customs inspector had branded him a smuggler.

In the early nineteenth century, Lake Ontario and the Upper St. Lawrence River were highways for contraband cargoes as smugglers operated in defiance of embargoes and taxes.

CUSTOMS MEN
THE SMUGGLERS' NEMESIS

The job of the modern-day customs officer is not easy. On one hand, he or she is on the front line of the war against criminals and terrorists who try to transport deadly contraband like narcotics and arms. When the officers catch those who engage in such nefarious traffic, they are heroes. On the other hand, to the ordinary commercial or pleasure traveller who wants to avoid paying excessive taxes on a bottle of booze or a souvenir trinket, the customs officer is a petty tyrant with all the appeal of a cop writing up a traffic ticket. The customs officer must be sharp eyed, patient and cool headed, while enduring sour faces, bad tempers and nasty words. The trials of the customs men in the nineteenth century, however, would be enough to make the modern officer blanch.

People living along the Canada–U.S. border in the nineteenth century felt that they had a God-given right to smuggle. The customs man, in their eyes, was a despised agent of the money-grasping government; a villain as despicable as any tax collector; a scoundrel with a license to steal; a pariah no more deserving of respect than a common thief. Evading him was a crime only if one allowed oneself to be caught.

Smuggling was often well organized, and the smugglers frequently operated in armed gangs. As author Dave McIntosh explains in his in-depth history of the Canadian customs service, *The Collectors*, the job of the customs man was lonely, thankless and frequently dangerous.

Customs men were threatened, beaten up and sometimes shot at. One officer who was on the receiving end of a bullet was saved when the lead ball couldn't penetrate the 13 layers of clothing he was wearing to keep out the cold.

Smugglers would ferry their goods—tea, tobacco, alcohol, salt, silk, gunpowder (anything which had an import duty on it)—across the St.

Lawrence River or the lakes, and land at someplace far from a customs house. Then they would load it onto horse-drawn wagons for transport to market. Merchants were only too glad to profit from stocking their shelves with cheap, smuggled goods. This meant that the customs officer could not just sit in his office. To be effective, he had to patrol the countryside in all kinds of weather to catch the smugglers in the act. When the officer did encounter smugglers, there was often more involved than the simple seizure of contraband.

John Verner, the Customs Collector at Maitland, Canada West, reported a typical confrontation in February 1846. Verner, on horseback with a servant following, encountered some men with a wagonload of goods on the road near Prescott. When he asked them if they had been across the river, the men answered only that they were going to Prescott. Verner advised them that they would have to report to the customs house at Maitland. The driver suddenly whipped the horse and tried to run Verner down on the road. The startled customs man wheeled his horse out of the way, pulled his pistol, and fired two shots at the smugglers' horses, wounding one of them. His servant raced up and handed him another pistol, which he pointed at the other horse's head. He told the driver he would shoot if he didn't stop. The wagon stopped, and the smugglers meekly accompanied Verner to his office.

As Verner's story indicates, a customs officer would rather shoot a horse than a smuggler. Only one smuggler was known to have been killed by customs men in nineteenth-century Canada. That occurred one night in December 1852, when a notorious smuggler named Chamberlain and several of his colleagues were surprised on the road near Brockville with a wagon full of contraband, by Officer Anthony Dixon and a posse of his assistants. The customs men recognized Chamberlain. Dixon called out, "Aha, Chamberlain; it is you, is it. You're a pretty fellow. Back again into a scrape already! But you must desist and give up that property."

Chamberlain cried, "By Jesus Christ, I never will!" He was armed with a six-shot pistol. At least one other smuggler had a gun, and the rest were armed with clubs. Suddenly one of the smugglers cried, "Shoot them! Blow them to hell, goddamn them!"

The confrontation erupted into a melee of gunfire and swinging clubs. Two bullets hit Dixon. He staggered, but kept on his feet. Chamberlain stuck his gun against the head of an officer and cried, "I'll blow your goddamned brains out!" But when he squeezed the trigger, the gun misfired. Dixon shouted, "Fire on the villains!" By the time the smoke cleared and the crack of pistol shots had echoed away, Chamberlain had been clubbed to the ground and was begging for mercy; Dixon had been wounded, though not seriously; and a young smuggler named Henry Smith lay dead on the ground with a gun in his hand and a bullet in his body.

An inquest was held, and it took the jury only a few minutes to exonerate Dixon and his men. The Toronto *Globe* reported,

> From the evidence it would appear that the officers did their duty with courage and coolness and that the unfortunate fate of Smith was caused by the mad opposition of the offenders against the law. The deceased is said to have been an unoffending young man, who was seduced into the smuggling attempt by others. His fate should be a warning.

It was not just the smugglers who detested the customs men. The community in general also despised them. After all, smuggled goods were cheaper than merchandise imported legally, so the average citizen tended to see the smuggler as a friend and the customs man as the foe. Residents of a community would sign petitions to rid their town of a customs officer who was too diligent in his duty, or go out of their way to make life miserable for him. In one Upper Canadian community the newly appointed customs collector could not find a place to live because no one would rent him a room. Another agent in Upper Canada, Malcolm Cameron wrote: "The whole agricultural population is in favour of the smuggler... they have lost sight of the evils and sinfulness of smuggling—forgetting that it leads to falsehood, perjury and sometimes to assaults and even murder...." He went on to suggest that more moderate duties would make smuggling less worthwhile.

The trials and tribulations of the customs man are well documented in the story of John James Kerby, the Collector at Fort Erie from 1834 to 1854. To hold such a job for twenty years called for a man of considerable mettle, and that James Kerby was. He had fought in the War of 1812, rising to the rank of colonel of militia. Twice awarded the Sword of Honour, he was the most decorated native-born Upper Canadian to have served in that conflict.

Kerby became the customs man for Fort Erie in September of 1834 when the man who had previously held the post was dismissed for embezzlement. James had a twenty-mile stretch of Niagara Frontier to patrol, every foot of it friendly ground for smugglers. He was on the job for the full twenty

Buffalo, as seen from Fort Erie.

years, except for a ten-month leave in 1837-38 when he went with his militia regiment to fight William Lyon Mackenzie's rebels. During that short period his deputy collected the duties— and then stole them.

The zeal with which Kerby tried to enforce the Revenue laws earned him the hatred of both his countrymen and the smugglers from Buffalo. He was charged time and time again with trespassing and illegal seizure. Petitions for his removal and letters of complaint about him poured into the office of the Lieutenant Governor of Upper Canada. Kerby spent as much time writing letters defending himself from "false imputations so injurious to my character..." as he did patrolling the frontier. He was shot at more times in the line of duty than he ever was during the war.

Kerby made his first seizure two days after taking the post. One John Tidy of Ancaster submitted a false claim on the weight of some tea and cheese he had brought over from Buffalo, so Kerby confiscated the tea and the cheese, as well as Tidy's horses and wagon. (As much as two-thirds of the tea consumed in Canada was smuggled.) In March 1835, Kerby seized two barrels of smuggled salt from Johiadah Schooley, and also confiscated Schooley's horses and sleigh. Schooley had tried to get by the customs by crossing the ice from Buffalo at a place six miles from the customs house. The enraged Schooley went around town denouncing Kerby to one and all until Kerby threatened to formally charge him with defrauding the Revenue. Kerby was eventually

Fort Erie, as seen from Buffalo, c. 1811. Canadian Customs collector John James Kirby was hard pressed to keep up with the contraband crossing the water, but his dedication to his duty earned him the hatred of smugglers on both sides.

obliged to give Schooley back the horses and sleigh, one of many instances in which the government failed to back him up in his performance of his duties. But this in no way deterred Kerby in the execution of his job. He seized smuggled cargoes of everything that might appear on a pioneer family's shopping list, from whiskey to ginger to matches.

All this, of course, roused the ire of his neighbours. A local newspaper, the St. Catharines *Journal,* reported in February 1846, "Many attempts have been made to injure Col. Kerby," but none were as "cold blooded [and] fiendish" as the ambush one moonlit night in which Kerby was shot from behind with a shotgun. His back and his neck were peppered with duckshot. Kerby was fortunate that the gun must have been discharged from some distance. Had it been fired from point-blank range, the blast could have cut him in two. The assailant was never arrested, though Kerby had a good idea of who it was.

The citizens of Fort Erie were quite resourceful in their ruses to thwart Kerby. When goods he had confiscated were put on the auction block, they agreed not to bid against each other so the person from whom they had been seized could buy them back at a low price. If the opportunity arose, they simply stole the goods back. The captains of the two ferries operating between Fort Erie and Buffalo, the *Waterloo* and the *Water Witch,* made life difficult for Kerby by landing at a dock a quarter of a mile from the customs dock. Kerby retaliated by seizing the *Water Witch.* People began to bring lawsuits against Kerby. He appealed to his employer, the provincial government, for help, and got none. He went broke paying lawyers and would have had his property seized by the sheriff for non-payment of debt had his brother not come to the rescue with some money.

> My whole trouble and misfortune is that I acted fearlessly to the best of my humble ability in the just protection of the rights of the crown... I have thus been made a sacrifice to the gratification of these people when I know and feel that Government in justice to me as a faithful servant ought to support and bear me out.

Early in 1854, Kerby seized 12 barrels of contraband whiskey. It was one of his last big hauls. In July, John Kerby died. The smugglers rejoiced, and few of Kerby's fellow citizens mourned his passing. Not until they had experienced the incompetence and corruption of those who replaced him at the post would people realize what a sterling customs man John Kerby had been.

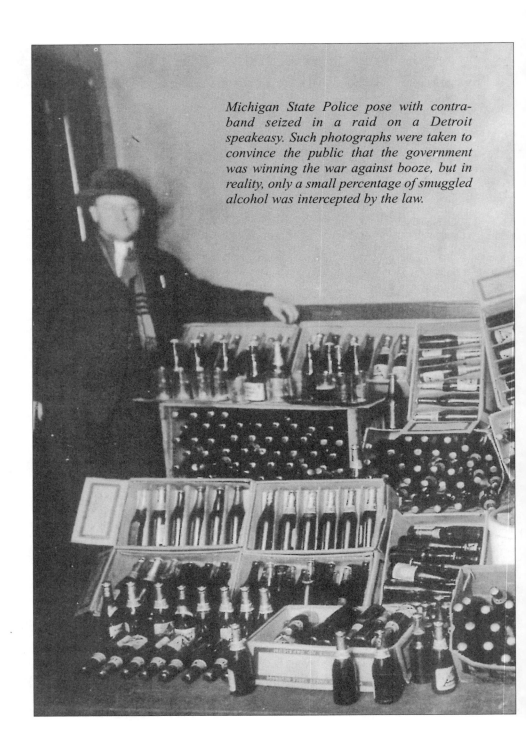

Michigan State Police pose with contraband seized in a raid on a Detroit speakeasy. Such photographs were taken to convince the public that the government was winning the war against booze, but in reality, only a small percentage of smuggled alcohol was intercepted by the law.

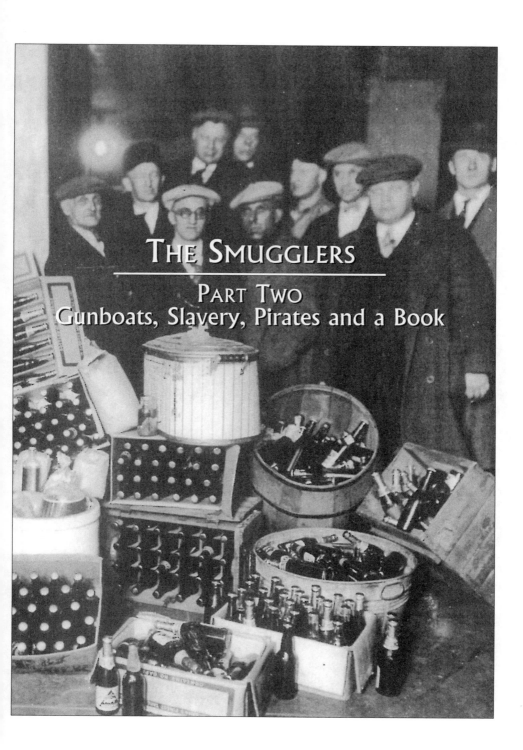

THE SMUGGLERS

PART TWO
Gunboats, Slavery, Pirates and a Book

The USS Michigan, *a state-of-the-art gunboat and the lone American warship on the Great Lakes, was a weapon in the fight against smuggling.(Below) Loggers at their meal in a Michigan lumber camp. The smuggling practices of American lumber barons brought men like these into conflict with the U.S. government.*

THE USS *MICHIGAN*
TIMBER WAR ON THE GREAT LAKES

From the mid-nineteenth to the early twentieth century, the steam frigate USS *Michigan* was the lone American warship patrolling the Great Lakes. In that time an appreciative public gave it the nickname "Guardian of the Lakes." Launched at Erie, Pennsylvania, on December 5, 1843, the sidewheeler was the first iron-hulled vessel in the United States Navy. It was 176 feet long, 27 feet in the beam (not counting paddlewheels) and carried 236 tons of iron armour. The *Michigan* was capable of a cruising speed of 14 knots, making it the fastest ship on the Lakes and, at that time, one of the fastest in the world. It could mount a total of 18 guns, but in keeping with a treaty between the United States and Britain, the *Michigan* usually carried just one eight-inch gun. It had a crew of 106 officers and men. The *Michigan* was originally constructed as a response to Britain maintaining a five-ship fleet on the Lakes, including the iron-hulled steamer *Mohawk*. But because London and Washington had learned, after the War of 1812, to settle differences diplomatically, it never fired a shot at a British or Canadian vessel. The principal duty was assisting vessels in distress, whatever colours they flew. In its many years of service, however, the *Michigan* would be called upon to help with surveys and police trouble spots, to guard Rebel prisoners during the Civil War, to thwart an act of Great Lakes piracy by Confederate agents, and to deal with smugglers. One of the most unusual incidents in which it played a role was the Timber Troubles of Lake Michigan.

In 1817, 1822 and 1831, the government in Washington passed laws designed to protect vast tracts of Great Lakes woodlands. Wishing to preserve a supply of timber for the Navy, Congress made it a felony to cut down oak, cedar and white pine in the protected areas. The laws were immensely unpopular with frontiersmen moving into what had once been called the Old Northwest, who felt that they had a God-given "title to the trees."

The Navy, which first had the responsibility of protecting the forests, did not do a very good job of it. Nor did the Treasury Department when it took over. It just wasn't possible to police such a large and remote frontier region. The few people who were caught cutting timber illegally faced only paltry fines—penalties that were little more than licences to commit larceny. For good timber was in high demand, and there was money to be made by those who could smuggle it out. There *were* places where timber could be cut legally, but the privilege cost money; stealing was more profitable. Timber poachers became big-time lumber barons, and the stealing and smuggling of wood from federal reserves had all the aspects of large-scale organized crime including corruption, violence and murder. The lumber barons established themselves in the boomtowns of Chicago and Milwaukee, and soon had newspaper editors and local politicians—not to mention gangs of lumberjacks who would double as hired thugs—at their command. They also exercised considerable pull with the Great Lakes merchant fleet, which was making a tidy profit smuggling contraband timber.

The biggest victim of the ruinous attack on the woodlands was the young state of Michigan, whose hills were being stripped bare by timber gangs from Illinois and Wisconsin. The Detroit *Daily Free Press* railed against them, while the Chicago *Tribune* warned federal agents to keep out if they valued their "personal welfare." Rapine, it would seem, went hand in hand with "Life, Liberty, and the Pursuit of Happiness."

In 1853, The Department of the Interior, now the custodian of the forests, sent revenue agent Isaac J. Willard to investigate the depredations in Michigan as well as similar outrages in Minnesota. With him were fellow agent Harvey W. Henry and U.S. Marshal George W. Rice, both of them Michigan men. What Willard saw appalled him. He witnessed logging gangs defy the law and threaten agents and potential informants. The timber men burned government boats and other property, all under the guise of "defending their rights." One night Willard narrowly escaped death when arsonists set fire to the inn where he was sleeping. He and his colleagues carried on with their jobs in spite of threats, and the ranks of their enemies grew.

Since roads were few, they travelled hundreds of miles in an open boat, gathering evidence and informing "any persons in possession [of illegal timber] that it was claimed by the General Government." Willard's greatest difficulty was finding people to guard the timber he had declared seized. He wrote in his report, "It is impossible to find a resident of the district who would not betray me." He probably knew that a deputy federal agent had been murdered only a year earlier while trying to seize some pirated timber in Iowa.

In one incident, Willard and his men surprised a logging crew run by a man named Benjamin Bagnal. They confiscated 26,000 board feet of lumber, 3,000,000 shingles and 3,000 cords of shingle bolts. Many of the loggers fled into the woods and Bagnall himself escaped by boat, but Willard managed to collar others, including the captains of several vessels.

Angry timbermen held a meeting at Grand Haven, Michigan, to organize armed resistance to the government. Backed by the lumber barons and the bosses of the merchant fleet, they threatened violent rebellion. On land or on water, they promised, they would resist any government men who stood in their way. To demonstrate their point they burned some seized timber and federal boats. When Willard attempted to sell his confiscated timber at auction in Chicago, he was driven away by a mob of armed men.

But Willard had tenacity. He obtained arrest warrants for the leaders of the smuggling gangs and had them served. Unfortunately, the marshal who did the serving was in cahoots with the timber pirates, and after "arresting" them, he released them on their own recognizance. Some of the merchant captains were arrested by Michigan authorities, only to be "sprung" by their crews. Two who were being held on a chartered ship got away when they used threats and intimidation to convince the ship's crew to release them.

While the timber barons and their marine confederates were spreading anarchy to defend their "right" to pillage and smuggle, the USS *Michigan* was hundreds of miles away in Erie, preparing for the first spring cruise. The captain, Commander Abraham Bigelow, had been told nothing of the troubles in the Northwest. He and his crew were anticipating a routine cruise to the Upper Lakes. Bigelow had no reason to keep the date of his departure from Erie a secret, or to double the sailing watches. He had

Timbermen hauling logs. Timber barons defied laws against rapacious logging practices. Sometimes rival crews battled over logging "rights."

had no contact with the only other vessel that might have interfered with the timbermen—the tiny, sail-powered, revenue cutter *Ingham*. The *Ingham* was a tub that had long since seen its best days, and its skipper discreetly kept away from the trouble brewing on Lake Michigan.

Late in April, the *Michigan* cleared Erie for Buffalo, then crossed Lake Erie heading for the Detroit River. Captain Bigelow had no way of knowing that the steamer *Buffalo*, the largest propeller-driven ship on the Lakes, had left Lake Michigan with a full load of timber. The *Buffalo*'s skipper intended to ram the *Michigan*. With the weight of the timber in his hold, he was certain he could buckle that iron hull and send the Guardian of the Lakes to the bottom. Neither the timber barons nor the smugglers wanted the Navy sticking a bowsprit into their crooked business.

The *Michigan* passed Detroit on the afternoon of May 5th, went through Lake St. Clair and up the St. Clair River, entering Lake Huron in the early evening. The running lights were lit, and the gunboat went onto the lake under a bright moon on a clear night. Visibility could not have been better.

At about 2:15 on the morning of the 6th, the watch on deck saw the lights of another ship about 12 to 14 miles ahead. The *Michigan* was just off Point Aux Barques, Michigan. The duty officer gave an order to steer north by northwest, away from the oncoming vessel. This should have given the *Michigan* and the unknown vessel plenty of room, but half an hour later it appeared that the stranger was bearing down on the *Michigan*. The Navy men still had no cause for alarm. They were not at war with anybody, and no common thieves, such as those who plagued the Mississippi and the Missouri Rivers, would dare attack a federal gunboat. The oncoming ship must have a man asleep at the watch, or drunk. The *Michigan* swung to port to keep out of the fool's approach.

The big ship, however, matched the *Michigan*'s every manoeuvre. By three o'clock it was only a few hundred yards away, but looked as though it would glide by on the port side. Suddenly, the stranger swung ninety degrees and was aiming all her tonnage directly at the *Michigan*'s port bow. The officer on deck, Lieutenant George Ransom, yelled to his helmsman to turn hard a' port. Then he picked up his megaphone and called to the crew of the monster surging toward him to turn hard a' port, as maritime law dictated. He still didn't believe that the other ship was deliberately trying to *ram* them.

No one answered his warning. The *Michigan* veered to starboard, but it was too late. As Ransom sounded general quarters and crewmen tumbled from their bunks and rushed to their stations, the big ship bore down on the naval vessel like a giant torpedo. It struck the *Michigan*'s port quarter, shattering one of the ship's boats, crushing the plate armour, and staving in the *Michigan*'s side. The massive jolt from the collision sent woodworking in the ship's interior crashing down. Captain Bigelow, who had been sleeping, now clambered over wreckage to get on deck, which was strewn with debris. His engineers reported that the *Michigan* was "much broken below," but was not in danger of sinking. It wasn't even leaking. In his report, Bigelow would say, "Had the *Michigan* been built of wood instead of iron, there is no doubt but that she would have been cut down below the water's edge and sunk."

Having bounced off the *Michigan*, the big propeller ship continued on its course without even slowing down. Angry that the other vessel had

The harvest of the woodland. Short-sighted logging policies denuded the hills of the Great Lakes states. Timber barons used politics, violence and smuggling in their pursuit of life, liberty and the pursuit of fast money.

not stopped to offer assistance, Bigelow gave chase. In spite of the damage to the port bow, and even though the other ship was going at top speed, the *Michigan* easily overtook it.

From below the other vessel's stern, Bigelow hailed the deck watch and asked if they needed assistance. For some minutes there was no answer. Then someone gruffly replied that they needed no help. When Bigelow demanded identification, he was refused. He ran the *Michigan* alongside the port of the other ship so he could see the vessel's name—the *Buffalo*. Still ignorant of the trouble in timber country, Bigelow believed the collision had been the result of negligence on the part of the *Buffalo*'s watch, and he let the big ship go. He didn't know that the *Buffalo* had been going at top speed after the ramming because the captain had been certain that the still floating *Michigan* would open fire. The *Buffalo* had sustained some damage to the bow and was leaking, though not seriously, and the skipper wanted to make port quickly.

In spite of Lieutenant Ransom's suspicions that the *Michigan* had been rammed on purpose, Captain Bigelow wrote in his report, "As I cannot suppose that the Propeller was run into the *Michigan* intentionally, I am led to conclude that there was no lookout on board of her." But things just didn't add up. Why had the *Buffalo* made that sudden turn to port? Even if the collision had been an accident, why hadn't the captain stayed to assist a stricken vessel—part of both the written and unwritten codes of the sea since ancient times? And why had the crew refused to give identification?

In Chicago, while the *Michigan* underwent two months of repairs, Bigelow began to find answers. Another ship, the *Republic*, had been nearby when the *Buffalo* rammed the *Michigan*, and its captain saw the whole thing. There was no doubt in his mind that the attack was deliberate, and when he reached Chicago he put his account in writing. Bigelow also learned of the "Timber Rebellion" and of the lumber barons' threats. He filed a formal protest and recommended that the owner of the *Buffalo*, a Mr. Wallbridge, be sued for damages due to the "careless, wanton, and culpable" conduct of the *Buffalo*'s crew. However, as the evidence was circumstantial, the suit never reached court. Oddly, no one was charged for other breaches of maritime law, such as leaving the scene of the collision.

Isaac Willard, meanwhile, was still trying to fight the good fight against the timber thieves. Knowing he did not have the resources to go after the hordes of loggers and sailors involved in cutting and smuggling, he concentrated on the lumber barons, the mill owners and the ship owners. But he found himself stonewalled at every turn. The Chicago press kept the public stirred up against him and his fellow federal agents with inflammatory editorials that denounced the "tyranny" of the government. Contraband timber he had confiscated was stolen back by the smugglers because he could not adequately guard it. Judges and politicians sympathetic to the lumber barons and their partners in crime stalled on bringing indictments against those Willard mentioned in his reports. However, the worm was about to turn.

The Secretaries of the Interior and of the Navy decided that something had to be done. They sent confidential orders to Captain Bigelow, who had returned the *Michigan* to Erie. He was to sail to Kalamazoo, Michigan, and assist U.S. Marshal Rice "in pursuing and arresting certain depredators upon the public lands." This time the *Michigan* left port without the foreknowledge of the lumber barons and the voyage was not marred by any attempt at sabotage.

On August 30, to the delight of Isaac Willard, the warship arrived at the mouth of the Manistee River on the east shore of Lake Michigan. Marshal Rice went aboard and joined Bigelow and his crew in a raid on a lumber camp at the Herring River. The lumberjacks escaped into the woods, but the captain of a merchant vessel was arrested. Two boats that had come to steal back a load of confiscated shingle bolts turned tail and fled at the sight of the *Michigan*. The merchant captain and some other men were sent to Detroit to stand trial. The *Michigan* then paid a surprise visit to Chicago where Marshal Rice arrested more of the lumbermen and packed them off to Detroit before crooked local judges could free them.

The *Michigan*'s next call was Milwaukee, where Rice hoped to apprehend logging boss Benjamin Bagnall, who had evaded arrest earlier.

Bagnall still proved to be a slippery character. He was arrested by a Wisconsin Deputy Marshal, who immediately put him on parole, allowing him to escape.

The noise the *Michigan* was making on Lake Michigan, however, carried all the way to the White House. President Franklin Pierce personally authorized Bagnall's arrest and removal to Michigan for trial. Bagnall was arrested and—protesting all the way—hauled aboard the *Michigan.* The Milwaukee press called the arrest "A High Handed Outrage." "There is no longer any security or safety for the liberty of the citizen" one hypocritical editor thundered.

While Bagnall's rather sensational trial was in progress, the *Michigan* patrolled Green Bay and other timber hot spots, and rounded up more of the timber thieves. Things went so well that Captain Bigelow was able to report, "The marshal and timber agent find a favourable change in their position since this vessel has been ordered to cooperate. The tone of the marauders is changed, and they have ceased to abuse those employed by the government to protect the timber."

Bagnall was found guilty and fined, and all of his contraband timber was seized and sold at auction. In mid-October, the *Michigan* was ordered back to Erie. The Chicago *Tribune,* smarting over the defeat of the lumber barons, decided to play a nasty prank. It reported that the *Michigan* was lost in a storm on Lake Michigan. The story reached the New York newspapers and shocked the country. Captain Bigelow had to explain to the Navy Department that, "a low newspaper, the Chicago *Tribune,*" had made the false report because of "the ill will and resentment of a class of men who have grown rich from the profits of this nefarious business... The reported loss of this vessel is from their malice."

Unfortunately, the *Michigan*'s victory was short lived. The timber barons used their money and power to influence Congress and get rid of pesky honest men like Isaac Willard. They managed to restructure the administration of federal lands so that enforcement of laws was next to impossible. Soon they were back cutting trees and smuggling timber with a vengeance. Not until the turn of the twentieth century were they stopped, when the destruction of the woodlands was all but complete. The *Michigan* had won a battle, but this time the smugglers won the war.

James Jesse Strang, Mormon "King" of Beaver Island. He tried to stop whiskey smuggling, and was himself accused of smuggling timber.

THE STRANGE SAGA
OF JAMES JESSE STRANG

While the Timber Rebellion was shaking up the Lake Michigan region, trouble of another sort was building up to what would become known as the Beaver–Mackinac War. This strange conflict would draw the *Michigan*, the lone American naval vessel on the Great Lakes, into a conspiracy that climaxed in assassination. The series of events which led to the death of the United States of America's only "king" began in Nauvoo, Illinois, in 1844 when Jesse James Strang (no connection with the Missouri outlaw of the post-Civil War years) met Mormon leader Joseph Smith.

Strang, who would switch his names around to James Jesse, was originally from New York State, but had moved to Wisconsin. He had been a teacher, a Baptist minister, a postmaster and a lawyer. He was a gifted public speaker and believed that the greatest thing a man could achieve was fame. He wrote, "Fame, fame alone of all the productions of man's folly may survive." He had a great fear that he might die before doing something for posterity.

Strang's wife Mary was the sister-in-law of a Mormon named Moses Smith. Strang was fascinated by the new religion and, in 1844, he went to Nauvoo to meet the founder of Mormonism, Joseph Smith. He converted to the Mormon faith, and so impressed Smith with his skills as an orator that he was almost immediately made an elder of the church. Then on June 24, 1844, Joseph Smith was lynched by a mob in Carthage, Illinois.

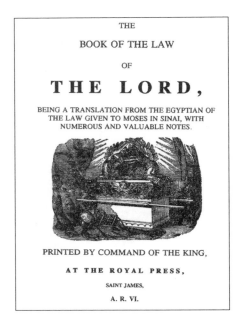

THE

BOOK OF THE LAW

OF

THE LORD,

BEING A TRANSLATION FROM THE EGYPTIAN OF
THE LAW GIVEN TO MOSES IN SINAI, WITH
NUMEROUS AND VALUABLE NOTES.

PRINTED BY COMMAND OF THE KING,

AT THE ROYAL PRESS,

SAINT JAMES,

A. R. VI.

"Printed By Command of the King." Strang took his role of monarch and religious leader seriously, printing this "Book of the Law" for his followers. (Right) The town of St. James on Paradise Bay, Beaver Island, was the heart of "God's Kingdom on earth."

A power struggle erupted in the Mormon congregation. Brigham Young assumed leadership, but James Strang claimed that Joseph Smith had appointed *him* heir, and produced a letter he said had been written by Smith to prove it. The majority of the Mormons supported Young, and would eventually follow him to Utah. Strang was excommunicated, but he, too, had followers. He declared himself the true leader, and excommunicated Young.

In September of 1845, Strang claimed to have had a vision. On his instructions his disciples dug at the foot of a tree and found some brass plates with mysterious inscriptions on them. Only Strang could "interpret" the script. He said that the writing confirmed that he was a "Prophet and Seer of God" and the "holy viceregent" on earth. More of the Mormon congregation came over to Strang's side, among them, those who did not want to make the arduous trek to Utah.

American society in general viewed Mormonism with suspicion and persecuted its adherents, so Strang looked for a place where he thought his people could live in peace. He chose Beaver Island at the northern end of Lake Michigan, arriving there in June of 1848 with about 25 followers. Beside the island's beautiful natural harbour, which they named Paradise Bay, the Strangites founded their new village, St. James. They built a mission for the conversion of the "Lamanites" (Indians) and made preparations for the arrival of the rest of their Mormon brethren.

By the summer of 1850, there were fifty Strangite Mormon families living on the island in a scattering of farming communities. They were

expected to pay one-tenth of all their earnings to the church. They had built a sawmill and their own schooner, and had constructed a road. Due to their location near the western end of the Straits of Mackinac, they were in a good position to dominate local trade. The island became a regular stopover for steamers needing to buy firewood.

James Strang founded and edited the community newspaper, the *Northern Islander*. He was the people's spokesman in dealings with the "Gentiles"—non-Mormons. Then, in 1850, he did something that went totally against the grain of American society. Citing instructions from a new set of mysterious brass plates, he proclaimed himself "King of the Kingdom of God on Earth." He published books and pamphlets defending his "Divine Right" to rule. He made an about-face on the controversial issue of Mormon polygamy. Previously he had been against the practice, and had denounced the much-married Brigham Young. Now he embraced it, taking a second wife. (He would eventually have five.) He told the men in his community that they must have at least two wives each, but only about twenty obeyed this edict. Strang had a tin crown and a wooden sceptre, and he called his frame house "The Castle." July 8th was to be celebrated as "King's Day." It all struck the Strangites' neighbours as unChristian and unAmerican, and inflamed the people against the Mormons.

Strang said that he was king only over his own followers, but began to extend his autocratic rule over some "Gentile" fishermen who also lived on Beaver Island. He insisted that they, too, pay a tithe to his church. There were rumours that he had those who refused to pay flogged. Then he

ordered the Treasurer of Mackinac County, of which Beaver Island was a part, to turn one-tenth of the taxes collected on the island over to him.

Not far away from Beaver Island, at the other end of the Straits of Mackinac in Lake Huron, was Mackinac Island. Among its residents— mostly Irish fishermen and a few traders—resentment towards the Mormons on Beaver Island grew. Religious bigotry was only part of it. Up until the arrival of Strang and his people, Mackinac Island had been the dominant centre for trade in the region. Now that monopoly was threatened. Since their island also belonged to Mackinac County, the people there objected to Strang's claim to what they considered an undue share of the tax money. They didn't like Strang's "bullying" of their fellow fishermen on Beaver Island, and it angered them when Strang made critical comments about the United States' recent war with Mexico. The Mackinac Islanders were quite willing, therefore, to join the Beaver Island fishermen in an attempt to forcefully drive the Mormons away.

The confrontation, which took place on July 4, 1850, was a fiasco. The fishermen and traders assembled at a trading post on a part of Beaver Island called Whiskey Point. While the "Gentiles" passed around the liquid courage, the Mormons hauled up a cannon they had procured in case of an emergency, and lobbed a few rounds in the general direction of the foe. No one was hurt, but the cannonfire and the sight of the Mormons assembled

(Page left) The light-house on Beaver Island was built on Whiskey Point, named for a former fur trader's opera-tion. (Right) Irish-Catholic fishermen were not pleased with the influx of Mormons to Beaver Island.

under arms were enough to put the fishermen to flight. Thus ended the Battle of Whiskey Point.

Thwarted on the field of honour, the Mackinac Islanders now attacked the Mormons through the courts. They had been joined by a disaffected Strangite named George Adams who claimed that Strang had threatened his wife. Among Strang's unusual rules was one that required the women to wear bloomers instead of long skirts, and some of the women objected to it. Strang was arrested by the county sheriff, but the case was thrown out of court.

For some time the fishermen and traders of Mackinac Island, and their colleagues on Beaver Island, had been engaged in a frontier bootlegging operation. They brewed up a concoction called "Indian whiskey" which they traded to the Natives for furs and fish. This firewater was a delightful blend of diluted cheap whiskey, tobacco and cayenne pepper. It cost five cents a gallon to manufacture, and sold for fifty cents to a dollar a gallon. Selling alcohol to Natives was illegal, so in April of 1851, when a Strangite constable caught some of the fishermen at it, he confronted them. The result was a gunfight. Again, no one was hurt, but the Mormons' foes tried to take them to court on bogus charges of theft. Once more, they were unsuccessful.

A month later, two of the Beaver Island fishermen assaulted a Mormon. When the Mormon sheriff and a posse attempted to arrest the assailants, there was a shoot-out. One fisherman was killed and two men, including the sheriff, were wounded. Of the two fishermen who committed the original assault, one was captured and the other escaped.

Now that there had actually been bloodshed, the whole region was in an uproar. The press accused the sheriff and his posse of murder. There were absurd accounts of outrageous crimes committed by the hedonistic Mormons. Lurid stories were carried in the newspapers of Chicago, Detroit and Buffalo. They came to the attention of President Millard Fillmore himself when he visited Michigan. The President ordered the U.S.S. *Michigan* to the trouble spot.

On board as the ship steamed into the fray was District Attorney George Bates with fifty armed men to support the ship's regular complement. Bates first arrested a Strangite judge, J.M. Greig, at the Mackinac County courthouse, and placed him in irons on the *Michigan*. Then the warship steamed through the Straits for Beaver Island, arriving there at 2:00 a.m. on May 24. Bates told Greig to point out Strang's house or he would hang him from a yardarm. Soon a boat with muffled oars was pulling toward shore, its landing party armed with pistols and cutlasses. They surrounded Strang's house and caught the whole family fast asleep. By morning Strang was a prisoner on the *Michigan*. Bates then tricked Strang into luring one hundred of his people aboard. They were all taken to Detroit.

Strang and his followers were charged with mail robbery, tax evasion, smuggling timber, counterfeiting and treason. Strang conducted the defence himself, and with his brilliant oratory he demolished one charge after another. The prosecution had no evidence other than biased hearsay. The Mormons walked away from the three-week trial victorious. The following year, 1853, they elected Strang to the Michigan State Legislature. The Mackinac Islanders tried, and failed, to keep him out of government by having him arrested on more trumped up charges.

As an officially elected representative, Strang successfully had Beaver Island made part of a new county, Emmett, separate from Mackinac Island. Then he instigated a crackdown on the bootlegging. The whiskey sellers from Mackinac Island were told to get out of Emmett County and stay out. Furious over the prospective loss of a large source of their revenue, the merchants and fishermen of Mackinac held a meeting. They denounced "The Mormons of Beaver Island" for robbery, piracy, denial of access to fishing grounds, and the alleged destruction of some fishing shanties. Then

Strang and his followers were charged with various offences including counterfeiting and treason

they declared war on Beaver Island, without informing the Mormons.

On July 12, a Mormon sheriff and 13 other Beaver Islanders went to the mainland of Emmett County to find jurors for a sitting of the circuit court. At the fishing village of Pine River they were ambushed by a large number of armed men. Six Mormons were wounded in the opening volley, but they all managed to pile into their boat and make for open water. Beaver Island, however, was 25 miles away, and three boatloads of Mackinac men were in pursuit with murder in mind. Just as they were about to overtake the exhausted Mormons, a sailing vessel, the *Morgan*, providentially arrived on the scene and interceded, almost certainly saving the lives of the sheriff and his men.

Down in Chicago, Captain Bigelow of the *Michigan* received a letter from a Mr. Smith, pleading for assistance. Smith claimed that his family and others were old residents of Beaver Island who were being terrorized by the Mormons. Bigelow got underway for Beaver Island, but before he arrived there he learned that "Mr. Smith" was a Mormon who had become estranged from Strang's church. He decided that he would not interfere in what he considered a Mormon internal affair.

The Battle of Pine River was the last shooting incident for a while, but the situation in northern Lake Michigan remained tense. In 1854, Strang's opponents accused him of padding the census count of his congregation in order to obtain a larger share of state funds. Rumours kept circulating that the Mormons were bandits and pirates who plundered up and down the Michigan and Wisconsin shores. The *Michigan*'s new captain,

Thomas Bedford and his wife. After Strang had him flogged for the crime of adultery, Bedford plotted Strang's assassination.

Charles McBlair, took the many complaints made against Strang and his flock to be true. Strang responded by being openly critical of the American form of government for not protecting honest, innocent people. The Mormons were, in fact, becoming quite prosperous, and thereby fuelling the flames of envy in their neighbours.

Within the Mormon community, discontent was growing over the rule of King James. Many were unhappy with the harsh punishments inflicted for minor infractions of church rules. A dozen men renounced their faith and dropped out of the church. There were probably others who were opposed to King James, but kept quiet out of fear. One of Strang's opponents said that those who broke with the church "incurred the odium and ill will of the sect to a degree which they think threatens not only their property but their lives." There was no solid evidence, though, that Strang ever threatened anyone's life.

Then, early in 1856, a man named Thomas Bedford was caught in the act of adultery with another man's wife. Bedford received the punishment laid down in church law, 79 lashes on the bare back. After his ordeal Bedford harboured a deep hatred for Strang and plotted revenge. He may have drawn as many as forty people into his conspiracy. He began practicing with a pistol.

On June 5, 1856, two of Bedford's ringleaders met Captain McBlair in Chicago and sang a litany of woes about the suffering of the people of Beaver Island under Strang's "tyranny." The captain decided that he had better take the *Michigan* to the island "and render such assistance to those

Strang's assassins sought refuge aboard the USS Michigan.

citizens threatened by the hostility of Strang." En route to Beaver Island McBlair had to make a stopover in Milwaukee, which gave his two visitors time to get back to the island a few days ahead of him and inform Bedford.

On June 16 at about 1:00 p.m. the *Michigan* docked at a wharf on Paradise Bay. Captain McBlair sent his pilot to fetch Strang to the ship so they could talk. Whether the captain was at all involved in what happened next is uncertain. As Strang and the pilot walked down to the wharf, Thomas Bedford and another dissident, Alexander Wentworth, ambushed Strang and cut him down with pistol fire. The king was shot in the face, the back and the back of the head.

The assassins and many of their confederates sought refuge aboard the *Michigan.* Captain McBlair would not turn them over to the Beaver Island authorities, claiming he was fearful that Strang's followers would lynch them. He took them to the sheriff at Mackinac, who immediately released them. They were hailed as heroes.

Strang died 23 days after he was shot, on July 8, "King's Day." With their leader dead, the surviving Mormons on Beaver Island could not hold out against the foes howling around them. Gangs of "drunken ruffians" descended on the island and drove the hapless people from their homes. They were forced aboard passing vessels with little more than the clothes on their backs. The homes and property they left behind were seized as the spoils of war. Captain McBlair and the *Michigan* were cruising Lake Superior while this atrocity was going on. The Guardian of the Lakes returned only in time to prevent the victors from killing each other over the booty. The Strangites were gone from Beaver Island, but the legend of the sect became part of local lore—along with a story about an island cache of Mormon gold, which nobody ever found.

Fugitive from slavery. Professional slave catchers used dogs to run their quarry down. (Right) Early nineteenth-century caricature of a runaway slave. Slaves were told that running away from their master was a crime against God and the state.

THE UNDERGROUND RAILROAD

The black man sat with his head in his hands, afraid to look up, afraid of drawing attention to himself. If the slave catchers saw him, they didn't even have to know who he was. Just the fact that he was black and on the train approaching the bridge linking Niagara Falls, New York, to Niagara Falls, Canada, would arouse their suspicion. He knew that they watched the border crossings like this one, scrutinizing every approach, every conveyance. They could stop the train, arrest him and haul him back to the South to cruel punishment and a life of bondage. He knew that others had made it this far, with freedom within their grasp, only to be snatched back at the last moment.

The black woman sitting next to him stared quietly ahead. She had gone this route before and knew well the dangers. If *she* were caught, there would be much more than a return to servitude in the South—there would be a hangman's noose and a $40,000 reward for the slave catcher who apprehended her. She kept a pistol hidden in her belongings and she had long ago resolved never to be taken alive.

The train rolled onto the bridge, then passed the midway point. They were in Canada! The woman gave the man a nudge and said, "You done shook the lion's paw." That meant he was free, and safe. He jumped to his

Plantation slave family in South Carolina. Slaves had no legal rights. Family members, including children, could be sold away on the master's whim.

feet and cried, "Oh, go and carry the news! One more soul got out safe!"

It was the mid-1850s, and the man—whose name was not recorded, though his story is true—was one of some three hundred runaway slaves escorted to freedom in Canada by the most famous of all the "conducters" on the Underground Railroad, Harriet Tubman.

The Underground Railroad was a loosely organized, ever-changing system of routes and way stations used for the smuggling of the most unusual of all cargoes—human beings. It existed wherever a fugitive slave was trying, with the help of sympathetic men and women, to escape servitude. Sometimes its operators used actual trains, as Harriet Tubman did on this occasion, but they also used woodland paths, rivers, boats, wagons—any and every means possible. The people who operated the Railroad were black, white, and Native. Their ranks included Quakers, Jews, Roman

Slave catchers and their hounds capture a runaway. The Underground Railroad was fraught with danger. Recaptured slaves were brutally punished. Laws against excessively cruel treatment of slaves were routinely ignored.

Catholics and Protestants. Some offered their services only occasionally; others dedicated their lives to it. All risked extreme penalties if caught.

Not all runaway slaves headed for Canada. Many went to the Free States in the North, where they hoped to remain hidden from the dreaded slave catchers. Others went to Mexico, to the Caribbean, to wild and remote places within the Southern states, to lands still held by the Indians, even to England and Europe. But for the majority of the runaways, perhaps as many as 40,000, Canada was "The Promised Land."

There had, in fact, been slavery in Canada under both French and British rule, but the "peculiar institution," as it was politely called, never took hold the way it had in the American South, largely because the land and the climate did not lend themselves to plantation agriculture. In the 1790s and early 1800s, anti-slavery laws were passed in Upper Canada, and while a few people did own slaves, the institution became socially unacceptable. Slaves arriving in the colony were automatically free and given the full protection of British law. Slavery was outlawed throughout the British Empire in 1834, but there were probably no slaves in Upper Canada

Southern slaves heard that there was freedom in Canada, but often did not know how far away Canada was. Slave owners told them wild tales of savage animals and vast distances. Whites who smuggled slaves to freedom risked severe penalties. (Right) Slave owners posted rewards for the capture of runaways. The bounty money was attractive to "poor whites" and even to other slaves.

by 1820. Slaves from the United States began slipping over the border to freedom. When the Americans invaded in the War of 1812, a "coloured regiment" fought alongside the British regulars and the Canadian militia to prevent the conquest of Canada. American soldiers from the South returned home after the war, and undoubtedly (and unintentionally) carried news of a place "up north" where there were no slaves.

But Canada was a long way off, and few tried to attempt the journey. Fewer still made it. In 1823, one man tried to cross the Niagara River on a wooden gate. He was swept out into Lake Ontario, where he was picked up by the steamer *Chief Justice Robinson*. When the captain told him he was on a Canadian ship, the man fell to his knees and said, "Thank you, Lord, for delivering me to Canaan!"

Few people today could understand just how barbaric slavery in the South was. While some slaves worked at trades or in households, the vast majority was subjected to long hours of back-breaking labour in the fields.

$100 REWARD!

RANAWAY

From the undersigned, living on Current River, about twelve miles above Doniphan, in Ripley County, Mo., on 3rd of March, 1860, A NEGRO MAN, about 30 years old, weighs about 160 pounds; high forehead, with a scar on it; had on brown pants and coat very much worn, and an old black wool hat; shoes size No. 11.

The above reward will be given to any person who may apprehend this said negro out of the State; and fifty dollars if apprehended in this State outside of Ripley county, or $25 if taken in Ripley county.

APOS TUCKER.

Slaves' living quarters were usually unsanitary, disease-ridden hovels. Slaves had no rights; they were not even considered human. Horses and dogs were given better treatment. Some slave-owning states had laws that were supposed to protect slaves from excessive cruelty, but they were largely ignored. In fact, masters who were known for being "kind" to their slaves were harshly criticized by their peers for "ruining the niggers." Opponents of slavery accused the "kind" masters of being the worst of the lot, because their benevolence glossed over the basic brutality of the institution.

A slave could be beaten, whipped, branded, starved, confined, tortured in any sadistic way imaginable just on a master's whim. For female slaves there was the added horror of sexual abuse. The slave could be sold away from his or her family at any time. Slaves were forbidden: to gather in groups of more than five (when not working); to hold religious services without a white person in attendance; to learn to read and write; to be off the plantation without a pass; or to have drums (the whites thought they would use them to transmit secret "African" messages).

The white population of the South was paranoid in its fear of a slave uprising, especially after the revolution in Haiti in which the black slaves of that Caribbean colony rose up against their French masters, killed many of them, and formed a Black Republic. Insurrections in the South were savagely crushed.

The other thing the slave owner feared was the runaway. The escape of a slave meant a monetary loss, but it also inspired others to do the same. For this reason, the slave owners installed strict measures to discourage

The Fugitive Slave Act of 1850 allowed slave catchers to pursue fugitives in the Free States of the North. Legally free Blacks were often seized and taken South. Only in Canada was there real safety.

escape attempts. Slaves were forbidden to leave their cabins at night without permission. Armed men patrolled the roads; any black person they found off the plantation without a pass was whipped and taken into custody. But the two most effective means the slave owners employed were fear and ignorance.

A slave knew that captured fugitives suffered frightful punishments: flogging, branding, castration, ear-cropping, tearing out of toenails were just a few of the torments meted out to captured runaways. The slave might be "sold down the river" to the dreaded slave markets in New Orleans. Or he might be turned over to a brute whose profession was "correcting" slaves who were "wrong minded."

Though a few slaves managed, secretly, to learn to read and write, most of them were illiterate. They were forbidden to have books, maps, or calendars. Slaves had it drilled into their heads from infancy (as did white children) that slavery was "right," that blacks were by nature inferior to whites. They were told that a runaway slave committed a crime against his master, the state, and God. Most slaves were woefully ignorant of the world outside their plantation or community. Their masters exaggerated the distances a person had to travel to get to the North or Canada. (One escapee said his master had told him the Detroit River was three thousand miles wide.) They told them terrifying tales of the cold, wild animals, and evil white men who would skin them alive and devour their children. Slaves who had run away and been recaptured or who had even travelled in the North with their masters were often kept away from other slaves out of fear that they might "contaminate" them.

If, after all this, a slave did the unthinkable and ran off, the master did everything in his power to have the culprit brought back, dead or alive. The countryside would be plastered with wanted posters bearing the runaway's description. The master might go after the slave himself, or he might hire a professional slave catcher who was paid a bounty for every escaping slave he apprehended. Slave catchers were armed and mounted, and often used specially trained "negro dogs" to hunt down runaways. These dogs would tear a victim apart if their master didn't call them off in time.

The slave owner also had the law on his side, especially after the passing of the Fugitive Slave Act in 1850. This law permitted a master or a slave catcher to go anywhere in the country, including the Free States in the North, to apprehend runaways. There were fines and jail terms for anyone, black or white, caught giving assistance to escaping slaves. In the Slave States, the punishment was death. The Fugitive Slave Act was a threat to free blacks as well. A slave catcher did not have to prove that a black person he had seized was an escaped slave. All he had to do was get one unscrupulous white person to swear that the victim was a runaway slave. The court was then bound by law to turn that person over to him. In this way, many blacks, who had gained their freedom legally or had never even been slaves, were kidnapped into bondage. There were white victims, too. Many slaves were of such fair complexion that they could pass for whites, and indeed, used it as a means of escape. Some slave catchers reversed this by seizing a white person—usually a recent immigrant—claiming that he or she had Negro blood, and dragging the victim down South to be sold into slavery. Thus, there were slaves in the South with Irish or German accents.

No one was more vilified in the South, or more of a thorn in the side of the slaveholder, than the abolitionists, black and white alike. Abolitionists were outspoken in their condemnation of slavery. They denounced it from pulpits, from political platforms, from lecture podiums and in newspaper editorials. When the slave-holders quoted Biblical passages, which they interpreted as being supportive of slavery, the abolitionists found other passages that damned it. When the slaveholders claimed that the American Constitution guaranteed them the right to have slaves, the abolitionists said that such a constitution was a "Covenant with Death and an Agreement with Hell." The Slave States passed laws against the distribution of abolitionist literature. The constitutional right to freedom of speech stopped at the Mason Dixon Line. To so much as utter an abolitionist sentiment in the South was to invite the wrath of the law, or worse, a lynch mob.

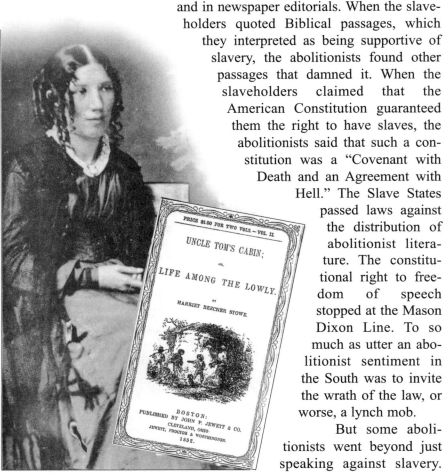

Abolitionist Harriet Beecher Stowe, author of Uncle Tom's Cabin. *The anti-slavery novel fed the fires of abolition everywhere, except in the South, where it just fed fires.*

But some abolitionists went beyond just speaking against slavery. They attacked it right on its home ground. One was Harriet Beecher Stowe, whose novel *Uncle Tom's Cabin* took the nation, and then the world, by storm. In 1850s America the melodramatic story about the sufferings of a Kentucky slave family hit like a bombshell. Northerners who had been indifferent to slavery in the South were weeping as they read the tale. They added their voices to those already demanding abolition. The novel crossed the border into Canada where it strengthened the resolve to keep the colony open to escaping slaves. Then it crossed the Atlantic to England, and was read by Queen Victoria and Prince Albert. It was translated into 22 languages including Welsh (*Caban F' Ewythr Twm*) and Italian (*Il Zio Tom*)—though the Vatican banned it as subversive. Everywhere it was published it fed the fires of abolition. In the South it just fed fires. (In Maryland a free black man was sentenced to ten years in prison for having a copy of *Uncle Tom's Cabin* and some abolitionist literature in his house.) Southern reviewers denounced the novel as a vulgar exaggeration. But Stowe said she had based much of the story on real events narrated by escaped slaves.

One Canadian who was moved by *Uncle Tom's Cabin* was Doctor Alexander Ross, an esteemed physician and naturalist. He travelled to the South, where he was welcomed into the mansions of wealthy slave owners as a distinguished foreign visitor. Under the cover of pursuing his studies of birds and butterflies, he was free to wander the countryside and the fields. At every opportunity he would talk to the slaves. He would tell them about the North and Canada, dispelling the falsehoods told by the slave owners. Ross gave them maps, knives, compasses, money and information on how to get to the first safe houses on the route. Sometimes he guided them personally. Whenever he left a district, there would be a rash of escapes. On one occasion he was accused by an angry planter of helping a slave escape, and was surrounded by an ugly crowd who were howling for retribution. This might have meant having the letters "SS" (for "slave stealer") branded on his hand with a red-hot iron, being tarred and feathered, or being hanged. Fortunately for Ross, the slave he had helped to escape heard of his predicament and, in a show of true gallantry, came back. He told his master a story that convincingly explained his absence, thereby saving Ross. He later made a successful escape, and Ross continued with his perilous work in the South.

An unfortunate myth grew in which runaway slaves were all helpless, child-like beings who would never have been able to make the dangerous journey without the help of whites. Nothing could be further from the truth. Whites did help, of course, and for that they were ostracized, fined, jailed, beaten and killed. To do what they did took courage. But perhaps the greatest courage was shown by those former slaves who, having reached freedom in Canada, turned around and went back to help others escape.

Harriet Tubman, the former slave who became the most celebrated "conductor" of the Underground Railroad. Sworn never to be captured alive, she always carried a pistol. There was a $40,000 reward on her head. (Right) Tubman (far left) with people she guided to freedom in Canada. Her proud claim was that she never lost a passenger.

There were many of them, but the Underground Railroad conductor who most infuriated the slave owners with her persistence, her bravery, and what they would have considered her audacity, was Harriet Tubman. It wasn't just that she was black, she was a *woman!* And yet she eluded the slave catchers with their horses and guns and dogs time and time again. Born in Maryland, Harriet had escaped to Canada with the help of a white neighbour, upon learning that she was going to be sold. When she was a girl, her drunken master had struck her on the head with a blunt object for showing defiance. The head injury left a visible mark, and for the rest of her life she was plagued by sudden, unpredictable "sleeping spells." The woman the slaves called Moses may have made as many as 19 trips to the South. Every journey was fraught with danger, but Harriet was confident, resourceful, and utterly without fear. She used disguises, bluff and an uncanny ability to adapt to any situation to get her people through. She carried opium to quiet crying babies, and a pistol, which she used to threaten any of her passengers who got cold feet and spoke of going back. To allow one to do so would endanger the rest. Her "trains" always began on a Saturday night because Sunday was the slaves' only day off and the escapees wouldn't be missed until Monday. After preliminary arrangements had been made, there would be a quiet knock on a slave cabin door, and a voice in the darkness would say, "It's me, Harriet. It's time to go No'th." It was her justifiably proud claim that she never lost a passenger.

Not all slaves who took the Underground Railroad had conductors to guide them. Many went on their own, with only the knowledge that they should follow the North Star and that there were safe houses marked in special ways, where they could hide and be fed. Some had only a song for a guide. "Follow the Drinking Gourd" (the Big Dipper) was allegedly composed by a man known as Peg Leg Joe. No one knows just who Joe was. In one story he is an old white sailor, and in another, he's a black carpenter. He taught this song to slaves under the very noses of the overseers, who didn't suspect that it was a coded set of instructions for escapees who would have to cross the Tombigbee, Tennessee, and Ohio Rivers. It went, in part:

If you follow the drinking gourd
When the sun comes back
And the first quail calls
Follow the drinking gourd
For the old man is awaiting
To carry you to freedom
If you follow the drinking gourd

The riverbank makes a very good road
The dead trees will show you the way
Left foot, peg foot, traveling on
Follow the drinking gourd

Whatever means the runaways used, they all faced the nerve-racking danger of being caught at any moment. Any suspicious person could inform on them. Even other slaves were known to turn runaways in, out of fear or in hopes of reward. Agents of the Underground Railroad warned them to be wary of con artists, black and white, who would offer to guide them for a fee, then take their money and leave them stranded or inform on them.

Then there were the patrols, often made up of poor whites who had no slaves of their own, and harboured a deep resentment towards the only people lower on the social ladder than they were. These men not only earned money for patrolling the roads and capturing runaways, but they could also violently demonstrate their "superiority" over their unfortunate captives.

In the early to mid-1820s, one of the worst threats to slaves in Maryland and Delaware was the Patty Cannon Gang. Described as a wild, vicious woman, Cannon was, ironically, Canadian born, and arrived in

Maryland about 1802. She murdered her husband and established a gang of ruthless cutthroats who preyed mainly on black people. They captured runaways, sometimes by luring them (with the help of other blacks) to supposed safe houses. They would also kidnap slaves from plantations, then deliver them back, claiming them to be runaways. Free blacks, too, were snatched by these marauders and sold into slavery. Cannon was eventually convicted of murder (of a white man) and imprisoned. She committed suicide in her jail cell.

Once the escapees made it to the Free States in the North, they still faced that last giant hurdle, the international border. Some went by sea to Nova Scotia and others crossed by land from the New England States into New Brunswick and Quebec. But most of those who had opted for Canada chose the province of Upper Canada (later Canada West). The soil was better for agriculture, there were numerous associations that helped former slaves get settled, and from there they could more easily keep in contact with family and friends in the United States. The Great Lakes were a barrier, though, with but three main crossing places: Kingston at the eastern end of Lake Ontario, the Niagara Frontier, and the Detroit River.

Some were able to cross the lakes by ship. Fugitive slaves who reached Chicago or Milwaukee, or other posts on Lake Michigan would try to find passage with sympathetic captains who would take them to Canadian ports like Collingwood, Sarnia and Windsor. William Wells Brown, who would win acclaim as America's first black novelist and playwright, was born a slave in Kentucky. He escaped to Canada and found a job as a steward on a passenger ship on Lake Erie. He became an active member of the Underground Railroad, hiding fugitives on board his ship and smuggling them across to Canada. In one year he took 69 people to safety this way.

There was heavy smuggling of runaways across Lake Ontario, too. Oswego, New York, was a busy port of embarkation, especially after the passing of the Fugitive Slave Act. Escaped slaves and free black people who did not feel safe in cities like New York, Philadelphia and Boston, fled to Oswego to find passage to Kingston. Residents of Oswego hid people in their homes until arrangements could be made with sympathetic captains. Three captains from Oakville, to the west of Toronto—Robert Wilson, James Fitzgerald and a man named Morden—frequently transported escapees in the grain holds of their vessels. Smuggling slaves out of the U.S. was not as perilous for these Canadians as it was for American skippers,

Escaped slaves in Windsor, Canada. Former slaves were protected by British law, but they still faced bigotry. There were occasional attempts to kidnap them back to the United States.

who faced jail terms if caught, but a Canadian captain did run the risk of having his boat confiscated.

The Detroit–Windsor and Niagara Falls crossings were at first glance the easiest, but were in fact the most dangerous because they were so closely watched by the slave catchers. Those enterprising men haunted the docks, patrolled the rivers in boats, and lay in wait along the approaches to the bridges at Niagara. More than one desperate runaway, trying to avoid the conventional crossings, drowned trying to get to the Canadian side in some flimsy craft or by swimming.

One young woman taking the Detroit route made it through thanks to a clever ruse devised by her guides. They dressed her in respectable looking clothes, complete with a veil for her face, and put a borrowed white baby in her arms. The teenaged daughter of one of the Underground Railroad guides accompanied her as a "servant." When the young women boarded the train, the runaway was horrified to see her former master sitting in the same car. For the whole trip she kept her head down and focused her attention on "her" baby. At the Detroit dock the master was going through the crowd of people waiting for the ferry, obviously looking for her. He did not suspect what appeared to be a white mother and child. The women boarded the ferry, then just before the gangplank was raised, the "servant" took the baby and disembarked. As the ferry pulled out into the river, the escaping woman took off her veil and waved to her furious master on the dock, calling out her goodbyes. The other people on the boat raised a cheer.

The suspension bridge at Niagara Falls must have been a tantalizing sight to fugitives with hundreds of miles of hardship and fear behind them. No boats necessary; one just had to *walk* across. But if a person were apprehended so much as a foot inside the American line, he or she could be dragged back. Caution, therefore, was of vital importance. One pair of men, who had fled from Virginia, had enough money to buy a set of fine clothes and then bribe a penniless white man to wear them. They "borrowed" a horse and carriage, and then drove across the bridge as a gentleman's driver and footman. There was a New York undertaker who smuggled people across in his hearse, and a travelling bookbinder who hid them in a false bottom in his wagon.

Patrick Snead of Georgia made it to Niagara Falls, Canada, and after some time thought that his trail would be cold enough for him to go back to the New York side and take a job as a waiter in a hotel. He was, as he put it, "as white as my master." Then, in the summer of 1853, five constables from Buffalo showed up at the hotel and seized him. He put up a struggle as they nearly strangled him with his own cravat, and tried to put shackles on him. The other waiters, all of them black men, rushed to the rescue. They pulled Snead free of the constables and dragged him down to the dock. They bundled him into a small ferry boat and told the boatmen to take him to Canada. The boatmen pulled on the oars and were more than halfway across when the constables on the American shore shouted out that Snead was a murderer. Upon hearing that word, the boatmen stopped. Then a man on another ferry, apparently their superior, called out to Snead's boatmen, ordering them back. Snead was handed over to the constables. But all was not lost. A good lawyer disproved the fake murder charge, and a sympathetic judge purposely delayed drawing up the "fugitive" warrant, giving Snead time to escape to Canada.

Slaveholders, of course, did not appreciate Canada giving asylum to runaway slaves. Southern politicians like Henry Clay and John C. Calhoun repeatedly demanded that the colonial governments in Canada send escaped slaves back to the United States. They argued that slaves were property, which should be returned to their rightful owners, and criminals who had violated the laws of the United States. They were thieves, said the slave owners, because they had stolen *themselves.* They were also accused of stealing other property from their masters, usually food and clothing. One was even accused of stealing the chains he was wearing at the time of his flight. But the Canadians would not send the former slaves back. The Americans then turned to Britain, demanding that the mother country tell the Canadians to return the slaves. The British said no. In fact, Queen Victoria announced that every fugitive from slavery was under the protection of British law the moment he or she set foot in her domains anywhere in the world. The Royal Navy hunted down slave ships the same as it did pirates. That Canada was a bastion of this British anti-slavery policy led Southern slaveholders to bitterly denounce what one of them called "the vile, sensuous, animal, infidel, superstitious Democracy of Canada."

Unfortunately, not everybody in predominantly white Canada welcomed the former slaves. The new arrivals encountered bigotry just as they did in the Free States of the North. Even the leaders in the black communities were divided as to whether their people should be integrated into white society or live in segregated settlements. But under British law they were free and equal with their white neighbours. They could vote, own land, go to school, and seek redress in the courts. They had difficulty adjusting to the cold climate, and many of those who had laboured all their lives cultivating cash crops like cotton, sugar, tobacco and rice, had to learn how to grow food crops for their families and for market. Many newcomers became disillusioned, but a common sentiment was expressed by a former slave named John H. Hall who wrote to a friend:

> I wants you to let the whole United States know we are satisfied here because I have seen more pleasure since I came here than I saw in the U.S. in the 24 years that I served my master... It is true that I have to work very hard for comfort but I would not exchange with ten thousand slaves that are equel [sic] with their masters. I am Happy, Happy.

John Anderson of Missouri killed a slave catcher in self-defence during his flight to freedom in Canada. His extradition case became an international incident.

Yet, in spite of the protection of British law, the newcomers in Canada still had to be on guard. The pro-slavery faction in the U.S. was always looking for ways, however devious, to reach across the border. There was a sensational case involving John Anderson of Missouri who, during his flight to freedom, had killed a slave catcher in self-defence. American authorities tracked Anderson down to a village in Canada West and began the procedure for extradition on a charge of murder. What began as a hearing before a judicial tribunal in Toronto became a highly publicized international incident. Its tremors were felt in the White House and in the highest courts of Britain. Anderson was eventually released, but his vengeful master in Missouri sold his wife and child into slavery's oblivion.

There were always rumours about Southern slave catchers sneaking into Canada to kidnap runaways and free blacks and smuggle them back into the U.S. Usually the stories were nothing more than rumours, but they stemmed from real incidents. In 1830, a former slave named Andrew was working on the farm of the Baby family of Sandwich (Windsor) in Upper Canada. Andrew's old master tracked him there and offered to buy him back for two thousand dollars. Charles Baby turned the offer down. Then the master said that Andrew had to go back because he was a horse thief. Andrew denied the charge, and Baby believed him. The master returned to the United States, but came back to the Baby farm with five slave catchers. They came on a Sunday morning, when the family would be at church, but were surprised to find that Charles had stayed home. He and some neighbours fought the would-be kidnappers and drove them off. Then they gave Andrew some money to go to Toronto where he'd be safer.

But not even Toronto was beyond the reach of the slave catchers. In 1840 two Americans armed with bowie knives tried to seize a black man there, claiming he was their slave. A local newspaper, the Toronto *Patriot*, reported that the pair was fined five pounds "for the brutal and cowardly practice of carrying bowie knives."

There were two recorded incidents involving slave catchers in the town of Chatham, which had one of the largest black communities in Canada West. One began in London, where former mayor Elijah Leonard saw a young black boy being forced onto a train by a man whose accent gave him away as American. He suspected that the boy was being kidnapped, but the train pulled away before he could do anything about it. He spoke to a black friend named Anderson Diddrick. They knew that the Windsor-bound train would stop at Chatham, so they telegraphed ahead. When the train rolled into Chatham, a hundred black men and women armed with clubs swarmed aboard and rescued the child. Leonard later said, "Mr. kidnapper was very glad to get off with a whole skin."

The other involved Mary Ann Shadd, the first black woman to publish and edit a newspaper (The *Provincial Freeman*) in North America. When Shadd saw a black youth struggling with some white men on the main street of Chatham, she seized the boy and tore him from their grasp. Before the startled slave catchers could react, Shadd hustled the boy to the town courthouse and began ringing the bell. A crowd of people, black and white, responded to the alarm, and the would-be kidnappers fled.

The American Civil War and Abraham Lincoln's Emancipation Proclamation of 1863 brought an end to slavery and the need to smuggle people over the border into Canada. During the war, many of the black men who had fled to Canada went back to the U.S. and joined the Union Army. Some wanted to be part of the crusade to vanquish slavery once and for all. Others went because the welcome they had known in Canada had cooled somewhat. Many white Canadians felt that with the death of slavery in the U.S., there was no reason for the former fugitives not to go back. After the war, with the Confederacy defeated and slavery at long last abolished, two-thirds of the former slaves living in Canada returned to the U.S. Most wanted to find the family and friends they'd been forced to leave behind. Those who went back to the Southern states probably did not foresee that the rights they had gained would be chipped away and replaced with oppressive laws which would deny them the equality they had known in Canada. It would take more than a century of struggle and sacrifice to win them back. The descendants of the courageous people who had travelled the Underground Railroad would one day follow their own quest for justice on the Freedom Road.

A pirate's challenge: "Come back tomorrow, you tubercular brat, and I'll give you another lickin'."Roaring Dan Seavey was the terror of Lake Michigan.

ROARING DAN SEAVEY

Captain Dan Seavey was an anachronism. He would have been more than comfortable looting the Caribbean with Henry Morgan's buccaneers, or pillaging the eastern seaboard of America with Blackbeard's pirates. For Dan Seavey *was* a pirate, a smuggler, a poacher and a lot of other things; but his era was not the Golden Age of Piracy, when freebooters of his ilk ruled the seas, it was the late-nineteenth and early twentieth centuries. And his domain was not the briny sea, but Lake Michigan, where one would think a piratical career would be short lived. Yet, Dan Seavey not only lived the life of a swashbuckling marauder in the heart of North America... he *got away* with it!

Roaring Dan, as he came to be known, was born in Portland, Maine, on March 23, 1865. As a boy, he loved ships and the exotic tales of the old salts down at the harbour. Like many a New England lad, at the age of twelve or thirteen he ran away to sea. He sailed on tramp steamers and then, when he was old enough, he joined the United States Navy. He soon found, though, that taking orders wasn't much to his liking, so when his enlistment was up he left the Navy and headed west. He worked for a while with the Bureau of Indian Affairs in Wisconsin and Minnesota, and among other duties had to apprehend bootleggers bringing whiskey down from Canada. But the lure of the open water was too much for Dan. He became a commercial fisherman, married, and had a daughter. Then, in 1898, the news of a gold strike in Alaska swept across the nation. Dan apparently had friends in high places, because Captain Frederick Pabst, the Milwaukee brewing tycoon, asked Seavey to accompany him on a gold-mining expedition in the north. The adventurer in Dan couldn't resist, and he was off to the Gold Rush, leaving behind his wife and child. The rough, tough mining camps would have appealed to Seavey, who had a reputation as a hard drinker and a brawler, but he did not strike it rich. He was penniless when he returned from Alaska.

Sometime just before the turn of the century, Seavey wandered into the rugged town of Escanaba on Michigan's Upper Peninsula. It was a community of loggers, miners, and iron workers, but going to work for a company boss didn't appeal to Dan. He acquired a little two-masted, forty-foot schooner, the *Wanderer* (there seems to be some doubt as to whether he came by it honestly), hired a few men as crew, and set himself up in the freighting business. He said he would ship any cargo anywhere on Lake Michigan. The freighting company, however, was just a cover. Seavey's real business was larceny.

Seavey would sail into a harbour at night without his running lights on, and pillage wharves, unlocked storehouses and untended boats. Lumber, foodstuffs, liquor, manufactured goods—Seavey took it all. On one of his raids he even took a pair of live oxen. Sometimes he hauled his loot to Escanaba, his home base, but usually he disposed of it in Chicago where he had underworld connections—black marketeers, who would take anything he brought them and ask no questions. Dan also made himself and the *Wanderer* available to gentlemen involved in the business of smuggling whiskey (or anything else the chaps in the revenue cutters might be interested in).

Seavey used every trick in the book and never let an opportunity to steal slip by. If he came across a vessel that had been disabled by a storm or some accident, he plundered it. Sometimes he created his own "salvage" by luring ships onto reefs or into shallows with fake navigation buoys, an old-time form of piracy known as "wrecking." When the crew of the stricken ship escaped in their lifeboat, Seavey and his boys would swoop down on the prize.

When Dan wasn't stealing and smuggling, he was poaching. He would go to Summer Island off Michigan's Garden Peninsula, or to nearby St. Martin's Island, where he had a homestead. Both islands had herds of deer, and Seavey would engage in some illegal hunting. He would pack the venison on ice in the hold of the *Wanderer* and smuggle it into Chicago, where it fetched a good price on the black market. The hoodlums to whom Seavey was selling the contraband venison once got the notion that they would cut him out of the operation and increase their own profits. They sent a boatload of ruffians to Summer Island to shoot the deer themselves. Seavey and his crew confronted them, but were outnumbered and forced to retreat. There was no way Seavey was going to let a pack of Chicago hoods muscle in on his territory, however. He put a cannon on the deck of the *Wanderer* and caught up with the interlopers partway down the lake. The hoodlums might have run the tough streets of Chicago, but out on the water, they were in Roaring Dan Seavey's domain. He opened fire and sent their boat to the bottom. There is no indication that he picked up survivors.

While Seavey was colourful, to say the least, he was also dangerous, and could stoop to the lowest forms of crime. He transported prostitutes around the lake to the bordellos of various ports. He would sometimes anchor off isolated lumber camps and use the *Wanderer* as a floating brothel. It was *rumoured* that he lured men onto his schooner, took them out onto the lake, robbed them, and then threw them overboard. Not as dramatic, perhaps, as making someone walk the plank, but just as effective—and dead men tell no tales. But rumours aren't facts, and one of the difficulties with Dan Seavey's story is separating truth from legend. This is well illustrated in the accounts of the taking of the *Nellie Johnson*.

Probably Seavey's greatest single act of piracy was stealing the *Nellie Johnson*, a forty-ton schooner which made the run between Beaver Island and mainland ports. The *Nellie* had once been owned by Seavey's old pal Captain Pabst, and Dan had even worked on it as a crewman. We have two accounts of what happened: the legend, and the facts as reported in the press at the time. First the legend.

On June 11, 1908, Seavey sailed the *Wanderer* into Grand Haven, Michigan, and entered a saloon where he found the crew of the *Nellie Johnson*. He started drinking with them and was still standing when they were all passed out. With the *Nellie*'s crew out of the picture, Seavey went back to the dock and boarded the schooner. He overpowered the captain, who was alone, and bound him with chains. Then he set sail for Chicago, dumping the captain overboard along the way. In Chicago he sold the *Nellie Johnson* and its cargo for a tidy profit, but this time the authorities got wind of this outright act of piracy.

The law had tried to catch Roaring Dan before, but he had hideouts at numerous places along the shores. And given his reputation as a fighter, it was said that the police and the revenue men weren't *too* anxious to lay hands on him. Once, when he had stolen a small schooner from a wharf at Chicago, the authorities chased him across the lake. He raced into the harbour of Frankfort under full sail, ran the boat aground, hopped ashore and disappeared. This time, they were determined to make Dan Seavey face the music. They set up a trap to catch him.

Seavey never turned down an opportunity to make a dollar—even an honest one—so when a man of some means offered to pay him to sail his private yacht to Mackinac, Dan accepted. The yacht owner, who was working with the revenue men, let them know where Seavey was going and when. He was taking quite a risk, because Dan could well have sailed almost anywhere, and added a fine yacht to his list of prizes.

But this time he was on the up and up, and set sail for Mackinac. As he rounded a place called Point Betsie, he found the steam-powered revenue cutter *Tuscarora* waiting for him. Seavey made a run for it. It was dusk and he thought that if he could stay ahead of the *Tuscarora* until nightfall, he could lose it in the darkness. But the revenue cutter stayed right on his heels, having all the advantage of steam over sail. When Seavey saw the light of a harbour buoy just outside the port of Frankfort, he shot it out and rigged a decoy, a barrel with a lantern on it. The *Tuscarora* fell for the trick and ran aground. But the ruse didn't work entirely. A shift in the wind foiled Seavey's chance to escape. The *Tuscarora* fired a shot across his bow, and Dan had to surrender. He was clapped in irons and taken to Chicago to stand trial for piracy. But all was not lost. Nobody knew just what had happened to the captain of the *Nellie Johnson*—only that he had disappeared. In court, Seavey claimed that the captain had gotten drunk and had given him the *Nellie Johnson* and the cargo to pay off a debt. Since the only person who could have denied the story wasn't around, Seavey was released.

That's the story the old freshwater salts of Lake Michigan like to tell, and it has appeared in several written accounts. But the report in the Chicago *Daily Tribune* on Tuesday, June 30, 1908, differs somewhat. In that article, there is no mention of Dan drinking the *Nellie Johnson*'s crew under the table, or dumping the chained captain overboard. According to the *Tribune*, it was the owner and skipper of the *Nellie Johnson*, R.J. McCormick, who went to the authorities to complain that his boat had been stolen by John [sic] Seavey and two others. Seavey's partners both disappeared sometime after the hijacking. Seavey tried, and failed, to sell the schooner and its cargo of cedar wood and then anchored the boat near his home at Frankfort.

Meanwhile, Captain Preston H. Ueberroth, commander of the cutter *Tuscarora,* was searching every bay and port of the Michigan coast for Roaring Dan and the pirated vessel. Worried that Seavey would be warned of the hunt and take to the hills, he was very cautious with his enquiries. When necessary, he swore his informants to secrecy. Just when it seemed the manhunt was going nowhere, Ueberroth was informed that the *Nellie Johnson* was at Frankfort, moored in the river right by Seavey's house, and that Dan planned to sail out across the lake in the *Wanderer* the following morning.

Ueberroth took the *Tuscarora* out to where he could intercept the *Wanderer*, and waited all night. In the morning, Seavey came out, clipping along under full sail and with a stiff breeze. The steam-driven cutter gave chase to the tall-masted schooner. As Ueberroth stated in his report: "He had a good start and it was an exciting race, but we finally overtook Seavey and ordered him to lay to. The arrest followed and I delivered the prisoner at Chicago." Exciting race indeed! In the chase to catch the *Wanderer*, the *Tuscarora* had all the paint burned off its smokestack.

Seavey could have been charged with piracy, which carried the death penalty, but the charge was that of stealing a vessel on which he had been employed. Had he been found guilty even of that lesser charge, he would have faced a $10,000 fine and ten years in prison. As it turned out, a good lawyer got him off.

It is known for certain that Dan loved to drink and fight. Seavey would fight anyone, anywhere. If someone had a reputation as a scrapper, Dan would challenge him just to see if the tough guy deserved the notoriety. He had a rule of no guns or knives, but aside from that it was no holds barred. Biting, eye-gouging, ear-ripping, and stomping with hob-nailed boots were all allowed. The combatants would often take a break from the carnage to gulp down the type of whiskey affectionately called "coffin-varnish" and then go back at it. At a bar in the town of Manistee, Dan locked horns with a man reputed to be one of the toughest lumberjacks who ever trod leather. The two men ordered everyone else out of the bar and then squared off. According to the newspaper accounts, by the time the police arrived to spoil the fun, they had practically demolished the place.

One fight Seavey lost was to a much smaller man who showed up in Escanaba looking for *him*. Seavey relied on brute strength, savagery, and raw toughness in a fight, but this little man seemed to fight scientifically. He was unbelievably fast on his feet and threw hooks and jabs with blurred speed. Dan could hardly lay a hand on him. Seavey finally fell to the ground, his face pounded to hamburger. It turned out that some of Roaring Dan's friends had decided he needed to be taken down a peg or two, so they had hired a professional prize fighter from Chicago. Dan thought it was a damn good fight just the same. "Come back tomorrow, you tubercular brat, and I'll give you another lickin'" he allegedly said.

It wasn't *all* boozing, brawling, and pillaging with Dan. He was known for his bizarre practical jokes, such as lining a bar with human skulls (heaven knows where he got them) to frighten drunks into sobriety. He once had a stint as a movie double, standing in as a diver for an actor. He also accompanied a team of archaeologists from the University of Wisconsin on an expedition to Lake Nipigon in Northern Ontario. He would then boast that he had "professors" for friends.

When the *Wanderer* was in port, children were always welcome on board. Seavey gave them fruit, told them stories, and taught them sailor's lore. There is one story that sounds apocryphal but could be true. An Escanaba father objected to his young son keeping company with a disreputable man like Seavey. The man went down to the dock one day and saw the boy on board the *Wanderer*—forbidden territory. When the boy came off the schooner, his father was waiting for him on the dock. It was a time when most parents firmly believed in the adage, "Spare the rod and spoil the child." The father seized his son, put him over his knee and began to give him a public spanking. Seavey went after the father and gave him the same punishment, warning him to "Leave my shipmates alone!"

After Dan beat the rap for the theft of the *Nellie Johnson*, the authorities found a creative way to put an end to his criminal activities. They pinned a badge on him and made him an honorary United States Marshal. They convinced him to join them in putting a stop to the whiskey smuggling, venison poaching and theft on the Great Lakes. Maybe Dan's close call with the *Nellie Johnson* had something to do with it, but whatever his reasons, he took the job and did it well. He had the advantage of knowing people and places the more conventional lawmen did not. Moreover, the other desperadoes knew *him*, and not many cared to have Roaring Dan Seavey after them. The crime rate in the Lake Michigan region dropped, largely because Dan himself had stopped stealing, but also because he was now on the side of the law.

One miscreant, however, did not take the threat of Marshal Seavey very seriously. The man was a notorious thief and whiskey smuggler who had been peddling booze to the Indians on the Upper Peninsula. The law wanted him and sent Dan to bring him in. Seavey found the man in a bar in the town of Naubinway. When he told the smuggler he was under arrest, the outlaw replied, "If you can drag me outside, I'll board your schooner for Chicago." It was like waving a red flag in front of a bull.

The marshal and the wanted man had the obligatory belts of whiskey, then tore into each other. The battle was Homeric, with the warriors stopping from time to time to toss another shot past bloodied lips and cracked teeth. Finally, Seavey slammed his opponent into the bar and then dropped him to the floor. Dan needed another drink of whiskey, but didn't want to risk letting his man get back up while he poured one. So he used the bar's piano to pin the man to the floor. After downing his dram, Dan removed the piano. The smuggler didn't get up. He didn't move at all. The next day he died. Seavey turned the body over to his superiors along with his report. There was never any investigation into Seavey's method of making an arrest.

In 1918, the *Wanderer* was destroyed by fire, and Seavey replaced the old sailboat with a 45-foot motor launch. The extra speed and space would have come in handy, because with the onset of Prohibition, marshal or not, Seavey got back into bootlegging. Running booze down from Canada was probably even more lucrative than piracy.

At the age of sixty, Dan Seavey was still issuing his "come one, come all" challenge to anyone who wanted to try him in a fight. And he still liked kids. He actually admonished some boys he caught stealing apples from a boat. "Don't swipe," he told them. He wept when his efforts to rescue a boy from drowning at Escanaba failed.

Seavey was believed to have made a fortune from his criminal exploits, as much as a million dollars. People said, though, that he gave much of it away to the poor and to charities that benefitted children. Whether he was indeed a Robin Hood, or he simply blew the money on whiskey and women, Roaring Dan was a pauper when he died in a nursing home in Pestigo, Wisconsin, in 1949, at the age of 84. A long life for a pirate!

Irish author James Joyce, whose novel Ulysses *became the most notorious banned book of the twentieth century. "An Odyssey of the sewer," said one critic. (Inset) Joyce with Sylvia Beach in the office of Shakespeare and Company, the launching place for "the greatest novel of the twentieth century."*

THE SECRET JOURNEY OF *ULYSSES*

Booklegging—the smuggling of banned books—is almost as old as writing. Ancient Hebrew patriarchs didn't want their people exposed to the idolatrous scribblings of pagan writers, so they forbade them to read anything but scripture. If an Israelite wanted to read the false-god infested epics about Troy and the wanderings of Odysseus, he'd have to smuggle Homer into the Promised Land in a jar of olives, and make sure the tent flaps were tightly closed before he extracted it. The ephors (elders) of ancient Sparta permitted only literature that glorified war. Anything else, they feared, might undermine the Spartan fighting machine. So, if a Spartan hoplite (foot soldier) wished to peruse the erotic poetry of Sappho, he'd have to sneak it into town when he returned home from campaign, and relax (sort of) behind the barracks with his forbidden scroll. Discovery would not result in a severe beating, the usual Spartan punishment. It would mean having half of his beard shorn, making him an object of ridicule—a terrible punishment for booklegging, as far as a Spartan was concerned.

The early Christians banned almost everything written before the time of Christ (and quite a bit that was written after) as heresy, blasphemy, idolatry or any other label they could come up with. It is thanks to the courage and resourcefulness of ancient and medieval bookleggers who were willing to risk fire, dungeon and sword that anything at all remains of the writings of Plato, Aristotle, Cicero, and an entire Humanities and Classical section-full of other great writers.

This policy of ecclesiastical book banning (and subsequent booklegging) was carried on through the centuries. The leaders of the Roman and Greek churches—and later the Protestant churches—condemned not only the works of each others' scholars, but also the writings of anyone from their own ranks who did not tow the dogmatic line. Secular governments got in on the act, adding to the lists of the forbidden any literary works that were considered to be subversive. So, by the Age of Enlightenment, Europe was ablaze with burning books and roasting authors, not to mention careless bookleggers.

When Europeans crossed the ocean to the Americas, taking with them slavery, alcohol, smallpox, gold fever, land hunger, guns, rats, religious intolerance and notions of white superiority, they also took along the idea that some things some people wrote were bad. And so book banning and booklegging came to what are now Canada and the United States. By "banning" we aren't talking about just keeping the novel *Candy* out of the hands of giggling adolescent boys. We're talking about governments telling entire populations that they are forbidden to read specific works. It is moral censorship run amuck. Among the books which have been banned at various times and in various places are Voltaire's *Candide*, Chaucer's *Canterbury Tales*, Walt Whitman's *Leaves of Grass*, Mary Shelley's *Frankenstein*, Ana Sewell's *Black Beauty*, and Henry David Thoreau's *Civil Disobedience*. Other authors whose works have been subjected to selective banning make up a veritable all-star list from the Literary Hall of Fame: William Shakespeare, Mark Twain, Oscar Wilde, Margaret Laurence, Jack London and D.H. Lawrence. Banned works by anonymous writers have included the Bible, *The Arabian Nights* and *Little Red Riding Hood*. (In one version of the beloved Brothers Grimm tale, Red has a bottle of wine in her basket of goodies for Grandma; some school boards objected to the presence of alcohol in the story.)

Book banning has, of course, continued right up into modern times, and the bonfires of Nazi Germany were but the most stupidly spectacular example. Ontario residents may recall the hubbub that was generated back in the 1970s by the illustrated sex-education book *Show Me*. And the world witnessed book banning in its vilest form when Iran's Ayatolla Khomeini put out an assassination contract on author Salman Rushdie because of perceived anti-Islamic insults in the novel *The Satanic Verses*. Even in this twenty-first century (not the thirteenth) there is a voice (though happily feeble) calling for a ban on the *Harry Potter* stories on the grounds that they glorify witchcraft.

One might wonder what all this has to do with smuggling in the Great Lakes region. It is simply to establish some historical background for an episode in which one of America's great writers took it upon himself to sidestep his government's ban on a work by another great writer, and smuggle copies of the book into the U.S. via the Windsor–Detroit "whiskey funnel" in the days of Prohibition. It was one of the twentieth century's most unusual booklegging exploits.

Irish author James Joyce has been described by biographer Richard Ellman as "the bizarre and wonderful creature who turned language and literature on its end." He was eccentric, courageous, and in the opinion of some of his contemporaries, a little mad. Yet even Joyce, as he spent an estimated 20,000 hours writing his masterpiece, *Ulysses*, could not have imagined that the novel would become one of the most celebrated "banned" books of all time. Nor would he have thought that the book would be selected by the Modern Library as the greatest novel of the twentieth century—something which must have those who branded it as "filthy" spinning in their graves. But he must have had an inkling, as he laboured over the text, that there would be problems. Some of the people he hired to type the manuscript quit after reading certain passages. The husband of one typist read some of the chapters and threw the manuscript into the fire.

Ulysses is a 900-page "stream of consciousness" tale about one day in the lives of three Dubliners, one of whom is tormented by his wife's infidelity. Each episode in the story corresponds to an episode in Homer's *The Odyssey*, hence, the title. (*Ulysses* was the Roman name for the Greek hero *Odysseus*.) The novel had a mixed reception among Joyce's literary peers. Ezra Pound loved it. Ernest Hemingway called it, "a most goddamn wonderful book." Virginia Woolf dismissed it as the work of "a queasy undergraduate scratching his pimples," and said that it was "reeling with indecency." Poet Alfred Noyes called it, "The foulest book that has ever found its way into print." George Bernard Shaw said, "It is a revolting record of a disgusting phase of civilization; but it is a truthful one." Among the other critiques which found their way into reviews were: "a dirty masterpiece," "an Odyssey of the sewer," "the product of a frightened and enslaved mind," "rotten caviare," "literature of the latrine" and "enough to make a hottentot sick."

To those who had set themselves up as the censors of literature in the English-speaking world, *Ulysses* was just plain dirty. The story has some sexual content, which is mild by today's standards, but was considered quite shocking in the 1920s. The novel was banned in Great Britain, Canada and the United States. When the American literary magazine *The Little Review* published the novel in serial form, its editors were convicted on obscenity charges and fined. Editions of the magazine that contained installments of the offending chapters were seized by the United States Post Office and burned. When a British literary magazine, *The Egotist*, tried to run it in serial form, many of its subscribers threatened to cancel their subscriptions. Nothing could have brought the novel greater publicity, but when *Ulysses* appeared in book form in 1922, distribution seemed all but impossible.

Hemingway hatched a scheme to smuggle what he called "a most god-damned wonderful book" into the United States via Canada.

Sylvia Beach, proprietor of the Shakespeare and Company bookstore in Paris, had published a limited edition of two thousand copies, which she planned to sell by subscription. But postal authorities in Britain, Canada and the U.S. would have none of it. *That book* wasn't going to cross their borders if they could help it. The United States Post Office seized four or five hundred copies (all private property) and burned them. British postal authorities swooped down on an equal number of copies, which then mysteriously disappeared. Canadian postmasters "standing on guard for thee" were issued a directive to seize any copies that came to their attention, but there does not seem to be any record of a mass confiscation (though it is quite likely some individual copies were intercepted and destroyed). Embarrassed by all the fuss, Joyce's own family lent out the copy he had given them so it wouldn't be in the house. In Paris, the visiting Prince of Wales allegedly complained of seeing *Ulysses* displayed in a bookstore window.

A result of all this controversy, of course, was that people wanted to read the notorious bookcsome for the wrong reasons. It became fashionable to own a copy of the book with the "swell dirty passages," as one person called them. (The average working guy who paid good money for a smuggled copy so he could read the "dirty bits" was in for a disappointment and, in many cases, those who were not well read found the story too perplexing to follow.) People returning from France to countries that had banned *Ulysses* began smuggling in individual copies. In fact, it became a daring thing for Americans visiting Paris (especially young women) to pick up a copy of *Ulysses* at Shakespeare and Company or some other Paris bookshop, just for the thrill of smuggling it into the U.S.

In his critical study *ReJoyce*, Author Anthony Burgess recalls cutting the book into sections and hiding them all over his body to get it into England—a method used by many bookleggers. Others hid it in hat boxes or wrapped it up in lingerie. There is a story about a Dubliner who sneaked a copy into Ireland in an empty Guinness stout barrel. (Joyce's native land would actually be the last country in the Western world to lift the ban.) One person (oh, the sacrilege) disguised a copy as a Bible. The first mate on an American freighter managed to sneak a boxful past American Customs, and

Joyce and Beach in the doorway of Shakespeare and Company in Paris. The Prince of Wales complained about seeing Ulysses *displayed in the window of a bookstore in Paris.*

probably turned a tidy profit. Some copies were cut up and hidden in newspapers. Others were shipped through the mail disguised with false covers. Booklegged copies that made it to British, American and Canadian bookstores were kept discreetly under the counter and offered only to trusted customers.

It is the true but seldom told tale of one shipment of *Ulysses* that deserves a place in the annals of smuggling on the Great Lakes. The slickest plan to smuggle *Ulysses* into the United States was hatched by none other than one of the book's first admirers, Ernest Hemingway. In 1923 Papa Hemingway, whose own novels would establish him as a macho icon of American literature, was a top reporter for the Toronto *Daily Star.* He was not happy in Canada and wrote to his friend Ezra Pound that he was reading *Ulysses* "to cheer me up." (He also complained of having to buy a box of chocolates from "bootleggers" because the stores were not allowed to sell candy on Sunday.) Hemingway was a friend of Sylvia Beach, who had tied up a lot of money in her publication of *Ulysses*, and was having a difficult time selling the copies abroad. People were reluctant to place an order when there was a good chance the book would be confiscated and burned. Hemingway decided to combat the ennui of life in Toronto the Good by helping his friend Sylvia.

Prohibition was in full swing, and it was no secret that thousands of gallons of booze were crossing the border from Windsor to Detroit every day. Hemingway got the idea that if whiskey and beer could be smuggled into the U.S., why not books? The rum-running epidemic would, in fact, be the perfect diversion. The customs men at the leakiest border crossing on the continent would be so intent on intercepting liquor, they might not even notice a shipment of banned books.

First Hemingway contacted yet another friend, Barney Braverman, a former Chicago newspaperman who had just taken a job with an advertising agency in Windsor. Braverman lived in Detroit, and commuted across the river everyday. Braverman had also made a close study of the methods bootleggers used to sneak whiskey across the border.

Hemingway told Braverman to rent a room in Windsor. Then he contacted Sylvia Beach in Paris and ordered forty copies of *Ulysses*. Beach sent the copies to Braverman's Windsor address. Braverman was able to convince the Canadian customs agent that the carton contained cheap novels valued at only fifty cents each. Thus, he not only got the forbidden books into Canada, but he also avoided paying three hundred dollars in duties on the real value of the expensive, limited-edition books. A few days later, Braverman wrapped up a copy of *Ulysses* and took it with him when he boarded the ferry to Detroit. The ten-minute boat ride seemed to take forever, and Braverman couldn't have felt greater anxiety if he'd been carrying a dozen bottles of Canadian Club.

As Braverman passed through U.S. Customs, an officer looked suspiciously at the package and told him to unwrap it. Braverman unfolded the wrapping paper, certain that he was about to be charged and fined, and the precious book carried off to the incinerator. But he kept his composure and played innocent, just the way he had seen the bootleggers do. The officer glanced at the book... and then waved Braverman on through. The man *had not recognized* the infamous title. The book that had New York customs officers rifling through suitcases and emptying shipping crates apparently meant nothing to the boys in Detroit. Senior postal and customs authorities had evidently expected to stop all incoming copies of *Ulysses* at eastern ports and had not considered the Canadian back door. Braverman smuggled all forty copies of *Ulysses* into the country that way and mailed them off to eager recipients—the internal American postal system not being subject to the same scrutiny as mail coming in by foreign post. Braverman later boasted that he had "put one over on the Republic and its Methodist smut-hounds." Hemingway evidently felt that the significance of his accomplishment would be lost on the rather conservative Toronto of the time, but would be praised by later generations. He wrote to Ezra Pound from Toronto, "Someday someone will live here and be able to appreciate the feeling with which I launched *Ulysses* on the States (not a copy lost) from this city."

In 1933 (the year Prohibition ended), *Ulysses* was taken off the American list of banned books. A U.S. publisher, Random House, had undertaken to publish *Ulysses* in the United States and took the matter to court. Judge John M. Woolsey found the book to be not pornographic. Indeed, in his ruling he praised it. Morris Ernst, a lawyer who represented Joyce and other literati commented, "We may now imbibe freely of the contents of bottles and forthright books." But the novel's notoriety remained for a long time. In the 1953 film *From Here To Eternity*, it was the "dirty book" which the drill sergeant found in the misfit Prewitt's footlocker. In the 1962 Cold War thriller, *The Manchurian Candidate*, it was one of the books strewn about the room of the nightmare-haunted Ben Marco. Audiences had only a quick glimpse at the title, but that was all they needed to recognize *that book*.

June 16, the date in which the events of *Ulysses* are set, is now honoured in the Republic of Ireland as James Joyce Day or "Bloomsday" (after Leopold and Molly Bloom, the principal characters in the story). Joyce's admirers celebrate the novel with readings, literary contests and the obligatory glass of Guinness. The booklegging of the novel from Canada to the United States is part of the lore of the acclaimed greatest novel of the twentieth century.

The cities of Detroit and Windsor. Hemingway's booklegging plan was inspired by the bootlegging of Prohibition gangsters.

97

(Above) Detroit Police dispose of confiscated liquor in the Detroit River. With so much alcohol from Canada making it past American officers, the region became known as "The Funnel." (Right) Supporters of Prohibition called it "The Noble Experiment." Others called it an exercise in folly. During the "dry" years, 1920–1933, liquor poured into the United States, most of it from Canada.

THE BOOTLEGGERS

PART ONE
Boats, Guns and Rugged Individualists

War by illustration. In the temperance cartoons at the top, father wastes time and money in the saloon, surrounded by bad company (left) while his daughter is ridiculed for her ragged clothes (right). An anti-Prohibition poster distributed by a brewing company carries the message that lager is good for mothers and babies.

COMPLIMENTS OF
GEORGE H. GIES,
16 Monroe Avenue,
DETROIT MICH.

AGAINST PROHIBITION NO. 2.
Lager's amber Fluid mild,
Gives health and strength to wife and child.

A Prohibition Primer

The advocates of Prohibition—laws designed to stop the manufacture, sale, and consumption of alcoholic beverages—did not just wake up one day to a blinding, divinely inspired vision of a sober America. (Though some of them liked to *think* God was speaking directly through them.) In both the United States and Canada it took a long, hard fight before the "dries" had their way and imposed their well-intentioned but misguided legislation upon the general populations of the two countries. Drink was a powerful and well-entrenched adversary, with traditions, customs and a mystique going back to the earliest colonial times.

One could find beer, imported rum, or locally made whiskey or cider in almost every frontier household, and everybody, young and old, drank it. It was a common saying that "Beer is for children, wine is for women, whiskey is for men, and brandy is for heroes." A pitcher of beer often graced the family supper table simply because the local water was not safe to drink. Alcohol was the basic ingredient of numerous medicinal remedies, and many a mother put a cranky baby to sleep by adding a few drops of whiskey to its milk. For women in labour there was a potent brew known as "groaning ale." The average homesteader's cabin had a bucket or jug to which guests were free to help themselves. At "bees," where neighbours got together to raise barns, husk corn or do any of a number of tasks requiring many hands, jugs of whiskey were on the tables along with the platters of food.

Hell hath no fury! Militants of the Women's Christian Temperance Union demolish a saloon.

Pioneers reduced surplus corn and grain to "likker" because it was easier to transport and use in trade. For the sake of variety they made alcoholic beverages out of almost anything that grew, including onions, dandelions and goldenrod. Frontier hero Daniel Boone once ran a country store in which the two main items for sale were "whiska and bacca." When three-time member of congress Davy Crockett went "electioneering," he claimed he always took along a big plug of chewing tobacco and a big jug of whiskey to help him win votes. George Washington, Thomas Jefferson and Benjamin Franklin all brewed or distilled their own alcoholic beverages, and young Abraham Lincoln operated several taverns. In both the British and American militaries, a "tot" of rum or whiskey was part of the daily rations for soldiers and sailors. So strongly did frontiersmen feel about their booze that in 1794 the farmers of Western Pennsylvania almost went to war with the federal government over a tax on whiskey. President Washington himself had to lead an army of militia to put down the Whiskey Rebellion.

Prohibitionists often pointed to Dr. Benjamin Rush as the apostle of their movement. He actually preached moderation, not abstinence.

This is not to say that the settlers were all staggering sots. Even the man who could hold his grog with the best of them wasn't likely to prosper on the farm or at a trade in town if he were drunk half the time. Public drunkenness was, in most instances, socially frowned upon and could earn the offender a reprimand from the pulpit, a fine, a turn in the stocks, a flogging or banishment from the community. Religious leaders and people like Dr. Benjamin Rush pleaded for moderation, but not total abstinence.

Nonetheless, there were those who felt that alcohol was in and of itself, evil. There were early, localized attempts at Prohibition. The colony of Georgia tried it from 1733 to 1742, only to see a sudden increase in the number of illegal mountain stills. A temperance movement among Connecticut farmers in 1789 was the first prohibitionist activity in the new United States, though on a very small scale.

With the coming of the nineteenth century, territorial expansion and increased immigration, there was also a rise in the consumption of hard liquor as opposed to beer and wine. While many whites saw nothing wrong with using alcohol to cheat, debauch, and demoralize the Natives, the more conscientious took issue with it. Canadian explorer David Thompson actually smashed the kegs of rum he was supposed to use in Indian trade. Evidence began to emerge, too, that alcohol, once thought to have many medicinal properties, could actually be hazardous to health. Few stopped to consider that it was *overindulgence* that led to problems. Alcoholism was not recognized as a disease, but was seen as a serious flaw in moral character.

In the nineteenth century, a large influx of lager-drinking German immigrants brought about a revival in beer consumption. American brewers, many of them German or of German background, took advantage of new technology in transportation such as the railroads to open up chains of saloons across the country in which they could sell their own brands. Saloons sprang up on every street corner in the cities, while smaller communities with one church and one schoolhouse might have a score or more

Carrie Nation waged war on the saloons with a hatchet and a Bible. Bartenders welcomed "All Nations except Carrie."

of saloons. With competition high, the saloon owners resorted to a wide range of devices to keep as much booze flowing into as many bellies as possible. They placed hawkers on the sidewalks to entice men inside. They offered the first drink for free. They provided free (well-salted) lunches. While some saloons were impressively well decorated, respectable establishments, many were dirty, shabby eyesores—hangouts for bums, thieves, crooked gamblers and prostitutes—a far cry from the quaint inns and taverns of colonial times.

Alarm over the increase in drunkenness and the growing political power of the brewing and distilling lobbies led to a corresponding acceleration of the Prohibition movement. The American Temperance Society was founded in 1826, the Women's Christian Temperance Union in 1874, and the Anti-Saloon League in 1892. These were but three of many organizations dedicated to a total ban on alcohol. To give themselves greater legitimacy and moral leverage, they often crusaded arm in arm with other, more worthy causes, such as women's suffrage and the abolition of slavery.

The prohibitionists recognized no gray areas. To them there were no "moderate" drinkers. Either you drank or you didn't, and if you did you were doomed to ruination and damnation along with the gamblers, the fornicators and the godless foreigners. German beer barons were caricatured as Teutonic ogres preying upon the hapless masses. Women temperance fighters marched with banners reading, "Lips that touch liquor will never touch ours." Clergymen thundered that the "wine" Jesus and his apostles drank was only grape juice. From public hall stages and street corner soap boxes the temperance preachers ranted about the dangers of drinking: death by dropsy, death by self-immolation, blindness, insanity, poverty, children born sickly and already addicted to the devil's brew. They plastered walls and lampposts with illustrations of hopeless drunks staring in hollow-eyed despair at empty liquor bottles; ragged children standing outside the doors of a saloon while inside father is losing his soul as he squanders the grocery money. They dragged besotted derelicts out of gutters and hauled them on stage to be presented as "examples" of what the demon drink always did to a man. In the early twentieth century, the prohibitionists would even denounce alcohol as a cause of "Bolshevism."

A literary work entitled *Ten Nights in a Barroom*, which damned alcohol and saloons, became a huge sensation and was read in churches and schools across the continent. It was eventually made into a musical drama. One of the songs went, in part:

At dawn of day I saw a man
Stand by a grog saloon
His eyes were sunk, his lips were parched
O that's the drunkard's doom

His little son stood by his side
And to his father said
"Father, mother lies sick at home
And sister cries for bread"

He rose and staggered to the bar
As oft he'd done before
And to the landlord smilingly, said
"Just fill me one glass more."

One of the most colourful—and fanatical—crusaders of the Women's Christian Temperance Union was Carry Nation. Armed with a Bible and a hatchet (she called her visits "hatchetations"), she was determined to destroy the "wicked, riotous, rum-soaked, beer-swilled, bedeviled, publicans of Kansas." She would stride into a saloon and wreak havoc, smashing mirrors, windows, furniture and bottles. Bartenders took to hanging up

A driver representing "Old Man Ontario" rides a water wagon in a pro-tem-perance demonstration in Toronto. People who swore off alcohol were said to have gone "on the water wagon."

signs reading, "All Nations Welcome, except Carry." The more times she was arrested for destruction of private property, the more she seemed a mar-tyr to a holy cause.

The "wets," those who opposed Prohibition, made the mistake of simply ridiculing the prohibitionists, rather than taking them seriously. One parody went: "To drink, or not to drink, that is the question; whether 'tis nobler to suffer the slings and arrows of outrageous thirst or take up arms against the Temperance League and by besotting frighten them." Such levity was no defence against the self-righteous solemnity of the temperance move-ment. Strict "prohibitory" laws went into effect in Maine in 1851, Vermont in 1852, and New Hampshire in 1855. Kansas became a dry state in 1880, and as the late-nineteenth century rolled into the twentieth, state after state adopted Prohibition. At temperance rallies, converts would be encouraged to "take the pledge" to swear off alcohol, and upon doing so would be awarded with "Temperance pins" in the shape of a "T", hence the term "T-totaller."

Prohibition was on the move in British North America, too. Early in the nineteenth century, temperance societies were taking root in the Maritimes and Upper Canada, and to a lesser extent in Lower Canada (Quebec). Temperance was very much a Protestant phenomenon. In Catholic Quebec, while the Church condemned drunkenness, it never was solidly behind full Prohibition. New Brunswick went dry in 1856. In 1864 the Dunkin Act allowed counties and towns in the two Canadas (Ontario and Quebec) to decide by majority vote whether to be wet or dry. This option was extended to all of the provinces of the fledgling Dominion of Canada by the Scott Act of 1878. In an 1896 Royal Commission study on the liquor trade, the authors pointed out the "successes" of prohibitory laws in American states in which they had been in effect. After more than three hundred pages of "facts," figures, arguments and testimonies, the authors came to the conclusion that, "...the traffic in intoxicating beverages is hostile to the true interests of individuals, and destructive of the order and welfare of society, and ought therefore to be prohibited." In 1916 and 1917 all of the provinces except Quebec voted for Prohibition. Only for a brief period in the latter part of the First World War did Canada have national Prohibition.

In contrast, the Volstead Act, which brought about national Prohibition in the United States, went into effect in 1920 and lasted until 1933. It forbade all manufacture, transportation, importation and sale of alcoholic beverages. The making of small amounts of home-brewed beer and wine for personal consumption in one's own residence was permitted. Stores selling home-brewing equipment and supplies—sometimes called "sugarhouses"—opened up everywhere. Many of them did most of their business with bootleggers. Medicinal alcohol could be purchased at a pharmacy with a doctor's prescription—a loophole which many doctors and pharmacists exploited, until the government took steps to close it. The only other alcoholic beverage that could be legally sold was "near beer," which had an alcoholic content so miniscule that most drinkers didn't consider it worth the trouble.

Ontario went dry in 1916 and remained so until 1927. But Prohibition in Ontario was somewhat different from the American version. Ontario breweries and distilleries could still manufacture for export, and it was not technically illegal to export alcohol to the United States. It was just illegal for the American customer to import it. Ontario residents could, for a time, get booze by "mail order" via wet Quebec. This did not mean that postmen in Ontario communities were hauling around mailbags that clinked with every step. Because alcohol sales were legal in Quebec, mail-order merchants set up shop in that province. The Ontario customer would mail his order and payment to the merchant in Quebec. The merchant would forward the order to the brewer or distiller in Ontario, and send the receipt back to the customer. The customer would then use the receipt to pick up the order, or even have it delivered to his home. The out-of-province receipt was proof that the alcohol had not been "sold" in dry Ontario. An Ontario resident was also permitted to keep a certain amount of alcohol in the home as "cellar stock" for personal use. Just how much an individual needed for "personal" use sometimes became a matter of considerable argument, and many a bootlegger failed to convince police that the hundreds of cases of booze in the basement were just "cellar stock."

Today we can look back at the apostles of Prohibition and call them naive, self-righteous, deluded, etc. We can say that many of the politicians who supported them were hypocrites who simply jumped on the "dry" bandwagon and paid lip service to temperance in order to obtain votes. But the majority of the prohibitionists sincerely believed that their movement would usher in a wonderful new world of sobriety. Bank accounts would soar. Man-hours lost in the workplace would plummet. Crime would fall off so drastically that police forces could be trimmed down to the bare minimum and jails and prisons across the land could be closed. Poverty would be no more, and a major victory would be won over disease. Corn and grain which had been "wasted" in the manufacture of beer and whiskey would feed the hungry at home and abroad. Men who had staggered home drunk on Saturday nights would now be up bright and early Sunday mornings to accompany their wives and children to church.

But, as Oscar Wilde once put it, "You can't make people good by Act of Parliament." Prohibition did not stop anybody from drinking. In fact, it made drinking the "in" thing to do, simply because it was not allowed. Young people who might otherwise have been satisfied with their sodas and lemonade now found that it was "smart" (early twentieth-century slang for "cool") to carry a hip flask. Legitimate drinking places closed down, but "blind pigs" and "speakeasies" (illegal drinking places) proliferated—32,000 in New York City alone. As one man put it at the time, "Anybody who says they can't find a drink ain't trying."

A Prohibition agent smashes kegs of beer. Confiscated alcohol had to be destroyed quickly, or bootleggers would steal it back.

By outlawing booze, prohibitionist governments made criminals out of millions of otherwise law-abiding citizens. In doing so, they seriously undermined the general respect for law and order, a fact that was reflected in a little verse penned by an anonymous poet:

Mother's in the kitchen
Washing out the jugs
Sister's in the pantry
Bottling the suds
Father's in the cellar
Mixing up the hops
Johnny's on the front porch
Watching for the cops

Worst of all, they handed the underworld a golden opportunity to haul in riches beyond their wildest dreams. All of the tainted money gained by robbery, prostitution, loansharking, bookmaking, extortion and the other crim-

Booze on ice. Tin Lizzies pick up smuggled Canadian liquor from a boat on frozen Lake St. Clair.

inal rackets paled in comparison to the bonanza of bootlegging. Coarse, semi-literate thugs like Al Capone became powerful bosses of organized crime. Even more frightening, *syndicated* crime (crime carried out on a national, corporate scale) evolved, eclipsing even organized crime with the scope of its evil. So, far from wiping out crime, Prohibition gave it conditions under which it could fester and spread. Court systems became clogged. Jails and prisons filled up—often with people who had never been in trouble with the law before Prohibition. Trusted politicians and officials in high places were corrupted. More police had to be hired, and Prohibition agents and Coastguardsmen. More Coast Guard vessels were needed. Ordinary citizens, who under normal circumstances would never have had any sort of criminal dealings, found themselves rubbing shoulders with hoodlums. The drunken violence associated with seedy bars was nothing compared to the mayhem erupting in city streets as gangsters battled for control of the bootleg trade. The horrific consequences would be felt long after Prohibition ended, as criminal empires, which had bloated on bootleg money, wormed their way into a thousand other avenues of North American life. Many of the notorious bandits of the Dirty Thirties—men like George "Machine Gun" Kelly, Charles "Pretty Boy" Floyd, and Lester Gillis (alias Baby Face Nelson)—were graduates of the bootlegging school of crime.

The rate of disease and death related to alcohol rose too, simply because the gangsters who had taken over the booze business weren't very concerned about quality control. Their most well-heeled customers could be more or less sure that they were buying real scotch from Britain, real rum from the Caribbean and real rye from Canada. But for the majority, it was a case of *caveat emptor*—let the buyer beware. Gangsters disguised

Weekend tourists returning to the U.S. from Canada came up with ingenious methods for sneaking liquor past customs officers.

moonshine, bathtub gin, and industrial alcohol with food colouring and flavouring and shipped it out with nary a thought for the consequences. The "good stuff" from Canada and elsewhere was frequently watered down and spiked with raw alcohol. Death and blindness from alcoholic poisoning became almost epidemic.

About a third of the illegal alcohol entering the United States came from Rum Row, a flotilla of "mother ships" from Europe and Canada lurking off the Atlantic seaboard just outside U.S. territorial waters. These ships supplied smaller vessels, which ran the booze into centres like New York and Boston. Almost all of the remaining illegal liquor came directly from Canada. The Great Lakes and the St. Lawrence River, as we have already seen, had a long history of smuggling before the advent of Prohibition. These vast waterways, separating two sovereign nations and so difficult to patrol, had been used by smugglers to thwart laws and tariffs in the transport of contraband as diverse as potash, alcohol, timber, silk and food. Now they were about to become the highways of illegal bootleg commerce during the years of the folly called Prohibition.

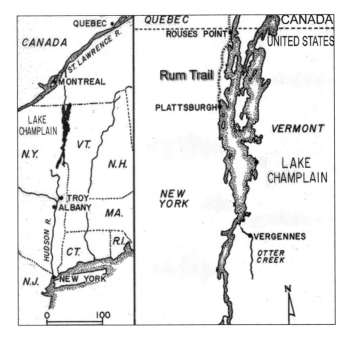

(Left) The Lake Champlain Rum Trail. With its northern tip conveniently in Canada, the lake provided bootleggers with a back door to New England and New York City.

(Lower) Rum cars seized by police being sold at Rouses Point, New York. Bootlegging led to a sharp increase in auto theft.

LAKE CHAMPLAIN'S RUM TRAIL

While the kingpins of the bootleg trade were sending boatloads of liquor across Lake Ontario, Lake Erie, and the Detroit and Niagara Rivers, bootlegging on only a slightly smaller scale was being carried on a short distance to the east, through the valley of Lake Champlain. The "Rum Trail" began at Saint-Jean-sur-Richelieu in Quebec and ran down the Richelieu River by both water and highway to Rouses Point, New York, a small community on Lake Champlain just inside the U.S. border. From there the smuggled alcohol would go to customers in Plattsburg, Saratoga, or other upstate New York communities, or it might be taken all the way to New York City.

Most of the bootleggers were tourists and weekend visitors who tried to sneak a few bottles of liquor or beer past customs officers. (A popular "Canadian" souvenir was the American-made hip flask, available at United Cigar Stores, where it actually outsold tobacco.) They were of little more than nuisance value to the customs men, and when caught were usually fined a few dollars after having their alcohol confiscated. Some of them did try very hard, though, to get away with it. Bottles would be stashed in what people hoped were secret compartments in their cars. A favourite ploy was to hide the bottles inside women's clothing, on the presumption that male officers wouldn't search the ladies. Some customs officers foiled this tactic by taking their wives to work with them as unofficial deputies. Crossing the border with a car full of kids was another trick. The idea was to make it look like a "family" outing, and hope the customs officer wouldn't suspect that the children were sitting on a couple of cases of booze. An undertaker from the town of Mooers, New York, crossed the border several times in his hearse, supposedly to pick up someone's dearly departed. A supicious officer finally looked in the coffin, and found it full of liquor.

Border Station on the Rum Trail. Every car had to be searched not only for professional rum-runners, but also for American weekend tourists trying to smuggle a quart of whiskey or a case of beer.

Of far greater concern to the customs men and police were the professional booze runners—men like Francis "Sam" Racicot of Rouses Point. Racicot, who became a Rum Trail legend for the many times he successfully ran booze across the border, did not consider himself a criminal. He told historian Allen S. Everest in later years: "Most of the bootleggers considered that it was an unfair law and a law which had been foisted on us, which had no validity. We knew that it wasn't being supported by the general public... we didn't feel we were lawbreakers."

While Racicot may have considered himself a sort of Robin Hood and would have had a lot of public support in that, the American authorities did not agree. As far as they were concerned, bootleggers were desperadoes whose ranks included the likes of Charles "Muskrat" Robare of Keeseville, New York. Muskrat smuggled by both car and boat. He earned his nickname by swimming to freedom one time when officers were hot on his trail. Afterwards, he took to wearing a muskrat hat in honour of his exploit. Muskrat made fools of the lawmen time and time again, either outrunning them or beating them in court on technicalities. His luck ran out, though, and he did prison time in both Canada and the United States. He finally committed suicide after being convicted of murder.

The self-styled "King and Queen" of the bootleggers were Dick Warner and Dorothy Swartout of Saratoga, who operated with their Canadian partner, Tommy O'Connor. These three made numerous successful runs across the border, and quickly rose to the top of the "most wanted" list—all by the spring of 1920 when Prohibition was but a few months old. Warner and O'Connor were caught in 1920 and sent to prison. Two years later they were out and back in business, only to be caught again and jailed in Rouses Point. Dorothy, for whom the police apparently did not have a warrant, went to the jail to visit the boys. It isn't certain if she caused some sort of distraction for the officers on duty, but when the guards went back to the cell, they found it empty. The prisoners had removed a bar from a window and escaped.

With the help of Canadian police, American agents tracked the fugitives down to a farmhouse in Quebec. They were arrested and sent back to the U.S., protesting that they were Canadian citizens. O'Connor and Warner were lodged in the Plattsburg jail, and almost succeeded in another escape. A guard found that two bars on their cell window had been sawn through. How was a mystery. They had not been allowed visitors, and a search of the cell turned up no tools. They were transferred to yet another jail, then sentenced to prison terms. Surprisingly, Warner got only eleven months and O'Connor four.

A little more than a year later Dick and Dorothy were caught driving the scout car for a liquor convoy near Beekmantown, New York. A scout car was a vehicle that carried no alcohol, but went some distance ahead of the booze carriers to make sure the route was free of police and hijackers. This arrest was highlighted by a rare example of "bootlegger gallantry." Dick took the whole rap himself. To spare Dorothy jail time, he decided to "take the girl's medicine" as well as his own, and went to prison for two years. Reports say that the fallen king of the bootleggers took it all with a wave and a smile.

Dick Warner at least lived to tell his story. Not so fortunate was Wilbur J. Hunt, a cement contractor turned bootlegger. A daredevil who believed a fast car and the cover of night would keep him out of the clutches of the law, Hunt got into bootlegging early, but his career as a rum-runner was short. On the cold, rainy, windy night of October 12, 1921, 42-year-old Hunt and 29-year-old Lynn Maynard were in Hunt's car, transporting a load of booze. They were unaware that hijackers had been tipped off about their run. Near the town of Old DeKalb two trucks and a large touring car fell in behind the bootleggers and gave chase. When Maynard stepped on the gas, the pursuers opened fire. For 14 miles Maynard kept the car on the rain-slicked road while bullets ripped into it. One slug grazed his arm and struck the steering wheel, but he still managed to maintain control of the vehicle. Both men were carrying automatic pistols, and Hunt said that they wouldn't give up their booze without a fight. He pulled his gun, and had turned to fire at the hijackers when a bullet struck him in the neck. He gasped, "I'm done for now," and quickly bled to death. A minute later the

U.S. Marshal destroying liquor at Rouses Point, New York, during Prohibition. Because of its strategic location on Lake Champlain near the Canadian border, Rouses Point had a history of smuggling dating back to the early nineteenth century.

pursuing touring car skidded off the road and crashed into a telephone pole. The hijackers gave up the chase. Maynard stopped the car and hid some of the liquor in the bush at the side of the road. Then he drove on to Gouverneur where he reported the attack to the police. Officers found the liquor still hidden in Hunt's car, and later the stash at the side of the highway. Maynard was charged under the Volstead Act (see p.107). Hunt's killers escaped.

Outlaws like Dick Warner and Wilbur Hunt smuggled a lot of liquor and wine down the Rum Trail, but beer eventually became the contraband of choice, especially for bootleggers going to New York City. The Big Apple was getting most of its hard stuff from Rum Row (see p.111), but beer was always in demand. A journalist for the *New York Times* estimated that ten million gallons of Quebec beer was shipped into the U.S. in 1925 alone. A case of Molson's, Carling's, or Labatt's, which sold for $4.50 or $5 in Canada, went for $10 in Plattsburg and $25 in New York City. All one had to do was run the gauntlet of lawmen and rival bootleggers to get there. Hijackings were commonplace, so bootleggers tended to travel armed. They would usually go in pairs: one man driving and the other riding shotgun. Farmers rented their barns out as "way stations" where a bootlegger could hide in the daytime and get some rest. It didn't pay to be too trusting of *any-one*, though, because betrayal and the double-cross always lurked when there was money to be had.

Booze that had been seized by the law had to be disposed of quickly, or the bootleggers would steal it back. Sam Racicot "liberated" cases of liquor from the storage "strong room" of the Rouses Point customs house on three different occasions. Not until years later, when he had moved to Montreal, did Sam reveal to American police how he had managed to climb into the strong room through the transom over the door.

Destroying contraband alcohol was a problem in itself. It took time, and every bottle had to be guarded until it could be disposed of. Not even honest citizens passed up a chance to steal condemned liquor or beer. At first the officers poured the booze down the customs house toilet, but this wreaked havoc with the plumbing, as the alcohol ate away the packing that sealed the joints of the pipes. So they started dumping it in Lake Champlain—so much of it that environmentally minded citizens worried about the fish. Hundreds of thousands of bottles were smashed, creating a new problem: mountains of broken glass.

Smugglers soon learned that they didn't have to enter Canada empty handed. Those willing to take the risk smuggled silk, cigarettes, tobacco, and—most despicably—narcotics, into Canada. Raw alcohol was another profitable contraband cargo. It was produced in New York factories and brewed in rural stills, and could be sold to Canadian distillers who were hard pressed to keep up with the American demand for their products.

Rum-runners in the Lake Champlain Valley used every possible conveyance to get the booze over the border: trains, boats, sleighs, horses, cows, and their own strong backs. But the bulk of the smuggling was done in cars. One of the most notorious Canadian bootleggers, Conrad Labelle, was said to have kept a fleet of twenty. Though he regularly took booze to New York and raw alcohol back to Canada, he was never caught.

Rum-running was hard on cars. They had to carry heavy loads, often at high speeds, and frequently over suspension busting, unpaved back roads. They also got shot at a lot. Customs agents and police did not hesitate to open fire on rum cars that failed to pull over. They usually aimed for the tires or the gas tank, but many bootleggers were shot. Others were killed when their cars rolled over or crashed into trees after their tires had been shot out during a high-speed chase. There were casualties among the law enforcement officers, too, because many of the bootleggers shot back. The public and the press were highly critical of trigger-happy crooks and cops who engaged in running gun battles, with little apparent concern for public safety. One federal agent, commenting on the bootlegging in that region, said: "It is harder than trench warfare in France. Over there we could shoot them or grab them when we saw them, or go right in and get them. But here we've got to wait until they come over to our side of no-man's-land."

There were shootings in the border country almost every night. In June 1924 there was a week of what was called "guerrilla warfare" where the border meets Sully Township, Quebec, as hundreds of local lumberjacks took the side of the bootleggers in opposition to federal agents and American and Canadian police. In 1928 alone, 128 smugglers were killed in this area.

If a bootlegger couldn't outrun the law, he would usually abandon his car and flee into the woods. The police would destroy the captured booze, and put the car up for auction. This proved to be a boon for honest citizens, who could pick up a car cheaply at a government sale. Bootleggers rarely tried to buy their cars back because the vehicles were now known to the police. The high turnover in cars for the bootleg business led to a sharp rise in auto theft, with rings of car thieves busy on both sides of the border. Valleyfield, Quebec, actually became a black-market centre for stolen cars.

Some of the bootleggers believed Lake Champlain was the best route. For one thing, it cut many hazardous road miles off the run to New York City. At the beginning of Prohibition, the customs department had no boats on the lake, so bootlegging sailors had an easy time. In 1922 the customs men acquired their first boat, and eventually the Coast Guard took over.

The lake had other perils for the water-going bootleggers: storms, hidden reefs and the irregular shoreline. Boats coming down from the Canadian end of the lake could be held up by the railroad bridge which spanned the water near Rouses Point. It was a swing bridge, and all but the very smallest craft had to wait until it was open before they could pass. This made it a favourite place for customs officers to inspect boats. At Rouses Point all craft coming down from Canada were supposed to report to the customs office, but smugglers with fast boats often just roared right by. Others would bring their booze by land to a spot along the shore below Rouses Point and load it onto boats there. Small-time bootleggers would put a few cases of beer into a rowboat, and quietly slide down the lake with their cargo. But this wasn't suitable for the big operators. One of them, Billy Hicks, had a fifty-foot motorboat that held up to four hundred cases of beer. He painted it black, and made his runs only at night.

Unlike the automobile bootleggers, those who used boats couldn't just pull over and disappear into the trees when hotly pursued—though a few did try to swim for it. Several were caught when they developed engine trouble out on open water, but the customs men made their biggest hauls simply through being vigilant. A sharp-eyed officer once noticed that the barge *E. Daneau* was sitting too low in the water, considering that it was carrying a light load of lumber. Inspection revealed a hidden cargo space packed with two thousand barrels of ale. Other officers staged a raid at a time they thought the bootleggers would be off guard, and caught the steamer *Massagna* being unloaded. They seized the boat and 48,000 bottles of beer.

One device the bootleggers used to thwart the law was the "submarine." This was a low-lying craft, packed with booze, that was towed behind the smuggler's boat. If pursued by customs or the Coast Guard, the bootlegger would cut the submarine loose, and it would sink. The bootlegger could return later and, hopefully, recover his cargo. Unfortunately for a few rum-runners, it didn't always work. One submarine that didn't sink contained 5,000 quarts of ale. Another didn't sink quickly enough; customs officers "saved" it, and seized 4,000 quarts.

The lake rum-runners had coves and islands where they hoped to be safe from patrols and prying eyes. One, at a place called Rochester Point, was not only a depot for contraband liquor, but it also evolved into a sort of "summer camp" for bootleggers. There, the men could relax from the stresses and strains of their nerve-racking trade, and enjoy swimming, good food, a bit of their illegal booze, and the services of prostitutes brought down from Montreal. The bootlegging on the lake does not seem to have been as violent as its counterpart on land. Only one man, a customs officer from Vermont, was killed on Lake Champlain during Prohibition. He fell overboard during a chase and drowned.

More than a century before the Prohibition Era, the people of the Lake Champlain Valley had defied their own government to continue trading with Canada, even when the two countries were at war. Dollars, it seemed, mattered more than politics. The quantities of booze that flowed over the international line during Prohibition showed that this willingness to disregard an unpopular law was still strong. The attitude is expressed rather well in a bit of doggerel which actually found its way into the *Congressional Record.*

Four and twenty Yankees
Feeling mighty dry
Took a trip to Canada
And bought a case of rye

When the case was opened
The Yanks began to sing
"To hell with the President
God save the King!"

A Detroit River rum-runner loads up his speedboat at the Ontario shore. Most of the liquor would be watered down for sale in American speakeasies.

DEATH ON THE WATER

Bootlegging was not a game for the faint of heart. The risks involved in getting one's hands on the so-called easy money were enormous. There was always the possibility of being caught and sent to jail, or even of being shot dead by officers of the law. There was the even more chilling prospect of falling into the hands of hijackers, many of whom were as black-hearted as any cutthroat who ever skulked along a highway or sailed under the Jolly Roger. If bootlegging was a dog-eat-dog business, then the hijackers were the jackals, and the adage that dead men tell no tales was an integral part of their code of dishonour.

For those who bootlegged by water, there was the added danger of death by drowning or exposure. On the Great Lakes the perils were greater for bootleggers than for sailors legitimately employed, because the nature of the business demanded that the bootlegger work at night, without running lights, and in weather that kept other, less desperate mariners safely ashore.

Because secrecy was so much a part of the bootlegger's modus operandi, no one will ever know just how many lost their lives out on the dark waters—victims of ice, a sudden squall, a heaving sea, or a gang of murderous rivals. But some tragic incidents did come to the attention of both the police and the press.

One of the strangest stories is that of the *Sea Hawk*, sometimes called the *Mary Celeste* of the Great Lakes (in reference to the brig, which in 1872 was found abandoned but in perfect condition in the mid-Atlantic. The fate of the crew remains a mystery). The *Sea Hawk* was reputed to be one of the most seaworthy rum-runners on Lake Ontario. A fifty-foot cabin cruiser, it had a powerful engine and was well fitted with compass and other equipment. The crewmen were not greenhorns, but experienced sailors who had been in the rum-running business for about a year. Nonetheless, in November of 1927, the *Sea Hawk* was disabled in a storm and had to be rescued by the Cobourg–Rochester ferry. The men on board were half frozen. The bootleggers were fortunate that it was not the Coast Guard that came to their aid.

The *Sea Hawk* underwent extensive repairs in Rochester and on January 18, 1928, set out from Charlotte, Rochester's port of entry, on what was said to be a trial run. On board were three Americans: Donald Walker of Scriba, New York; and William McElhone and Norman Mallette of Oswego. The identity of the fourth man seems uncertain. The Toronto *Globe* identified him as G. Gunyawn of Oswego. He was listed as Harry Gunyo of Brighton, Ontario in the Belleville *Daily Intelligencer*. Yet another source says he was a Canadian named John Gunway. Understandably, it was common for bootleggers to operate under aliases.

The *Sea Hawk* did not return to Charlotte, nor did it put in at any other port on either side of the lake. Searches carried out by water and air along both the Canadian and American shores turned up nothing. By January 29, two of Donald Walker's brothers were in Kingston, arranging for aerial searches of the islands in the eastern end of Lake Ontario. They had contacted every community on the lakeshore in both countries by phone, and now hoped that their brother and his companions had been forced to seek shelter on an island that lacked a telephone. Bad weather and ice prevented any investigation of the islands by boat.

"Trial run," reporters were told when they asked why the four young men would set out on the lake at a time of year when weather was so hostile to navigation. But on January 30, the *Globe* was already suggesting that "There is some mystery as to the reason for the voyage." It was rumoured in bootlegging circles that the men were carrying over two thousand dollars in cash and that the "trial run" was actually a booze run.

For days the searchers came up with nothing. There was almost another disaster when one of the search planes broke a wheel while landing. Then, on February 2, a Prince Edward County farmer saw a wrecked boat frozen in the ice of Pleasant Bay along the Ontario shore. The boat was lying lengthwise, about eighty feet out. The farmer notified the police, who investigated.

At first it was thought that the wreck was not the missing *Sea Hawk*. It was the right size, but the wrong colour, and there was no name on it. The fact that the boat was deeply imbedded in the ice made immediate investigation difficult. But a day of mild weather caused the ice level to drop. Investigators found that the boat had been completely stripped of all fittings, including the engine. Close examination revealed that the outer coat of paint hid another colour—the original colour of the *Sea Hawk*. Police scraped away the new paint and found the words, *Sea Hawk of Rochester USA* on the bow.

The Walker brothers still hoped that Donald and his friends were safe on an island, but sadly, this was not so. On February 9 the search was called off. Spring thaw brought two of the bodies to the surface. The others were never found.

As in the case of the *Mary Celeste*, there are many theories about what happened to the *Sea Hawk*, but nothing that can be proven. Was it simply the victim of foul weather? Possibly, but not likely. The absence of the engine and other fittings indicates hijackers. It could be that the *Sea Hawk* was vandalized *after* being wrecked, but would mere vandals have gone to the trouble of disguising it with a coat of paint? Walker and his companions might have painted the boat themselves, but then it's unlikely they'd have been allowed to clear their home port in an unmarked vessel. The one certainty is that four rum-runners went for the easy money, and paid for their avarice the hard way.

Another notorious rum-runner, Stephen Wesley, went to a watery grave apparently unmourned. Originally from Chicago, where he supposedly had connections with some of the Windy City's mobster big shots, Wesley set himself up in Watertown, New York, on the doorstep of the Thousand Islands. Canadian booze was available just across the St. Lawrence River, and the labyrinth of waterways through the islands had been a smuggler's paradise for generations. This had been the haunt of Bill Johnston, the notorious nineteenth-century Pirate of the Thousand Islands,

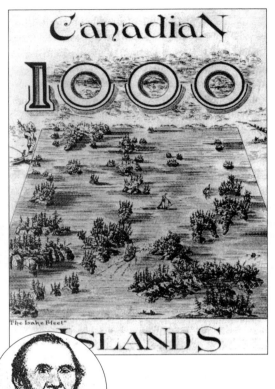

The Thousand Islands had been a smuggler's paradise for generations before Prohibition. But the St. Lawrence River could be treacherous in winter, as bootlegger Stephen Wesley learned. (Inset) Pirate Bill Johnston. (Page right) This comic image of a besotted American visitor in Canada did not reflect the view of American authorities. Washington constantly demanded that Ottawa crack down on the exporting of Canadian alcohol to the U.S.

who had supplemented acts of outright robbery with smuggling. Now it was a convenient crossing place for bootleggers like Wesley. All one needed, besides a boat, was nerve— and Wesley had plenty of that. His exploits in outwitting the police on both sides of the river as well as his knack for repeatedly pulling himself from the clutches of the mighty St. Lawrence itself earned Wesley the admiration of the bootlegging fraternity of Watertown.

Wesley made good money running whiskey and beer, and it showed. He wore silk shirts, had suites at the best hotels, and generally lived the high life, spending his cash as fast as he made it. But the admiration the other bootleggers had for Wesley was grudging, because most of his colleagues despised him. He was known to be untrustworthy, a swindler who looked out only for number one. He claimed that another bootlegger had stiffed him for $1,100 on a booze deal and took the man to court over it. Whether or not the man owed Wesley money, no self-respecting bootlegger

went whining to the law. There was a story about Wesley and yet another Watertown bootlegger getting together to haul a load of liquor to Chicago. They had no sooner sold their shipment than they were set upon by gunmen who took every cent they had. Something about the "robbery" didn't seem right to Wesley's partner. He believed the whole thing had been set up, and that Wesley and his Chicago friends had simply divided up his share of the liquor money.

Wesley's amazing run of good luck ended in the summer of 1928 when he was caught by American police while riding a motorcycle as "scout" for a truckload of booze. He already had a record for disorderly conduct (for firing a gun out of the window of a car) and was suspected of being a car thief. A year later he was caught smuggling booze, posted a $1,000 bond and then skipped bail. Weeks later he was caught again and tossed into the Jefferson County jail. It was autumn before he finally stood before a judge in a courtroom. Wesley pleaded poverty, and unbelievably, got off. The problem was, he really was broke. All of that fast money had run through his fingers like water.

Not being the most popular man among the rum-running crowd and with it being common knowledge that the police were watching him, Wesley had a tough time finding anyone willing to help him get back on his feet. The idea of looking for a real job was out of the question. Honest labour was for suckers.

Finally, someone did agree to stake Wesley to the bare minimum: a rowboat and enough cash to buy a few cases on the Canadian side. On a cold, rainy December day he took oars in hand and rowed over to Canada, where he bought his small load. He set out on the return trip as night was falling. The rain had turned to sleet, a strong wind was blowing from the northwest and the river was choked with ice. Sometime well after dark, soaked through and numb with cold, his clothing crusted with ice, Wesley landed on Grindstone Island on the American side of the line. An acquaintance of his had a home there, a place where he could eat, warm up and rest for a couple of hours.

After a short stay Wesley was ready to go again. The weather was deteriorating, and his host tried to convince him to wait until morning. But Wesley was determined to finish his trip that night. He climbed back in the little boat, and pushed off into the pitch black channel. He was never seen again. It became a matter of speculation: had the river claimed him, or had some associate he had once double-crossed been waiting for him on the mainland?

Bruce Lowery of Prince Edward County got into bootlegging reluctantly, but gained a reputation as a reliable and trustworthy rum-runner.

Three other Lake Ontario bootleggers, Tony Kane, William Sheldon and Bruce Lowery became legends in their own lifetimes. Kane was one of the most successful rum-runners on the lake, though he was also one of the first to undergo the indignity of being busted. A war veteran and a respected businessman in Syracuse, New York, Kane was almost always able to evade jail, either through bribery or sheer good luck. He did get sent to the penitentiary in Atlanta in April of 1930 after being caught with a load of Canadian ale, but was soon out on parole. His boats, the *Rene B.*, the *Blackjack,* and the *Firefly* were among the best in the rum fleet. Kane had one of his closest calls with the U.S. Customs, not for smuggling liquor, but for failing to pay duty on the *Firefly* (which he had bought in Toronto) when he took it to the United States.

One of the men who worked for Kane was William "Wild Bill" Sheldon, alias William Sheridan, alias John Woover. Wild Bill Sheldon was also an army veteran and had been smuggling for years by the time

Prohibition became law. He would smuggle anything as long as there was a dollar to be made. Wild Bill was a big man who loved to drink and spin yarns about his rum-running exploits. He had the distinction of being the most frequently arrested of the rum-runners and had spent time in jail. He did not carry a gun, but in the latter part of his career would keep sticks of dynamite handy to discourage Coast Guard vessels. On one of his escapades he was shot in the leg, and boasted afterward, "Hell, they'll have to do better than that to stop me. They'll have to shoot me in the head."

For awhile, Wild Bill was partners with Ulrich Meade, the only known black bootlegger on Lake Ontario. In May 1926, however, their boat, the *Jim Lulu*, was captured near Rochester after being shot up by a Coast Guard cutter. It did not help matters that Sheldon and Meade were already scheduled to appear in court on bootlegging charges that very day. They were each fined one thousand dollars and sentenced to six months. That was enough to make Meade seek other employment, but not Wild Bill. Since the western and central parts of Lake Ontario had become too hot for him, Sheldon moved his operation to the eastern end of the lake, where he met Tony Kane.

Bruce Lowery, the third man of the group, was one of many Prince Edward County residents who took to bootlegging, though he did so reluctantly. Hard luck of the worst kind struck Lowery when he was but twenty years old. A house fire took the lives of his father and two of his brothers, and left Lowery, his mother, and his younger brother (whom he had heroically rescued from the inferno) homeless and penniless. Lowery did a stint in the Canadian Army, and then worked as a commercial fisherman to support his family. He was a member of the Methodist Church, did not smoke and rarely drank. He became engaged to a young woman from a religious, staunchly prohibitionist family. However, Lowery was financially strapped. The price of fish was declining, and so were the catches on Lake Ontario. Against the advice of his family and without the knowledge of his fiancée and her family, Lowery decided to go to work for Dr. Hedley Welbanks. Doc Welbanks was a veterinarian who was also a known bootlegger. He was looking for a reliable man to run his boat, the *Rosella*. Everybody knew Lowery as reliable, responsible and one of the best sailors on the lake.

Lowery started running beer and whiskey in the spring of 1927. Everything went well until July 26, when the *Rosella* was confronted by a

Doc Welbanks, bootlegging veterinarian. When his boat the Rosella *was illegally seized and sold by the Coast Guard, Doc took it back at gunpoint.*

Coast Guard boat. Lowery did have a load of booze on board, but he was well inside *Canadian waters,* as witnesses on nearby islands would confirm. "Do you know where you are?" Lowery called to the skipper of the American vessel. "Never mind that, round up!" came the reply. With a machine gun pointing at him, Lowery had to comply. The *Rosella* was seized and towed to Oswego, where Lowery (giving a false name) was arrested.

Furious that his boat had been illegally seized, Doc Welbanks went to Oswego to protest and to reclaim his vessel. Lowery was released, but Doc lost the cargo of booze, and the *Rosella* was put up for auction in Rochester. Doc went there to buy back his boat, but was outbid by Dwight Palmer, owner of the Palmer Fish Company. Doc went back to Belleville with black thoughts forming in his mind. Palmer did some renovations on the *Rosella,* renamed it the *Verna,* and put it to work hauling fish.

On October 12 the *Verna* was in port in Brighton, Ontario, waiting out a storm. Doc Welbanks got wind of it. He went there, gun in hand, and seized his boat back. This caused a minor international incident. The Americans claimed that the boat had been legally confiscated and sold by the Coast

U.S. officers patrol the Detroit River. They stopped only a small percentage of the booze that flowed across the river. Truckloads of it also passed overhead on the Ambassador Bridge.

Guard, and was now the property of the Palmer Fish Company. Canadian Crown Attorney Bryson Donnan, speaking to the Toronto *Globe*, called the American seizure of a boat in Canadian waters, "high-handed piracy."

Eventually, title to the boat was restored to Doc Welbanks, though he was never compensated for the unlawfully confiscated liquor. Dwight Palmer was out the money he had invested in the vessel. Unfortunately for Lowery, his name appeared in the newspapers and his fiancée broke off the engagement.

Lowery continued bootlegging, and gained a reputation as a man who would get his cargo across no matter what the weather. He was also known as a man who would risk his own neck to help other sailors in danger from the elements, whether they were friends or total strangers. He worked for a while for Gentleman Charlie Mills, then bought his own boat, the 25-foot *Scout*. He armed himself with a rifle for defence against hijackers and for shooting out the searchlights of Coast Guard vessels.

By 1930 the ranks of the rum-runners on the Great Lakes had been somewhat thinned. Many had been scared off by an increasingly efficient Coast Guard. A new Canadian law forbidding the export of alcohol to the United States meant that the rum-runners also had to worry about the Ontario Provincial Police. Some bootleggers were cooling their heels in

Bruce Lowery (left) had to support his young brother Jimmy. His girlfriend Letty Hicks broke off their engagement when she learned that Lowery was a rum-runner.

American jails. The most unlucky had died with their boots on, victims of lawmen, hijackers or treacherous waters. But a core of tough, experienced die-hards still carried on. The money was just too good. Among them were Tony Kane, Wild Bill Sheldon and Bruce Lowery.

Two days before Christmas, 1930, Tony Kane and Wild Bill Sheldon left Bath, Ontario, with a load of beer for Oswego in Kane's 35-foot *Firefly*. By Boxing Day they had not reached their destination. The weather was terrible, and their buddies feared the worst. Several of them, including Lowery and another Canadian rum-runner named Cecil Phillips mounted a search by air, but a snowstorm forced the plane back to Kingston. They then set out in a motor launch for Main Duck Island, where they found Kane and Sheldon being entertained by Claude "King" Cole. The *Firefly* had developed engine trouble, and Wild Bill was making repairs. Relieved that his friends were alive and well, Lowery returned to Kingston, but Phillips chose to stay on the island. It was a fateful decision.

On New Year's Day, 1931, Kane and Sheldon shoved off in the *Firefly* to try to make Kingston. They battled the lake for five hours before they were forced back to Main Duck. The next day, in spite of high winds and heavy snow, they tried again. This time Phillips went with them. Two days later, in continuing bad weather, Lowery stopped off at Main Duck after making a delivery and learned that the *Firefly* had sailed on January 2.

He knew that it had not reached Kingston. He hurried back to the mainland and again initiated a search.

Engine trouble scuttled an attempted search by air, so a group of men went out in a motorboat. Heavy fog forced them back. Then the Kingston tugboat *Salvage Prince* took up the search. Despite horrendous sailing conditions, the tug prowled the waters around Wolfe Island, Pigeon Island, Main Duck and False Duck. The crew found nothing.

Four days after Sheldon, Kane and Phillips had last been seen, the weather was finally clear enough for a plane to go up. Meanwhile, Lowery took out a party of men in the *Blackjack*. Yet another group searching by boat became lost in the fog themselves for awhile. The American Coast Guard joined in the hunt, for a change engaging in their original task of search and rescue instead of gunning for bootleggers. Some cushions and pieces of wood were found floating near Amherst Island. Lowery identified them as wreckage from the *Firefly*. The Toronto *Globe* reported that there was not much hope for the "Sheridan party." In Syracuse, Kane's wife Lola and other members of the family were denying that Tony had gone to Kingston at all and were insisting that he was safe at home. His sister-in-law told a reporter from the Syracuse *Post Standard*, "I don't want to be discourteous, but I wish you wouldn't bother me any more."

On January 13, a body washed ashore at Cape Vincent, New York, at the headwaters of the St. Lawrence River. It was identified as that of Anthony Kane. The family had been trying to play down the news of his disappearance, out of concern for Kane's ailing mother. The corpse was found on Kane's 36th birthday. Cecil Phillips's body was found on Wolfe Island on April 18. The last of the doomed trio, Wild Bill Sheldon (or Sheridan, or John Woover) was found at Grenadier Island in May. Two days later it was revealed that his real name, after all, had been William Assman. No one ever knew what befell the *Firefly*. Those who knew the lake and the dead men surmised that they had probably been travelling too fast in water strewn with floating chunks of ice.

Bruce Lowery, perhaps reading the handwriting on the wall, quit the smuggling business and took on the less dangerous responsibility of running a still near Oswego. Late in 1931 he returned to Canada and was hired by the Gooderham & Worts distillery in Toronto. It was the least the company could do for a survivor of the bootlegging brotherhood which had kept its business alive.

Chicago streets. Throughout the Roaring Twenties the eyes of the world were on boozy, bloody Chicago. The blood was American, but most of the booze was Canadian.

THE IRON RIVER WHISKEY REBELLION
AND THE WAYWARD VOYAGE OF THE *ARBUTUS*

While the Lower Lakes, Erie and Ontario, bore the heaviest traffic of the bootlegging business, vast and remote Lake Superior witnessed its own dramas in the saga of Prohibition. There was a demand for alcohol in the domain of trappers, miners and loggers, and there were Prohibition zealots who were determined to keep the Superior country dry. One incident, which became almost comedic as the plot unfolded, was the "Whiskey Rebellion" in the tiny community of Iron River on Michigan's Upper Peninsula.

In February 1920, with Prohibition still new and bright with promise, an over-enthusiastic agent named Leo Grove seized barrels of home-made wine from members of the largely Italian village. The local State Attorney, Martin S. McDonough, told Grove that he could not confiscate the wine because he did not have a warrant. Furthermore, the wine was for the personal use of the people who owned it, and not for sale. Therefore, it was legal. Then he showed Grove the road out of town.

In a fury, Grove went to Chicago and complained to Major A.V. Dalrymple, the chief federal Prohibition officer for six Midwestern states, including Michigan. The picture Grove painted of Iron River was that of a "wide open" town where lawless men brazenly defied the federal government. He gave the impression that McDonough was the leader of a gang, which had prevented him from doing his duty and driven him from town.

Major Dalrymple bombastically told the press that he was going to take "as many men as are necessary from Chicago" to crush what he called a Whiskey Rebellion in Iron River. "I shall put respect and fear of the law in Iron County," he announced. He swore that he would arrest McDonough and "confiscate every still in the Upper Peninsula and destroy all bootleg liquor... Washington has told me to use my own judgement in this affair. My judgement is to go up and clean hell out of that district." The newspaper men grabbed the story and ran with it. A day later, headlines were screaming about a Whiskey Rebellion and defiance of the law in northern Michigan.

The people of Iron River were stunned—and scared. Many of them were immigrants and they did not want trouble with the government. Neither did they want to give up the homemade *vino* which was so much a part of their Old World culture. Most of the town turned out to help hide the barrels in old mine shafts, caves and the woods.

An army of journalists descended upon the little town, ready to write up lurid reports of a boozed-up frontier roost full of desperadoes. What they saw were white garments, towels and bedding hung out of windows—flags of surrender! The bewildered people thought that the army was coming and they were anxious to show that they had no desire to fight anyone. They professed their love for the United States, and one man proudly displayed the medals he had won in the Great War.

McDonough explained to the reporters that there was no Whiskey Rebellion, just a few Italian workers with some perfectly legal homemade wine. He also said that if Dalrymple came to make trouble, it would be *he* who would be arrested. McDonough knew that he had the local constabulary behind him.

Dalrymple did come, with 16 deputies and (he boasted) "600 rounds of ammunition." He said that he would deal with McDonough and his "confederates." They arrived on the night train, and the following morning, ignoring a request from McDonough for a meeting, set out to "clean up" the town. Learning that some barrels of wine were stored in the basement at the home of the local priest—undoubtedly a desperate character—Dalrymple went there with his posse of booze busters. They hauled the barrels out to the street and smashed them. Then they went to their hotel for lunch.

Disgusted that Dalrymple had refused to meet him to work out a peaceful solution, McDonough went to the hotel for a showdown. He strode in like an old-time gunfighter, stood in the middle of the room and said, "My name is McDonough." It did not bother him in the least that Dalrymple was surrounded by his men. There were police officers in the room, and reporters said that several hitched up their gunbelts. Then, with words rather than bullets, McDonough proceeded to cut Dalrymple down to size.

> I have read in the papers about various things which you plan to do to quell the whiskey revolt, as you call it. Now get this right—I will arrest you and your men and lock you up. Furthermore, if you or your men attempt to enter the homes of honest citizens here without due process of law, we likewise will arrest you and lock you up, and put you where you belong, Mr. Dalrymple.

Dalrymple grew red, stuttered, and blustered that he would continue his course of action and "see it through."

"You start something, and I'll see *you* through, Mr. Dalrymple— Major," McDonough replied. He went on to call shame on Dalrymple for the false things he had said in the press about the honest citizens of Iron River, and told him, "I don't believe you have quite as much guts right now as when you got off the train last night and dropped into this peaceful village."

The reporters took down every word. Dalrymple and his bully boys left town in a hurry, citing important business in Washington. With the departure of the "army of invasion," Iron River went back to being a quiet little town where Italian immigrants drank homemade wine with their meals. McDonough received telegrams from across the country, praising him as a hero.

A few months later, another bootlegging-related bit of burlesque had Michigan's Upper Peninsula in the news. The *Arbutus* was a 63-foot-long, leaky old steam tug, built in Wallaceburg, Ontario, in 1887. For 33 years it had been a workhorse, chugging through the cold, choppy waters of Lake Superior, hauling timber and other cargoes to Canadian and American communities on the shore of the world's largest freshwater lake. A tough little vessel in its heyday, the *Arbutus* even boasted steam-operated steering gear and an electric generator. It had been an honest worker, proving equal to all the tasks to which it had been assigned. Then came 1920 and

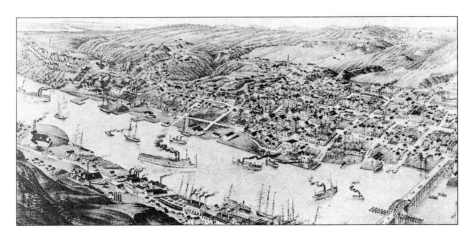

Houghton, Michigan, principal port on the Keweenaw Peninsula; the boozy crew of the Arbutus *missed it twice.*

Prohibition. Bootleggers who didn't mind taking the scenic route saw Superior as a convenient back door into the U.S.

On November 17, 1920, the *Arbutus* quietly cleared port at Port Arthur (now part of Thunder Bay), Ontario. According to the ship's manifest, it was carrying no cargo. Prohibition was not yet a year old, and this was a ploy already being used by bootleggers. The *Arbutus* was scheduled to go to Houghton, on Michigan's Keweenaw Peninsula. A couple of days out of port, engineer James Dampier became suspicious when he saw other crewmen moving crates on what was supposed to be an empty ship. Then he realized to his horror that those crewmen, M. McEacheron and John Dowd, as well as Captain George Stitt, were all intoxicated. Lake Superior in November is no place to be running a boat while under the influence. Moreover, the *Arbutus*, being navigated by drunks, was not heading in the direction of Houghton.

The Keweenaw Peninsula is 75 miles long and up to 50 miles wide, and boozy Captain Stitt almost missed it altogether. *Arbutus* steamed into port at Copper Harbor near the tip of the peninsula, many miles north of Houghton. At first Captain Stitt didn't even know he was in the wrong port. When he realized his error, he ordered the vessel to be turned around to head down the coast for Houghton. The lightkeeper at Copper Harbor noticed the unusual behaviour of the tug. Suspecting that it might be carrying liquor, he notified Thomas Coughlin, the deputy customs collector in Hancock, a town

The liquor-laden Arbutus *was destined for Houghton on the Keweenaw Peninsula. Instead, a drunken skipper and crew took the vessel into Copper Harbor, many miles to the north.*

just across the Keweenaw Waterway from Houghton. (The Keweenaw Waterway bisects the peninsula, making part of it an island.) Coughlin, in turn, telegraphed Leo Grove (of Iron River fame) in La Crosse, Wisconsin. If agent Grove had been anxious to deprive some Italian immigrants of a few barrels of home-made wine, he must have been on the verge of a stroke at the prospect of seizing a lakeboat full of liquor.

The *Arbutus* chugged on down the coast, and on November 20 arrived at Eagle Harbor. Once again, Captain Stitt mistakenly thought he was in Houghton. Again he realized his error, but as it was late he decided to anchor in the harbour overnight and continue the voyage in the morning. Then engineer Dampier made another frightening discovery. Where his coal supply should have been there were seventy cases of whiskey. The situation could hardly have been worse: a Canadian vessel full of booze, out of fuel, with three of its four men besotted, sitting in an American harbour! The captain decided they would remain at anchor for a few days and try to obtain fuel. They couldn't be arrested as long as the *Arbutus* didn't touch the dock. Somehow, word got to the captain that his boat was under suspicion, and scuttlebutt went around the community as to what was in the tug's coal bunker.

The following morning a party of federal Prohibition agents under the command of John Saul were on the dock, looking covetously across the water at the *Arbutus.* They couldn't touch the boat unless it pulled up to the dock, but it obviously wasn't going anywhere. Their wait ended at 2:00 p.m. when, to their surprise, the tug docked. Only two cold and hungry men were aboard, Dampier and Dowd—who were immediately arrested. Captain Stitt and McEacheron were gone. They were, at that moment, on a train heading for Canada. Not only had the two men given the Prohibition boys the slip, but the whiskey was gone, too!

Suspecting that the two remaining crewmen had dumped the liquor overboard, Saul sent a diver down to check Eagle Harbor's bottom. The man found nothing. Saul knew there was only one other explanation, since all that liquor didn't vanish into thin air. Eagle Harbor was only a small community, and it didn't take Saul long to find the whiskey—stashed away in almost every basement in town, including those belonging to some of the most important people in the community. During the night the good citizens had rowed out to the anchored *Arbutus* and bought every single bottle, and then had given Stitt and McEacheron a lift to shore. The captain's last order to Dampier had been to set fire to the *Arbutus* if it was in danger of being seized, but the engineer had a soft spot for the old tug and couldn't bring himself to destroy it. Besides, he wasn't about to compound his problems by committing arson.

On December 1 the *Arbutus* left Eagle Harbor with a captain, a Prohibition agent, and engineer Dampier on board, bound for Marquette farther down the Michigan coast. There the tug would be impounded at the government dock to await a court's decision as to its fate.

The trial got underway on January 17, 1921. James Dampier claimed that he had known nothing about the liquor on board the *Arbutus* until two days after leaving Port Arthur. He signed a 23-page statement detailing everything that had happened from the day they left port until the seizure in Eagle Harbor. He cooperated fully with the prosecution and was acquitted. Dowd was not there to testify. He had posted $1,000 bail and then skipped. Stitt and McEacheron had disappeared in Canada.

A number of Copper County, Michigan men were charged with a long list of offences including conspiring against the government, smuggling, importing whiskey and possession of contraband whiskey. Two prominent businessmen in Houghton (the town Captain Stitt had been too drunk to find) were said to have been the people who originally ordered the whiskey, which of course they denied. Some witnesses spoke of a major bootlegging conspiracy, complete with secret code words. A few men were fined $500, and most of the charges were eventually dropped.

Meanwhile, the old *Arbutus* was sitting on the bottom in shallow water, a disintegrating derelict. The Americans were going to burn the tug, but the Canadian government objected, pointing out that it was still Canadian property. The court said that the *Arbutus* could be released to the Canadian bank that held its mortgage, in return for $224 to cover the cost of seizure and storage. Almost a year after the *Arbutus'* fateful, drunken voyage across Lake Superior, two Canadians from Fort William, Ontario, Captain E.A. Fader and engineer Wilbert Toms, arrived in Marquette to take possession of the steamer. They raised the tug and spent ten days making repairs. On November 22, with two American sailors aboard as crew, Fader and Toms started the *Arbutus* on a homeward journey to Sault Ste. Marie. Two days later, off Grand Marais, they were struck by one of Superior's notorious "gales of November." They tried desperately to make harbour, but the churning seas ripped off the *Arbutus'* hatch cover and the tug began to flood. The four men launched their only lifeboat and abandoned the sinking *Arbutus* a mile from shore. No sooner were they in the rowboat than the lake capsized them. They clung to their overturned boat and drifted to shore. All of this was seen by the Deer Park Lifesaving Service on shore, but the would-be rescuers could not launch their boat, so angry were the seas. The shipwrecked men did finally make it to land—Captain Fader almost dead—and found shelter in a hunter's cabin.

A Coast Guard cutter in Grand Marais finally received word of the stricken vessel and set out into the teeth of the gale to find it. The cutter was almost wrecked itself in that steadily rising storm. As it was, the Coast Guard would have been too late. After a brief, inglorious career as a rum-runner, the *Arbutus* had gone to the bottom. The tug's story, like that of the Iron River Whiskey Rebellion, had been one of the less spectacular episodes in the annals of Prohibition.

Cash-strapped fishermen could earn good money smuggling liquor across the Lakes. The bottle on the bow of the boat at left indicates that the woman was quite aware of where the men went after dark.

HATCH'S NAVY

Prince Edward County, Ontario, is prime bootlegging territory. Joined to the mainland by a tiny neck of land (now cut by a canal, making the peninsula an island), it juts into Lake Ontario, separating the open waters of the lake from the Bay of Quinte. From overhead, it looks like a giant, natural wharf attached to the northeastern shore of the lake. In the days of the bootleggers, that's just what it was.

With 200 miles (325km) of shoreline, much of which is in secluded bays and inlets, Prince Edward County was the point of departure for thousands of boatloads of bootleg booze heading across the water to New York State. Because they could set out from land that extended well into the lake, the bootleggers had a relatively short run across open water. They also had the advantage of two distilleries right in their own backyard. Two enterprising Canadian brothers would capitalize on this accident of geography to build one of the most successful bootlegging operations in Canadian history, along with a beverage empire which thrives to this day.

Herb Hatch and his younger brother Harry were born in Prince Edward County in the 1880s. Their father, Bill, was in the hotel and saloon business, so the boys grew up gaining first-hand knowledge of the trade. As young men they tended bar for their father at the Oriental Hotel in Deseronto, a town just across the narrows on the Ontario mainland, and in a tavern on a nearby Indian reserve. In these establishments the bartenders had to be tough, because most of the customers were hard-drinking, working men who didn't shy away from a brawl. But Herb and Harry had a natural way with people.

(Left) Harry Hatch, c. 1925. The founder of Hatch's Navy developed a brilliant method for smuggling booze across Lake Ontario.

They were down-to-earth types who got along well with everybody.

Then Harry got married and, in 1911, opened a liquor store in Whitby. He did so well that two years later he and Herb became partners in a new liquor store in Toronto. The boys didn't know it yet, but they were on their way to the big time.

Harry was a brilliant businessman. He made important contacts with distillers in Scotland. As a travelling salesman covering the territory between Toronto and Montreal, he became familiar with everybody in the business and learned all the tricks of the trade. It wasn't often that Harry Hatch left an establishment without making a sale.

In 1916 the Ontario Temperance Act (OTA) forced the closure of bars and liquor stores in the province, so Harry and Herb moved to Montreal and went into the mail-order booze business. Liquor could not be legally sold in Ontario, but there was no law against ordering it by mail from Quebec. The Hatch brothers were extremely successful, thanks in large part to their many contacts in Toronto. They were briefly put out of business in 1918 when the federal government closed all distilleries as part of the war effort, but resumed making money off mail-order booze after the end of the First World War.

The brothers also made new partnerships. Harry linked up with Pud Woods, a man with solid connections in Ontario's racetrack circuit, to form Woods Limited. Herb and an Irishman named Larry McGuinness made the firm of Hatch and McGuinness. Both partnerships sold liquor in Ontario through the mail-order system, and to bootleggers in "dry" states south of the border. Harry also made the acquaintance of Sir Mortimer Davis, owner of the Canadian Industrial Alcohol Company, which owned the Corby distillery north of Belleville, and Wiser's distillery in Prescott.

In 1920, the Volstead Act brought the United States under national Prohibition, and a whole new world opened up for the Hatch brothers. Harry

In the early years of Ontario Prohibition, the Hatch brothers were in the mail-order business. Ontario residents paid for liquor in Quebec via the mail, and picked up the bottles in Ontario.

is alleged to have said, "Herb, that Volstead Act will make us millionaires." While the prohibitionists were still congratulating each other over the wonderful thing they had done, and toasting their great moral victory with buttermilk and sarsaparilla, the first illegal shots were being knocked back behind closed doors and bootleggers were gearing up to make sure the supply never ran short.

Most Canadian distillers had no twangs of conscience about selling alcohol to American bootleggers. Even when the Ontario Temperance Act was in force, making it illegal to sell liquor in Ontario, it was still legal to manufacture and export alcoholic beverages to other countries. As for the new American law, it did not touch Canadians on their own side of the international line. No laws were broken until the booze actually crossed the border. Sir Mortimer Davis, however, was a man who moved in exclusive social circles, and he was concerned about his reputation. He felt he couldn't risk becoming involved with bootleggers. As a result, sales of Corby's whiskey dropped, especially when the federal government outlawed the mail-order booze business in Ontario in 1921. The solution to Sir Mortimer's dilemma was the Hatch brothers. Harry became Corby's sales manager. Through him, whiskey would be sold to the firm of Hatch and McGuinness, who would then sell it on the American market. Under this neat arrangement Corby's sales skyrocketed from 500 gallons a month in 1921 to an astonishing 50,000 gallons a month in 1923, and Sir Mortimer didn't have to sully his image by dealing directly with rascally bootleggers.

For the Hatches, the shortest route to the American market was straight across Lake Ontario. They were fortunate that Corby's was close to the Bay of Quinte and Wiser's was on the St. Lawrence River. Contacts

(Left) Herb Hatch, c. 1951. Harry allegedly told his brother, "Herb, that Volstead Act will make us millionaires." (Right) J. Earl McQueen, seen here in 1942, was an experienced Great Lakes sailor and chief recruiter for Hatch's Navy.

helped a lot, too, and Harry and Herb had them on both sides of the water. They knew the residents of Prince Edward County who were willing to load up their boats with contraband liquor, and they knew the American bootleggers who wanted to buy it—and were willing to pay three or four times what it cost in Canada.

But it wasn't the Hatch style to do things in a haphazard way. They had a relative, Big Maudie Hatch, in Whitby. Big Maudie was a businessman who was a good friend to local fishermen. He had loaned money to a lot of them, taking out mortgages on their boats. Many of these mortgages were in arrears. Herb and Harry bought out Big Maudie's fishing boat mortgages, and then employed the fishermen as rum-runners. This was the beginning of "Hatch's Navy."

When an order came for a load of Corby's or Wiser's whiskey, the booze would be sent by rail to Whitby, where the fishermen picked it up. All the necessary government forms would be filled out. To avoid paying an excise tax the government levied on alcohol exported to the U.S., many bootleggers entered "Cuba" or "Mexico" on these forms. It did not seem to bother the customs officials that some boats were going to Cuba and Mexico two or three times a week. The Hatch brothers always admitted that their booze was going to the United States—which was not illegal—and paid the required duties. It galled the American government that the Canadian government not only allowed Canadian distillers and brewers to ship their goods to officially dry America, but also that Ottawa was making money off it.

As business picked up, Herb and Harry bolstered the Navy by hiring independent Prince Edward County boat owners. Their chief recruiter was Earl McQueen, an experienced Great Lakes sailor and a former lieutenant commander in the Royal Navy. Some of the Prince Edward County men who sailed for Hatch's Navy became bootlegging legends because of their daring exploits on the Lakes. Among them were: Earl's father, Captain John S. McQueen; Ben Kerr, "King" of the Lake Ontario rum-runners; Gentleman Charlie Mills; Archie Goyer, a barber who found that bootlegging paid better than cutting hair; and Jennie Batley, the only known Canadian woman rum-runner.

The bootleggers faced two dangers—the American Coast Guard and the lakes themselves. The latter was by far the more deadly, at least in the early days. The Great Lakes are, indeed, inland seas, and even Lake Ontario, with the smallest surface area, is no playground for amateur sailors. Treacherous currents, unpredictable winds and sudden storms have littered the lake bottoms with countless wrecks. Many an unlucky novice sailor, off on a bootlegging run for a lark and a few easy bucks, set out on those cold waters only to be washed ashore a corpse.

The American Coast Guard, on the other hand, was no great problem... at first. Established mainly as a life-saving and rescue service, it was ill equipped to deal with the flotillas of rum-runners coming across the lakes. The Guard had few boats, and those were too slow to catch most of the bootleggers. The Coast Guard on Lake Ontario received little help from municipal and state police, because New York Governor Al Smith was firmly against Prohibition. His attitude was: it's a federal law; let the feds try to enforce it.

Rum-runners crossing from Whitby or some cove in Prince Edward County would approach the American shore under cover of darkness. The boats, painted a dull grey (the Coast Guard called them "black ships"), were almost impossible to see. A pipe took the engine's exhaust underwater so there was no telltale noise. They might land at some lonely stretch of shore, where a flashing light told them the coast was clear. Farmers with shoreline property sold "landing rights" to American bootleggers. Or they might put

(Above) Port Dalhousie (now part of St. Catharine's, Ontario), one of several ports used by Hatch's Navy. Sailors who worked for the Hatch brothers were well paid and rarely had trouble with the law. (Left) Claude "King" Cole was a legendary bootlegger whose private domain of Main Duck Island was well known to most Lake Ontario bootleggers.

in at a dock where the lone customs officer on night duty had been bribed. One rum-runner, Claude Cole, whose base on Main Duck Island was a notorious bootleggers' lair, would even go up the New York State Barge Canal to Syracuse to unload. Once the booze had been delivered, the smugglers would turn their bows for home and disappear into the darkness.

The easy days came to an end, however, in 1924. The Coast Guard beefed up its Great Lakes fleet with fast, well-armed cutters, whose skippers would not hesitate to open fire on suspected rum-runners—a policy which led to some unfortunate "accidents." There was a purge of corrupt or incompetent officials and officers. Moreover, the American government, peeved at the lack of Canadian cooperation in discouraging bootlegging, had pressured the government of Prime Minister Mackenzie King into passing legislation that required Canadian customs officers to phone their American counterparts whenever a boatload of booze left a Canadian port for an American destination. Smugglers found ways around this inconvenience. One was to change the boat's name part way across. Thus, a boat, which left a Canadian port as the *Mary B.*, might enter American waters as the *Island Queen*. Still, things were getting dicey for the rum-runners now, as the Coast Guard actually started to catch some of them. A few were even being killed by Coast Guard bullets. The amateurs and the faint of heart now left the bootleg business to the professionals. Nobody was more professional than the brothers Hatch.

Before long, Hatch's Navy was operating out of Kingston, Belleville, Port Dalhousie, Whitby and the friendly harbours of Prince Edward County, as well as Port Colborne on Lake Erie. It was said that the brothers even had boats working Rum Row on the Atlantic Seaboard and a few on the Pacific Coast. Corby's was making so much money, Sir Mortimer Davis decided to expand his plant to keep up with demand. According to Harry Hatch, Sir Mortimer had promised Herb and him shares in the company, but when Harry raised the subject, Davis denied ever having made such an agreement. To the Hatch brothers, this was unacceptable, especially since it was they who had done all the work, ensuring that Sir Mortimer could keep his hands "clean." Harry and Herb decided to go into business for themselves.

Sitting in unused beauty near Toronto's waterfront was the old Gooderham & Worts distillery. The venerable firm, whose product had an excellent reputation among lovers of fine whiskey, had been closed for eight years and its equipment was antique. But to the Hatches it was a potential gold mine. Calling on friends in Scotland for financial help, Harry bought the old distillery in December 1923. Then he resigned from Corby's, taking with him his little black book of American contacts. To add insult to injury, he spirited away Corby's master blender, a man who would be difficult to replace. If Sir Mortimer was angry at losing Harry, the contacts and the blender, he must have been downright apoplectic at having to continue to sell through Hatch and McGuinness, knowing that their profits were going into the revitalized Gooderham & Worts, now a major rival.

The old Gooderham distillery did not have any aged whiskey in stock, and Canadian law stated that whiskey had to be aged at least two years before it could be sold. Harry had to get his product to market right

Gooderham & Worts Distillery, Toronto. Harry Hatch transformed the anti-quated whiskey mill into the cornerstone of a beverage empire.

away or face financial ruin, so his next coup was to talk the federal govern-ment into granting him an exemption from the two-year aging law. Newly distilled whiskey is inferior to aged whiskey, but Harry was certain this would make no difference to American drinkers. After all, they were happily buying up all the poor quality "swamp whiskey" the bootleggers could sell them, and not much of the "good stuff" from Canada made it through the pipeline unadulterated anyway.

Now Harry and Herb had to find a way to outwit the revamped American Coast Guard. They came up with a system that was brilliant in its simplicity. Most rum boat crews, when confronted with a Coast Guard cut-ter, tried to ditch the evidence by throwing their cargo overboard. This was time consuming, however, and if the Coast Guard caught up with the rum-runner before he could dispose of every single bottle, they had him. And even if the smuggler managed to deep-six all of his booze before the Coast Guard could get their hands on him, it still meant the loss of the cargo, which resulted in not only a serious financial setback, but also disappointed cus-tomers on the American side.

The Hatch brothers' first step was to fit out the fishing boats in their Navy with powerful engines, allowing them to haul bigger cargoes. Then, instead of loading the sacks of liquor *in* the boats, they packed them into nets which were slung *under* the boats. There were several advantages to this: the boat actually *looked* as if it was engaged in fishing; it could transport heavier loads because submersion in water reduced the weight of the cargo; and—if the Coast Guard did challenge the boat—the nets could easily be cut away, sending the evidence to the bottom of the lake. Even then, the cargo was not necessarily lost. Each load was equipped with a buoy and a heavy block of salt. When the salt melted, the buoy would rise to the surface, and the jettisoned whiskey could be retrieved. As an added precaution, when the "fishing fleet" sailed, fast decoy boats would be sent out to draw the Coast Guard away. Upon reaching the American shore, the rum-runners would cut the cargo loose on a shallow sandbar where American bootleggers could pick it up. This eliminated the danger of being caught while unloading. It also removed the risk of being ambushed by hijackers on shore.

This kind of savvy enabled Hatch's Navy to do something its rivals couldn't do: *guarantee* delivery. The independents on the Great Lakes found that if they wanted to survive in the business and stay out of jail, their best bet was to work with the Navy. They were welcome, provided they adhere to Herb and Harry's rules, which meant carrying only what was assigned to them and keeping their mouths shut. Rocco Perri, Southern Ontario's mob kingpin, was so impressed with the Hatch brothers' success that he put his own Lake Erie fleet of fifty rum-running boats in their capable hands. If liquor tycoon Sam Bronfman wanted to ship his product on the Great Lakes, he had to use Hatch's Navy.

Not all of the bootleg booze was destined for the American market. While the OTA was in effect in Ontario, some of the liquor would go to satisfy Canadian thirsts. Due to that peculiar law which allowed Ontario breweries and distilleries to export alcohol but not sell it at home, every case which left the manufacturer was under watchful government eyes until it was loaded onto a boat and cleared harbour, supposedly bound for a foreign port. To meet Ontario's demand for booze, some of it had to be re-imported, what was then known as "short circuiting." Landing a cargo back in Ontario could be just as tricky as landing it in the United States, because Canadian police had the same task as the American Coast Guard—to keep bootleg liquor out of their country—even if it *was* Canadian. Anyone they caught

smuggling it faced the same penalties they would on the other side of the water: arrest, confiscation, fines or possible imprisonment.

The Hatch brothers had a system for this phase of the operation, too. They purchased tiny Cedar Island just off the north shore of Prince Edward County, a few miles from Belleville. A rum-runner with a load of whiskey for the Ontario market would clear Belleville, then hide behind Cedar Island until after dark. He would then deliver his cargo to local bootleggers on the mainland.

The Hatch brothers were not satisfied with just being highly successful rum-runners. They had incredible foresight. In 1926 Harry Hatch negotiated one of the most astonishing business deals in Canadian history. The American-owned Hiram Walker distillery in Walkerville, near Windsor, Ontario, was up for sale. The Canadian government, at American urging, had set up a Royal Commission to investigate the liquor business, with particular

(Above) Walkerville, birthplace of Canadian Club whiskey. Hiram Walker set up business on the Canadian side of the river to avoid the condemnation of the American Temperance Movement. Ironically, his establishment became a major supplier of bootleg booze during Prohibition. (Left) The Walkerville Brewery. Beer manufactured here would run a gauntlet of cops and hijackers on its way to the warehouses of bootleggers like Al Capone and Dion O'Banion.

scrutiny given to smuggling. It wasn't likely that Ottawa would do anything to seriously interfere with what had become an incredibly lucrative export business employing thousands of Canadians, but questions were being asked at the hearings which could prove to be embarrassing to the distilleries' owners. The patriarch of the Walker family, Hiram Sr., had built his distillery on the Canadian side of the Detroit River in 1856 because of the growing temperance movement in the United States. He developed a mellow blend of whiskey that was to make Canadian rye famous around the world: Canadian Club. Now his heirs, Hiram Jr. and Harrington Walker, were worried that if they had to answer questions at a Canadian hearing, they could find themselves in trouble with American authorities. Like Sir Mortimer Davis, they were also concerned that their respectable family name could be tarnished. Associations with bootleggers just didn't go over well with the fellows at the country club. Therefore, the Walker brothers were anxious to unload their Canadian distillery.

Sir Mortimer was actually interested in buying Hiram Walker's, but in the end he walked away from the deal (to his subsequent regret). Sam Bronfman had just merged his liquor empire with the Distiller's Company Limited of London and Edinburgh, and had bought Seagram's distillery in Waterloo, Ontario, and so was not interested in Hiram Walker's. That left

The U.S. Coast Guard was not totally ineffective in its war against the rum-runners, as these pictures indicate. Four unlucky prizes are hauled into port by Guardsmen.

A Coast Guard vessel forces a rum-runner to heave to.

Barrels of beer sit on a Detroit dock, probably awaiting disposal.

the field wide open for Harry Hatch. He met with the Walker brothers and bought the distillery, plus its stock of four million gallons of aged whiskey for $14 million—about half its actual value. That the distillery was located right on the Detroit River and had its own export dock seemed almost too good to be true. Across the river was the city of Detroit, and beyond that the great thirsty American Midwest. The Coast Guard on the river was already overwhelmed with the liquor traffic pouring across from Canada, and Lake Erie wasn't far away. Harry Hatch was now at the helm of the biggest combined distilling operation in the British Empire, and Herb and McGuinness ran the biggest rum-running organization on the Great Lakes. Prohibition had indeed made their fortunes.

The Royal Commission investigating the booze business did bring about two setbacks for the Hatch brothers. Herb and Harry admitted under oath that they had been exporting alcohol to the United States. It wasn't illegal in Canada, and they had never denied it. But investigation revealed that they had also been re-importing liquor into Ontario. Consequently, they were stung for over $400,000 in unpaid sales taxes. And because American authorities were paying close attention to every word said at the Royal Commission hearings, Harry, Herb, and Frank McGuinness were indicted *in absentia* by a federal grand jury in Buffalo, New York, in December 1928. That meant they could not enter the United States without risk of being arrested. In a statement in the Toronto *Globe*, United States Attorney Richard Templeton said: "We are now striking directly at the heart of the powerful Canadian liquor-smuggling syndicates, and the results so far obtained may have far-reaching effects." This implied that the U.S. would be increasing the pressure on Ottawa to put a halt to the bootlegging. On the same page that featured the article in which this quotation appeared, there was another article about the death of a 21-year-old man from drinking "swamp whiskey."

In 1929, Harry handed the reins of the Hiram Walker–Gooderham & Worts empire over to Bill Hume, a new general manager he had lured away from Corby's under the nose of poor, put-upon Sir Mortimer, who must have rued the day he backed water on his old agreement with the Hatch brothers. Harry remained as chairman of the board, but devoted most of his time to his passion for breeding thoroughbred racehorses.

In that same year, the Mackenzie King government yielded to American demands. Boats carrying liquor destined for the U.S. were no longer allowed clearance from Canadian ports. This slowed down the bootlegging, but it did not stop it. The Hatch brothers and other distillers sent their booze the long way, via the French islands of St. Pierre and Miquelon off the coast of Newfoundland. And Hatch's Navy continued to slip across the Lakes and the Detroit River.

The new Canadian regulations, increased vigilance by the American Coast Guard, and the onset of the Great Depression after the stock market crash of 1929 made bootlegging a more difficult and less profitable game in the final years of Prohibition. Many of the Navy's old stalwarts quit the business while the quitting was good. In the early 1930s, it was evident to all but the most diehard prohibitionists that the "Noble Experiment" was a failure, and the Volstead Act would be repealed. Ever the visionary, Harry Hatch was ready for that. Even before Prohibition finally died in 1933, Hatch had begun construction on a big new distillery in Peoria, Illinois. It was completed in 1934, the biggest liquor mill in the world—and every drop of whiskey it sold would be perfectly legal. A monument, in a way, to a pair of Canadian brothers who started out as bartenders in Prince Edward County, Ontario, and to the sailors of Hatch's Navy.

Swashbuckling Ben Kerr as he appeared in 1906. Kerr was tough and absolutely fearless. In the end that would be his undoing.

BEN KERR
KING OF THE RUM-RUNNERS

Of all the Great Lakes rum-runners, Ben Kerr was one of the most swashbuckling and daring. In a nobler pursuit, he might have earned fame as an explorer or sailed to glory in international competition. But Kerr chose the sailor's version of the Old Outlaw Trail. His devil-may-care duel with the American Coast Guard and the dark waters of Lake Ontario, until that night when he mysteriously died with his boots on, earned Kerr the title, King of the Rum-Runners.

John Benjamin Kerr was born in Hamilton, Ontario, in 1884 on February 29, a day considered by many to be lucky. Unlike so many future bootleggers and rum-runners who grew up in poverty, Kerr had an upper-middle-class background. His grandfather, father, and uncle were all fish and game inspectors, so Ben spent much of his youth in the Great Outdoors, learning to hunt, handle boats and predict the weather by studying the sky. He was not a scholarly boy, but he loved music and became an accomplished pianist. He left school early and became a plumber, preferring the company of working men to that of high society. A strong believer in trade unions, Kerr had his first brush with the law during the long, violent Hamilton Street Railway strike of 1909. When soldiers enforcing a curfew barged into an ice-cream parlour in which Kerr was entertaining patrons with the piano, he stood up to them and allegedly felled two of them with his piano stool. Kerr was cleared of assault charges, but emerged as something of a local "working class hero."

(Above) Claude "King" Cole (left) on Main Duck Island, a popular bootlegger rendezvous. Cole saw Kerr face down hard case George Keegan. (Right) Hamilton, Ontario, where Ben Kerr was known as a bootlegger and something of a working-class hero.

In 1912, Kerr married Louisa May Byrons and a year later their daughter Helen was born. Married life would not sit well with him. His wife did not share his enthusiasm for the outdoors, and he would have at least one extra marital affair. With the coming of the First World War, he embarrassed his family by opposing the war, conscription, and the wartime profiteering of Canadian industrialists.

In 1910 Kerr had bought a waterfront lot along the Hamilton shoreline and started construction on a dock and fifty boat lockers. He continued working on it through the war years, and by 1918 was trying to make his way in the boat storage and rental business. With his friend, Jack Morris, he also started a speedboat-building company. Things did not go well, however, due to a post-war recession, and he later told a friend that "after the war, my family and I were nearly starving." Then came Prohibition.

Kerr had everything it took to be a successful rum-runner. He knew Lake Ontario well, he had nerve, and he had two boats to start out with—a 28-footer and a 30-footer. He started running beer and whiskey across the lake in April or May of 1920. By August he had paid off the mortgage on his boat storage property. He also began construction on a big new home for his family, and a second house to rent out.

Kerr was not breaking any Canadian laws by ferrying booze across Lake Ontario. Although the Ontario Temperance Act forbade the sale of alcoholic beverages in the province, it was perfectly legal to export it, American Prohibition notwithstanding. As one Canadian judge said, "There is no burden cast upon us to enforce the laws of the United States."

Kerr bought whiskey at Corby's distillery near Belleville, beer from any one of a number of Southern Ontario or Montreal breweries, and ran it across to Youngstown or Olcott, New York. The U.S. Coast Guard at this time was only equipped for life-saving and rescue operations. There were but 16 state troopers to patrol the whole northern border of New York State, and local police forces were not equipped to deal with rum-runners. The governor of New York himself was flat against Prohibition.

The biggest threat to smugglers (who preferred to call themselves "exporters"), aside from the lake itself, was hijackers. For protection, rum-runners hired "muscle" or went armed. Kerr carried a .45 revolver, a rifle, and a shotgun. He often stopped at Main Duck Island, a regular rum-runners' port o' call owned by Claude "King" Cole, himself a legendary smuggler. On one of his visits there, Kerr intervened in what could have been a tragedy. A couple of fishermen had pilfered some beer from bootlegger Gentleman Charlie Mills and his partner George Keegan. One of the toughest men on the lake, Keegan was a hard case who would one day work for New York gangster Jack "Legs" Diamond. Gentleman Charlie pulled a gun and seemed about to shoot one of the guilty fishermen when Kerr stepped

in and took the pistol from him. It happened so fast that Keegan, who was Mills' "muscle," barely had time to react. When he did make a move on Kerr, he found himself looking down the bore of the gun. Kerr then took the bullets out of the gun and handed it back to Mills. Kerr was now unarmed, but Keegan wanted no part of him. He and Mills walked away.

Soon Kerr was not only running booze to the U.S., but also "short circuiting" cargoes back into Ontario. This meant loading up with liquor supposedly destined for a foreign market, heading out onto the lake and then doubling back to land it on the Ontario shore, where it would be picked up by local bootleggers. For a lone wolf like Kerr, it was a form of double jeopardy. Southern Ontario was the "turf" of Rocco Perri, the province's biggest bootlegger. Perri had already eliminated most of his competitors, and Kerr's trespassing would not go unnoticed. But Kerr, the rugged individualist, carried on delivering booze to both shores, unconcerned that he might be living on a very narrow edge indeed.

By 1922, Kerr was running booze in the 35-foot *Evelyn* and a twin-engine speedboat. He hired two men, John Elliot and John Clark, to take short beer runs from Hamilton to Youngstown, while he made the longer trips from Belleville to a place near Rochester.

Ben Kerr's speedy rum boat, the Evelyn. *The man at the stern is Kerr's partner, Alf Wheat. He and Kerr would share the same mysterious fate.*

It was about this time that Kerr tangled with hijackers. Bootleggers were constantly stealing each other's wares, one obvious reason being that a stolen cargo could be sold for one hundred percent profit. The other reason was to scare off competition. The fewer bootleggers operating in an area, the greater the demand for whiskey and beer and the higher the prices. Hijackings could be violent, as the bootlegger had to rely on his own resources to protect his investment. He couldn't go to the police and complain that he'd been robbed.

As a precaution, Kerr made it a point never to actually land on the American shore. His buyers had to come out to his boat to get the cargo. This would give him a head start if the law—or someone worse—showed up. On this particular night he was a short distance from shore, passing sacks of ale to a man in a rowboat and to other men who had waded waist-deep into the water. Suddenly, as a rum-runner recalled in later years, "all hell broke loose, bullets were flying everywhere." There were gun flashes on the shore, and Kerr immediately grabbed his rifle and began firing at them. The men he'd been working with had scattered when the shooting started, but they regrouped as Kerr's fire drove the hijackers back. Then Kerr gunned his motor and took the boat about two hundred yards down the coast. He went ashore with his .303 rifle in one hand, his 12-gauge shotgun in the other, and his .45 pistol stuck in his belt. Outflanking the hijackers, he laid down a barrage of lead, shifting from one gun to the other to give the impression that more than one man was shooting. The hijackers fled. Kerr never knew if he had killed or wounded any of them. The close call moved him to make out his will.

In 1923, Kerr obtained the boat that became his pride and joy: the *Martimas*, a 42-foot cabin cruiser with a capacity for 1,200 sacks of whiskey or beer. It could do 15 knots and the hull was sheathed in steel, which meant

Hamilton crime boss Rocco Perri. Kerr did not like working for Perri, but was in no position to argue with him. Perri had a habit of bumping off people who crossed him.

that Kerr could brave the ice floes of winter, a season when even the Coast Guard vessels were in dry dock. *Martimas* was one of the largest rum-runners on the lake, and one of the most successful—facts which finally drew the attention of Rocco Perri.

Rather than have Kerr blasted into oblivion, the usual fate of Perri's rivals, Rocco decided to make him tow the Perri line. There is evidence that Perri went to Herb Hatch, through whom he bought whiskey from Gooderham & Worts in Toronto, a distillery owned by Herb's brother Harry. Rocco was the Hatch brothers' biggest customer, so he had pull with them. The deal was that Kerr had to stop running booze into Ontario, in return for which Perri put him in touch with Joe Sotille, an American bootlegger. Kerr would run Gooderham & Worts whiskey across the lake to Sotille, and would bring raw alcohol back to Canada. Raw alcohol had a variety of industrial uses and was unfit for human consumption. Bootleggers tried to "cook" poisonous impurities out of it, so it could be passed off as whiskey in bottles with forged labels. The gangsters who engaged in this nefarious business rarely had the chemical knowledge to do the job properly, so much of their fake whiskey was plain poisonous. Kerr may or may not have been aware of just how potentially lethal the rotgut was, but he was in no position to buck Perri.

By 1925 Kerr had three large cruisers on the lake. He captained the largest one, the *Martimas*, himself, with Elliot and Clark as crew. He hired other men to operate the smaller boats. Elliot was also a pilot and had a float plane which he kept near Kerr's Marine Garage. He quite likely used it to fly "reconnaissance," to watch the movements of the ever-growing American Coast Guard fleet.

One man working for Kerr was Alf "Gunner" Wheat, whom he may have met through Perri. Originally from England, Wheat was a decorated war vet who had been wounded at Vimy Ridge. Twice married, he now had seven children to care for. In 1920, like so many other men pressed for money, Wheat turned to bootlegging, running truckloads of beer from Kitchener to Hamilton. He had a friend on the Hamilton police force who kept him informed of police movements.

Like Kerr, Alf Wheat had had run-ins with hijackers, and had once been badly beaten up by them. He eventually found himself working for Rocco Perri under circumstances similar to those of Kerr. Perri was always looking for good men, and it would have been ill advised for Wheat to continue operating as an independent once Perri knew he was working in his territory. Alf Wheat became one of Kerr's staunchest friends, dividing his time between trucking beer overland for Perri, and taking Kerr's smaller boats for short runs across the lake. Wheat and Kerr got along extremely well, never arguing—which was unusual for men in a high-risk business. Wheat did have one big fault: he was an alcoholic.

One person with whom Ben did not get along was Bessie Starkman, Rocco Perri's "wife" (she had abandoned her real husband and her children to be with Rocco). Bessie was, in the parlance of gangsters, a "tough broad." She handled the books for Perri, and was the brains behind his bootleg empire. She had an abrasive personality, and was known to welch on financial agreements. Ben Kerr, a rebel who didn't like taking orders from *anybody*, would have been especially galled at being dictated to by a woman.

Nonetheless, with the American Coast Guard and the Ontario Provincial Police becoming more and more adept at catching bootleggers, Rocco and Bessie needed men like Kerr. For Kerr, even though he had to give Perri a cut, the money was still good. He expanded his Marine Garage, one of the additions being a secret room for storing booze. He built a dance studio for his daughter, and he was helping to put his younger brother Albert through university. Kerr was also sponsoring an industrial league hockey team, the Pals. Supporting a group of young men in the wholesome Canadian game of hockey provided a positive balance to the negative associations of his trade.

As the Twenties continued to roar, fuelled by bootleg booze, the American government pressed the government in London, England (which still controlled Canadian foreign policy) to make the Canadian government pass laws against exporting liquor to the U.S. Mother England didn't want to get *too* bossy with Canada, considering the huge contribution Canadians had made to the war effort. But for trade purposes she had to placate the Americans. Thus, it became illegal to ship booze to the U.S. on trains, shutting down an important bootleg supply line, and making the Great Lakes route all the more necessary. It was agreed that when a rum-runner left a Canadian dock, the customs service would notify authorities at the American port to which the boat was officially bound. Rum-runners got around this by giving false destinations, by changing the name boards on their boats in mid-voyage, or by laying over at Main Duck Island for a few days to throw the Coast Guard off. Some Canadian customs officers could also be bribed to simply look the other way when a rum boat was departing. For their part, the Americans improved on the quality and armament of Coast Guard vessels, and converted boats seized from rum-runners into vessels for their own fleet. They equipped their boats with radios, a technological innovation which smugglers like Kerr countered by installing radios of their own.

One advantage—if it can be called such—that Ben Kerr had was the willingness to cross the lake in winter. From mid-December until spring breakup, shipping on the Great Lakes would shut down. Lighthouses went dark; the Coast Guard went into dry dock. Ice and severe weather conditions made navigation so dangerous that one would have to be extremely brave or downright crazy to venture out onto the lakes. Ben Kerr did not consider himself crazy. He laid up his smaller boats for the winter, but made crossings in the *Martimas*, which was large enough to weather storms and whose steel armour protected it from ice.

By 1925 the American authorities knew who Kerr was, and they badly wanted to catch him, in the way that lawmen of an earlier age wanted to get their hands on Jesse James. Perhaps they had even heard of his boast, "I can outwit the feds anytime." His smaller boats, the *Evelyn* and the *Sparkley* could always outrun the Coast Guard vessels, but his flagship, the *Martimas* was built for capacity rather than speed. To avoid capture, Kerr had to be smarter than the Coast Guard men. He always made his runs at night and never when there was a full moon. In American waters he turned off his running lights, which was in itself illegal. He kept changing his drop days so the Americans could not establish any sort of routine in his movements, and he stuck to his policy of not landing on the American shore. All of this, however, could not protect him from an act of betrayal.

Dangerously working outside his arrangement with Rocco Perri, Kerr was making deliveries to John "Butch" Schenk and Mae "Happy"

Kerr's 47-foot cabin cruiser, the Martimas. *Losing this boat to the Coast Guard was a heavy blow.*

Goldstein at a place called the Oklahoma settlement just outside Rochester. Schenk was a major bootleg supplier for northern New York State and Goldstein was one of his top lieutenants. She was known to carry a .45-calibre pistol. One of their principal rivals was William Rund, owner of Rochester's Standard Brewery. Licensed to make near-beer, he was actually making real beer and keeping the law off his back with bribes. He, or someone associated with Standard Brewery, managed to plant a spy in the Schenk organization.

Sometime in the third week of May 1925, Kerr loaded the *Martimas* with 1,200 cases of beer for the Oklahoma settlement. John Elliot and John Clark were along as crew. Since the customs at Trenton had to notify the Americans that he had left harbour with booze, Kerr put in at Port Hope for a few days to keep the Coast Guard guessing. On May 26 he struck out across the lake. He did not know that the Coast Guard, the Customs Border Patrol, and the local Prohibition agents had been tipped off and had laid an ambush.

In the early hours of May 27, the *Martimas* was off the Oklahoma settlement shore unloading the beer into a rowboat, which was shuttling it to shore. American lawmen were patrolling the roads leading to the bootleggers' lair, and the Coast Guard was closing in by water. Before the unloading was completed, Kerr sensed danger. With three of the men from the unloading party still aboard, he gave the *Martimas* full throttle and roared for open water, heading for the Canadian side of the line. He was too late, though, and the faster Coast Guard picket boat was closing in on him.

As the men on the *Martimas* worked frantically to throw the rest of the sacks of beer overboard, the officer on the Coast Guard boat ordered Kerr to "heave to." Kerr ignored the order. Nor did he stop when the Guardsmen fired several warning shots over his bow. But when the Coast Guard machine gun put a round into his hull, Kerr had no choice but to give up. There were still some bags of beer on board the *Martimas,* so Kerr and his men were caught red-handed.

Back at the Oklahoma settlement the agents and patrolmen rounded up several members of the bootleg gang. One inspector approached a shadowy figure in the darkness, what appeared to be a man in a slouched hat and overalls. As the inspector drew near, the figure suddenly drew a gun. The inspector grabbed the weapon, and then saw that his "man" was actually Mae Goldstein, the gun-toting lady bootlegger. Strangely, she was the only one of those arrested to have the charges against her dropped, after which she quietly disappeared. This led to speculation that she may have been the informer.

The police raiders found plenty of evidence in the smugglers' hideout: money, guns, beer, liquor and wine. They tore the place apart expecting to find drugs, but found none. However, the elusive King of the Rum-Runners was in their hands at last. A journalist for the Rochester *Democrat and Times* wrote, "Kerr is the most daring rumrunner on the lake. For the past three years the Federal men have been laying for him at various points along the lake but always he would appear where they least expected him."

While Kerr was in jail waiting for bail to be arranged, Rochester got a taste of the kind of "bootleg war" violence usually associated with bigger cities like Detroit and Chicago when somebody dynamited the Standard Brewery. Kerr's bail was set at $10,000, but his lawyer had it reduced to $5,000. On June 16 he was released, and just before crossing the border back to Canada he brazenly announced to some astonished reporters that he was going right back to the "ale fleet." But for all his bravado, Kerr had taken a serious financial blow. Since he had no intention of returning to the U.S. to stand trial he would forfeit the bail money. He had lost thousands of dollars worth of cargo and, worst of all, he had lost the *Martimas*. The cruiser was turned over to the Coast Guard, who used it to catch other smugglers.

Even though one of Ben Kerr's rum-running colleagues said that Kerr "wasn't afraid of nobody," Kerr was very worried about going to prison. This concern was reinforced when, only a week after his return to Canada, his boat, the *Sparkley*, was captured by the Coast Guard. Alf Wheat and another man escaped arrest by fleeing into the woods with customs officers' bullets whizzing around them. Once again, the feds had been tipped off, possibly by someone from Standard Brewery, or possibly by Rocco Perri. Rocco and Bessie didn't like Kerr's independent ventures, and had already leaned on Gooderham & Worts to stop selling him whiskey.

Kerr's crewmen, John Clark and John Elliot, were caught and sent to jail for two months. Then it was revealed that one night, while running without lights in American waters, Kerr's boat had accidentally collided with a smaller boat and two Americans had drowned. The American officials wanted to charge Kerr with manslaughter. Meanwhile, the Coast Guard was catching rum boats with what was to the bootleggers, frightening regularity. One prize was yet another craft that might have belonged to Ben Kerr.

Kerr was, in fact, hiring men to take his shipments across the lake— small fry, the Coast Guard said whenever they caught them. The boats they used were inexpensive and no major loss. But the American authorities dearly wanted to get The King back in their clutches. When he didn't show up for his trial, they talked of extraditing him. When they seized a load of champagne at an inn near Rochester, they accused Kerr of being the rumrunner who had smuggled it across the lake. The Toronto *Globe* reported on December 5, 1925: "Customs men have had repeated warnings that Ben Kerr, who has styled himself 'King of Canadian Liquor-runners' has been landing large cargoes of champagne near Rochester for the holiday trade."

Kerr denied it, telling the press that he had not been in American waters since his capture on May 25. He offered to donate five thousand dollars to any Hamilton charitable institution if any American Prohibition officer could prove he had been in American waters since his arrest. "Tell the Coast Guard to put up, or shut up," he said. He added that he didn't even know what champagne looked like.

Kerr could have retired from the rum-running business. His house was paid for, as was the one he rented out. His Marine Garage was doing well. Moreover, his wife wanted him to quit. The booze business was getting increasingly dangerous, not only because of the law, but also because it was becoming more and more the territory of organized crime—a cash cow for the likes of Al Capone, Dutch Schultz, the Purple Gang... and Rocco Perri.

But something, be it avarice, stubbornness, or just the need to beat odds that were steadily increasing, the need to "live on the edge" drove Kerr to continue. But not until he had a boat that could outrun anything the Coast Guard could put in the water!

The *Pollywog* was forty feet long and seven feet in the beam. Its hull was sheathed in steel for protection from ice. It had twin 180-horsepower engines. The bow and hull were designed to make the boat plane at high speeds. At full throttle the *Pollywog* could reach an astounding (for the time) 40 miles per hour. Now Ben Kerr could leave the Coast Guard bobbing in his wake. But the Coast Guard wasn't playing games. In 1926 they opened fire on a Lake Ontario rum-runner named Leo Yott who refused to heave to. Over a hundred rounds poured into his 52-foot cruiser, the *Andy*. Yott was the first rum-runner to be killed by the Coast Guard on the Great Lakes. Not even the *Pollywog* could outrun bullets.

Kerr began making runs in the *Pollywog* in April 1926, very often alone, but sometimes with Alf Wheat. The *Pollywog* soon had the reputation of being the fastest boat on Lake Ontario, and Ben Kerr was becoming a legend. He was at the top of the Coast Guard's "most wanted" list, and the American government had a $5,000 reward posted for information leading to his capture.

Then came the poison booze scare of July 1926. A batch of almost pure wood alcohol got into the bootleg pipeline, courtesy of Joe Sotille, the

Kerr's last boat, the Pollywog, *seen here in Hamilton Harbour in the winter of 1925–26, could reach the astounding speed of 40 mph. But even the fastest boat couldn't out-run bullets.*

American bootlegger who was connected to both Kerr and Rocco Perri. Dozens of people died or were made blind. Sotille escaped to Sicily via Canada and Britain, but Kerr and Perri were among those arrested for manslaughter. They were held without bail for four months, but were finally released when police could not positively link them to the poisonous liquor. Kerr emphatically denied throughout that he had smuggled bad booze into Canada.

The poison liquor scare nonetheless had an effect on the bootlegging careers of both Perri and Kerr. It hastened the death of Prohibition in Ontario, closing down the province as a market for bootleggers. It eliminated Rocco Perri's source of American raw alcohol. It made association with Rocco Perri odious to Ontario distillers, who now declined to do business with him. Perri had to get his liquor from as far away as Vancouver. Kerr, however, could still buy from Ontario distilleries, and as far as he was concerned, Perri no longer had any kind of hold on him.

Kerr began working exclusively in the eastern end of Lake Ontario, buying his liquor from Corby's near Belleville, and running it to the New York shore between Rochester and Oswego. In winter he would operate out of Whitby. He hired Jack Morris Jr. as an extra crewman, because Alf Wheat's drinking was getting out of hand. Morris later related that the *Pollywog* was chased by the Coast Guard many times, but "they could never catch us."

When a Royal Commission was set up to investigate bootlegging, Kerr was one of those called upon to testify. He conducted himself coolly and intelligently on the stand, not incriminating himself, but also not perjuring himself—unlike Rocco and Bessie who lied when their turn came. Rocco Perri wound up serving four months in jail.

With his Ontario market pretty well dried up, Perri had to concentrate on selling more booze across the border. He bought a sixty-foot-long cruiser called the *Uncas*, which could hold 1,200 cases of booze, and began operating out of Port Hope. Perri, of course, hired men to do the actual smuggling, never going on a booze run himself. But he was in direct competition with Kerr, and Perri didn't like competition.

The odds against Ben Kerr were mounting. The Coast Guard was, in the words of another Canadian bootlegger, "awful desperate to catch him." On one occasion a Coast Guard boat spotted the *Pollywog* and immediately opened fire. There was no order to "heave to," no warning shot across the bow. With Jack Morris Jr. piling whiskey cases behind the pilot house to shield Ben from the bullets, Kerr gave the boat full throttle and got away. He later found eight bullet holes in the *Pollywog*. The Coast Guard had apparently adopted a shoot-on-sight policy for Ben Kerr. One day the Coast Guard even tried to get Kerr on his home ground. Three Coast Guardsmen went into the Bayview Hotel in Hamilton looking for Kerr and boasting what they would do to him once they found him. Kerr was present and happy to oblige them. He knocked out the first man with a single blow. A few more jabs and hooks, and the others fled.

The steadily increasing efficiency of the Coast Guard and the escalating violence of hijackings drove all but the most determined rum-runners off the lake. Ben Kerr was a big, tough man whose reputation was such that it was said no hijackers would mess with him. But some of those moving into the business had reputations of their own.

One such gang was the Staub brothers—Midge, George, Karl and Ed—who had moved to Rochester from Cleveland. The Staubs were a mean bunch by anyone's reckoning. They had tangled with the Purple Gang and come out on top. Ed had been a rustler in Nevada, where he killed a man in a gunfight. The Staubs soon took over the bootlegging business in

Rochester, eliminating rivals in whatever way was necessary. Their fifty-foot boat was even better armed than the Coast Guard vessels. The Staubs used their muscle and firepower to hijack at every opportunity.

The presence of the Staubs may have been the reason that Ben Kerr moved his winter base to Presqu'ile Bay. He was no coward, but he wasn't a fool either. From remote Presqu'ile he could operate relatively free of the Staubs and Perri. He had two independent bootleggers in Rome and Utica, New York, whom he kept supplied with beer and whiskey. Having severed his ties with Perri, Kerr would have nothing to do with the other mobsters who were gaining a stranglehold on the booze business. Just the same, Jack Morris Jr. quit Kerr in the fall of 1928. He felt that Kerr just took too many chances, especially in the treacherous conditions of winter.

On February 24, 1929, Ben Kerr and Alf Wheat set out in the *Pollywog* with a load of beer. They expected to be back the next day. They weren't. As the days passed, their families wondered—hoped—that weather had forced them to put in at Main Duck Island, where there was no telephone. No one could get through the ice to Main Duck until March 22. The caretakers there had not seen the *Pollywog*. Rumours began to circulate: Ben and Alf had been victims of hijackers; someone had gone after the $5,000 reward the Coast Guard was offering for Kerr.

Not long after, a man walking his dog along the lakeshore near Colborne, Ontario, found a man's hand and some human bones. A tattoo on the hand identified the remains as those of Alf Wheat. A few days later Ben Kerr's body was found floating just offshore. Later, some wreckage of the *Pollywog* was discovered.

The families of the dead men believed that they were murdered, either by hijackers like the Staubs or by the henchmen of Rocco Perri. Author C.W. Hunt, whose book *Whiskey and Ice* is the definitive biography of Ben Kerr, does not agree. He presents convincing evidence that the *Pollywog* ran out of gas and was trapped in the ice. It was crushed, and Kerr and Wheat died in the frigid water. Wheat's body was dismembered by the grinding action of the ice.

Ben Kerr knew Lake Ontario as well as any man alive, and for almost ten years it was his highway to riches. But in the end, it was the lake that claimed him.

"Gentleman" Charlie Mills and Jennie Batley. The young Englishwoman liked the air of adventure about the soft-spoken rum-runner.

Gentleman Charlie Mills

Charlie Mills was in many ways just the opposite of Ben Kerr. Canadian-born Kerr was forceful and cut an imposing, sometimes menacing figure. Mills, a native of Sanborn, New York, was slightly built, a man whose quiet, soft-spoken manner earned him the nickname "Gentleman Charlie." Kerr was a natural sailor. Mills was more at home in the cockpit of an airplane than he was at the helm of a boat. Two attributes Mills did share with Kerr, though, were nerves of steel and a desire to make lots of money fast.

Born in 1879, Charlie Mills grew up in an era in which people were fascinated with the idea of "flying machines," and was only 24 when the Wright brothers proved, in 1903, that mechanized flight was possible. Only a decade after that first feeble hop through the air, North Americans were being thrilled by a new spectator sport called barnstorming. Men in aircraft that were little more than wings and an engine held together with canvas and bailing wire performed death-defying stunts, to the astonishment of the crowds below. Actually, just going up in one of those hand-built contraptions was courting fate.

Among those few people brave (or foolhardy) enough to defy gravity and the gods was Charlie Mills. He became a pilot with a flying circus that performed at Niagara Falls. Mills would race his hydroplane against speedboats, or—even more dramatic—fly under the Niagara Falls suspension bridge. The latter was particularly hazardous because the downdraft of air currents in the narrow gorge of the Niagara River could easily

Mills' bodyguard, George Keegan, would one day work for New York gangster Jack "Legs" Diamond, shown here (at right) with his brother Ed.

drag a flimsy airplane into the murderous whirlpools below. Mills crashed his plane at least twice, and on the second occasion actually went down in the river, but was saved from drowning by his life jacket.

The money Mills earned as a stunt pilot was enough for a single man to get by on—just. He had a few ideas for aircraft design, which drew some interest from the American military, but not enough for Uncle Sam to grant any financial support. Mills didn't have enough money to develop his innovations. He quit flying for a living, probably took a factory job, got married, and fathered two children. When the United States belatedly entered the Great War in 1917, Mills was 37 and considered too old for service in the army. An Armistice was declared in 1918, the war officially ended in 1919, and in 1920 the Volstead Act became the law of the land in the United States. Suddenly there was a way for a daring, not-so-young man to make a bundle of money.

Mills arrived in Ontario's Prince Edward County sometime in the early 1920s. He was one of many attracted by the advantages this irregularly shaped peninsula offered to the bootlegging fraternity: close proximity to breweries and distilleries in Ontario and Quebec; a fishing population who knew boats and the lake; a relatively short run to the American shore; a convenient way station at Main Duck Island; and plenty of secluded, natural anchorages.

Before long, Gentleman Charlie was one of the best-known bootleggers in the eastern end of Lake Ontario and, from all appearances, one of the wealthiest. He had two or three cars, an airplane, a speedboat, and two big boats which he used for rum-running. He kept a room in a Belleville boarding house, and the landlady there said the top drawer of his dresser was always stuffed with money. He also had a house in Niagara Falls, New York, where his wife Maude lived. Mills always had a fat roll of cash in his pocket and had a reputation as a big spender. He loved to gamble, and it didn't seem to bother him when he lost heavily. He paid the men who worked for him very well although, unlike other bootleggers, he refused to pay bribes to customs officials.

Mills' biggest boat, the *Adele*, was 40 feet long and 11 feet in the beam. It was a workhorse with a capacity for up to a thousand sacks of booze, but was nicely fitted out with furnished sleeping quarters and a head. His second boat, the *Block*, was somewhat smaller and could carry a few hundred sacks. His speedboat was used for runs of a hundred sacks or fewer. Mills was aware of his inexperience as a sailor and his imperfect knowledge of the lake, so he hired men who knew what they were doing. Charlie's crews included: his son Bud; Babe Cole, the nephew of Claude "King" Cole who owned Main Duck Island; an experienced sailor known only as Spengler who was one of his best friends; and assorted fishermen from the Quinte area. Then there was George Keegan.

Keegan was a tough, experienced sailor who had survived two shipwrecks. More than just another deckhand, Keegan was protection. He was one of those hard cases few men cared to tangle with. In later years he would work for New York gangster Jack "Legs" Diamond. In spite of a gun-related incident involving Ben Kerr, and a couple of confrontations with a Belleville policeman, Mills was not fond of firearms. He did keep a rifle on the *Adele*, but the main reason no one ever tried to relieve him of the bankroll he liked to carry around was George Keegan. Better to leave the soft-spoken Gentleman Charlie alone than face the wrath of big George.

In the lucrative, early days of Prohibition, Mills would make three runs a week in the *Adele* and Bud would take the *Block*. They would load up at an Ontario port and sometimes lay over at Main Duck Island. Main Duck's King Cole, formerly a rum-runner himself, now found it profitable (and less risky) to stockpile booze on his island fiefdom and sell it to bootleggers. His island was a favourite haunt of both fishermen and rum-runners. Mills would then proceed under cover of darkness to his favourite destination, the city of Oswego, New York.

Mills' boat the Adele. *Charlie and Jennie had to abandon the vessel to the Coast Guard one night, and swim for shore. Mills later bought the boat back at auction.*

Canadian and American bootleggers alike loved Oswego. It had no Prohibition agents and the local police generally turned a blind eye to bootlegging. It was a wide open little city, with 11 hotels, 27 "ice-cream parlours," and an untold number of speakeasies, all of them dispensing bootleg hooch. Mills would land his cargo at a place near town called "the chimneys," sometimes picking up as much as seven thousand dollars for his night's work. Often, instead of going straight back to Canada, he would stay over in one of Oswego's hotels, blowing a bundle at the gambling tables. He was a high roller in those days, and it was all easy come, easy go.

During the years of the Ontario Temperance Act (OTA), Mills would also "short circuit" alcohol back into the province, landing it at a stretch of coast known as Booze Bog. One such delivery set off a series of events which could have inspired Mac Sennett, if the Hollywood maestro of silent film comedy had been aware of the goings-on in far-off Ontario.

One afternoon in April of 1925, Gentleman Charlie dropped off a load of Corby's whiskey at a place called Cressy Flats, near the southeastern

174

tip of Prince Edward County. The liquor was for Harry Yanover, one of the region's biggest bootleggers. As Yanover watched from a touring car parked nearby, the booze was transferred from the *Adele* to a horse-drawn wagon, then hauled up the slope to a waiting truck. As the truck lumbered down the road with the first load of whiskey, it got stuck in the gooey spring mud. Some helpful farmers came over to help push it free. While everyone concentrated on putting their backs and shoulders to the truck, no one paid any attention to the cases of liquor still in the wagon. Three farmers who had been watching from the bush saw a golden opportunity. They sneaked over to the wagon and escaped into the woods with six cases of whiskey. The bootleggers didn't see a thing. Now began the Tale of the Transient Whiskey.

At bootleg prices, a case of whiskey was worth up to two hundred dollars. The farmers, Stewart Powers and two brothers named Hicks, had twelve hundred dollars worth of liquor—pay dirt for men who made a thousand dollars a year through honest labour. Powers hid his two cases in a threshing separator. Earl and Ross Hicks stuffed theirs into a straw mow. Captain Kidd couldn't have done better with a chest full of Spanish dubloons. But some people just can't keep a secret.

The next day Earl Hicks, giddy with excitement over the biggest thing to happen to him since his first childhood visit from Santa Claus, went to the local general store and dropped some 26-ounce hints about what he and his companions had done. Willet Carson, his brother-in-law, was one of the lads lounging around the cracker barrel that day. He asked Earl a few innocent questions and soon figured out where the booty was hidden.

That night Carson and his pal Bill McCain sputtered up to the straw mow in a Model T Ford and did a little charity work in relieving Earl and Ross Hicks of their ill-gotten gains. Carson hid his two cases in a swamp, and McCain stashed his in his employer's barn. But all that whiskey travelling around the countryside untasted just didn't seem right, so the two decided to treat a few friends.

Meanwhile, the Hicks brothers went to the straw mow to check on their treasure and—in the words of country folks—there it was gone! They combed the countryside, creeping into neighbours' barns at night in search of the purloined booze (which they had purloined in the first place). Then they got word that brother-in-law Willet and buddy Bill had been pretty generous with their peers with some hard-to-come-by booze. Now they knew where their liquor had gone. Earl and Ross enlisted the aid of their cousin Ray Hicks, and Harold Powers (cousin of Stewart) for Operation Recovery.

Ross and Ray Hicks went to the general store where they found Bill and Willet, and engaged them in conversation, not letting on that they knew the pair for dastardly booze burglars. Earl and Harold, meanwhile, sneaked off to the barn where Bill McCain had hidden the two cases, and quietly reclaimed them. They loaded the cases into a buggy and took them to a merchant who dabbled a little in bootlegging, and exchanged them for hard cash.

But all of this mysterious movement of the demon drink around the peaceful Ontario countryside was generating rumour, and rumour always seems to find its way to the ears of the police. Frank Naphan, a behemoth of a man who was the county liquor inspector and a sworn foe of bootleggers, heard the whispers and passed on what he'd heard to the Ontario Provincial Police. The OPP began making enquiries.

Now there were cross-currents of whispers buzzing from farmhouse to general store to backroom card tables about phantom booze being moved in the night, and police sneaking around in search of it.

Then Stewart Powers heard that Willet Carson and Bill McCain had also figured out where his liquor was hidden and were going to steal it, so he moved his cases from the threshing machine to the basement of another Hicks—Nathan. When Carson and McCain arrived to plunder the threshing machine, all they got for their efforts was their hair full of hay. Unfortunately for Nathan Hicks, the latecomer to the gang, Inspector Naphan and three OPP officers raided the home of Nathan Hicks, found the booze, and arrested Stewart and him.

In their investigation, Naphan and the cops had leaned on some local farmers, a few of whom had committed the awful crime of drinking a little whiskey in a shed at the Hicks place. Had they said they had done the drinking *in* the house, they'd have been safe from the law. But as they admitted to drinking outside the house, they could be charged.

Meanwhile, Willet Carson still had his two cases of whiskey hidden in the swamp. Naphan and the cops knew those cases of devil brew were out there somewhere and were determined to find them. They also knew that Carson had been involved in spiriting spirits around the countryside. Naphan went looking for him.

Outside a neighbour's house, Naphan met Carson but didn't know who he was. He asked for directions to the Carson home, and Willet obligingly set him on the route to his own house. Then he took off for Kingston where he hid at his sister's house until things cooled down. The police never did find his cases of Corby's. Many people, including the bootlegger Harry Yanover, were charged and fined over this affair, which became part of Prince Edward County lore. But one who got away scot-free was Charlie Mills, who had delivered the booze in the first place.

Though Mills was doing well for himself as a bootlegger, all was not harmonious for him on the home front. His wife Maude objected to his heavy gambling, and the fact that he'd taken to chasing women didn't help matters at

Stewart and Ethel Powers. Ethel didn't know until the police came knocking that her husband had filched some cases of bootleg whiskey.

all. Then tragedy struck. Mills took their teenage son, Chester, on a bootleg run to Oswego. Out on the lake Chester became ill. Because it was the boy's

Belleville police officer, Fred Izzard. Mills threatened to "blow a hole" in him if he didn't stay away from Jennie Batley.

first time out, Charlie thought he was merely seasick. He wasn't. Chester was suffering an attack of appendicitis. He died before his father could get him to a hospital. Maude blamed Charlie for the boy's death, and left him.

Chester's death and Maude's departure left Mills lonely and depressed. George Keegan introduced him to Jennie Batley, a woman of somewhat mysterious origins. Batley was from England and had two sons. She claimed to be a widow, and said that her husband, Wallace, had been killed in a train accident. Mills apparently accepted the story of the late Wallace Batley, but when Jennie's descendants went looking for the burial place of this ancestor, they couldn't find it. Nor could Charlie Mills' biographer, Canadian author C.W. Hunt, find any documentary trace of him.

Whatever Jennie Batley's past before she met Mills, she was a survivor. It wasn't easy in those days for a single woman with two children to get by. She was ten years younger than Mills, but he liked her company and her sense of humour. She liked the air of adventure about the rum-runner, and the fact that he had money to spend on her. Unfortunately, she also liked a handsome, young Belleville policeman.

Fred Isard of the Belleville Police Department was seven or eight years younger than Jennie. He was big and, like her, he was English. Maybe Jennie thought there was something dangerously romantic about having boyfriends on opposite sides of the law. The triangle almost exploded into violence one night when Mills went down to the dock to check on the *Adelle*. What should he find on *his* boat but *his* girl in bed with the policeman. Mills pulled a gun. If it had been anyone other than "Gentleman" Charlie, Isard might have died with his pants off. As it was, Mills just warned Isard to stay away from Jennie. Then, perhaps to strengthen his relationship with Jennie, but maybe more likely to keep her where he could watch her, Mills bought a house for her and her boys.

In the mid-Twenties, more Prohibition agents and an improved American Coast Guard meant that bootleggers were getting caught with increased regularity. At some point one or more of Mills' hired men was captured and he lost the *Block*. He replaced it with the *Winnifred S.* Then, in the small hours of September 3, 1925, Charlie's turn came.

He and Bud were about five miles from Oswego in the *Winnifred S.* when they were spotted by a Coast Guard picket boat. Mills tried to make a run for it, but the Guardsmen opened fire with tracer bullets and a revolver. Charlie stopped the boat, and he and Bud were arrested and taken to Oswego. The Coast Guard officer, a Captain Jackson, wrote in his report:

> Mills Sr. stated it was his first load he had tried to land, but I have information that [he] has been operating at bootleg-ging for the past three or four years, and every effort has been made to get him... He is well informed and seems to know everyone that is connected with bootlegging in this section... I am sure it was an important capture even if the seizure was not large (50 cases) and Mills was somewhat of a leader in the business.

Father and son were released on bail, but the capture was a turning point in Gentleman Charlie's bootlegging career. One brief stay in jail was enough for Bud. He quit the business. Within that same month, Mills went home one night and found Jennie had gone out. He suspected that she was with Fred Isard, and he went downtown and got drunk. He got into his car and was careening around town looking for her, when he crashed through a fence and into a hedge. Two police officers showed up. Mills, not realizing they were cops, asked them to help him push his car back onto the road. Luck just wasn't with Charlie that night. The officers found a flask of whiskey on him. He was arrested again.

Since Bud was no longer in the family business, Jennie began to take an active part in the smuggling. The presence of the Coast Guard meant that Mills had to cut his runs back to one a week, but at Jennie's suggestion, he partly made up for lost revenue by smuggling American cigarettes into Canada on his return trips.

The Adele *in the Murray Canal. The Coast Guard opened fire on the* Adele *one night and killed Mills' partner.*

When Charlie and Bud failed to appear for trial in the U.S., Mills forfeited the $6,000 bail he'd paid. It was a severe financial blow. He had to sell the house and move Jennie into an apartment. Then, while he and Jennie were making a run, they were chased by the Coast Guard. Charlie couldn't risk being caught again. He and Jennie dove overboard, swam to shore, and escaped into the woods. Charlie lost his cargo, and had to buy the *Adele* back at auction.

This constant drain on his wallet forced Mills to increase his runs across the lake, which meant a greater chance of getting caught. One night he, Jennie, and Spengler were thirty miles east of Rochester when they were seen by the Coast Guard's big, new, 75-foot patrol boat CG-142. They tried to run for it and the patrol boat opened fire. A .30-calibre Lewis machine gun bullet hit Spengler in the chest. He was the second bootlegger to be killed on Lake Ontario by the Coast Guard. Charlie and Jennie made it back to the Canadian side and quietly had Spengler buried.

Bud decided to clear things up with the law on the American side of the lake. He was, after all, an American citizen and wanted to be able to go home. He pleaded guilty in court and was sentenced to thirty days in jail and a $5,000 fine. In October 1926, Charlie did the same thing, but the law wasn't going to let him off so easily. He was fined $10,000 and sentenced to a year and a day in the federal penitentiary in Atlanta, Georgia. Prison was hard on a robust young man. For the slim, middle-aged Charlie, it was hell.

When Mills was released the following year, he went back to Prince Edward County and resumed his relationship with Jennie. She had been seeing Fred Isard while Charlie was sweating it out in prison. Gentleman Charlie told the policeman he would "blow a hole" in him if he didn't stay away from his woman. Mills was broke and had to sell his beloved *Adele*. Prohibition in Ontario had ended, so now the only market open to the bootleggers was the United States, and *that* was quickly being taken over by large-scale mob operations. With a determination worthy of a better cause, Charlie got right back into the business. He bought another boat, an old rum-runner called the *Rosella,* which he rechristened the *Lucky Lindy* after his hero, aviator Charles Lindberg. It was only 25 feet long and could carry fewer than a hundred cases.

Charlie and Jennie resumed running booze across the lake, but the comeback was short lived. On July 5, 1928, they were spotted by a Coast Guard picket boat. (Whether Jennie was the person with Charlie on this occasion is uncertain.) When the bootleggers refused to heave to, the picket boat opened fire. Mills raced for shore under a hail of bullets. He beached his boat and ran into the woods as the guardsmen sprayed the beach with machine gun fire. Mills was not hit, but it was one close call too many. He and Batley got out of the business. They moved to Niagara Falls, New York. There the bootlegger who was believed to have gone through three million dollars in his heyday took up farming. It is not known if Charlie and Jennie were ever officially married, but she stayed with him until his death in 1943 at the age of 62. She later married and moved to Florida, where she died sometime in the late '60s. Gentleman Charlie Mills did do one sensible thing that Ben Kerr didn't. He got out of bootlegging while he was still alive.

(Above) The Reverend J.Q.L. "Leslie" Spracklin, a man of the cloth who picked up a gun and went out to fight the bootleggers. (Right) Billy Sunday, a popular Temperance "evangelist." blamed all of America's ills on alcohol.

THE PISTOL PACKIN' PARSON

While the Catholic Church never took a strong stand on the matter of Prohibition, there were clergymen of other denominations who did. On the American side of the line there was Billy Sunday, a one-time baseball star turned Presbyterian minister who called himself "the sworn, eternal, and uncompromising enemy of the liquor traffic. I have been and will go on, fighting that damnable, dirty, rotten business with all the power at my command." Sunday's on-stage theatrics (which would inspire generations of "evangelists") drew huge crowds. "Whiskey and beer are all right in their place," Billy would say, "but their place is in hell!" In a typical "water wagon" sermon, Billy would blame booze for all of the crime, poverty, insanity and misery in America. "The saloon is the sum of all villainies," he thundered. "It is worse than war or pestilence."

But for all his ranting, Billy Sunday confined his war against alcohol to the pulpit and the podium. He never pinned on a badge, strapped on a gun and went down into the trenches to do battle against the bootleggers. One Canadian preacher did,

Bev Trumble's Chappell House was a popular watering hole and the scene of a tragic confrontation.

though—with the backing of his government. In a few short months he would transform himself from an obscure, small-town minister to a temperance crusader whose quick trigger finger made him headline news.

J.Q.L. "Leslie" Spracklin became pastor of the Methodist Church in Sandwich (now part of Windsor), Ontario, in 1919. Just down the road from the church was the Chappell House, a hotel-saloon which blatantly disregarded the Ontario Temperance Act (OTA), dispensing booze at all hours. It was a popular spot, not only with Windsorites who liked to whoop it up, but also with drinkers from Detroit, just across the river. It was a rollicking place, noisy with shouts, laughter and music—not to mention the constant racket of cars coming and going. The proprietor of the Chappell House was Beverley "Babe" Trumble, a man the Reverend Spracklin had known all his life.

The Spracklins and the Trumbles were from Woodstock, Ontario, and the mothers of the two families were friends. Leslie and Bev, however, were not. Young Trumble was an extrovert who always seemed to be able to one-up Spracklin, who was more of a loner. Now Trumble was making money hand over fist selling beer and whiskey from his hotel, while law-abiding Spracklin was barely making ends meet as the humble pastor of a little church.

However, it wasn't Trumble's money that drew Spracklin's ire, as much as the fact that the Chappell House openly defied the law and the Sandwich police did nothing about it. On June 21, 1920, the angry parson went to a meeting of the Sandwich Town Council and, spitting fire and brimstone, blasted council members for allowing the deplorable state of affairs to go on. Spracklin complained that "the lowest element" of people came from the United States to the Border Cities—especially Sandwich—

looking for strong drink. He said that these people made the community unsafe for women and children with their "open debauch," while the police turned a blind eye. "At any time of night," he said, "you can hear men passing your street door using the most obscene language; drunken, rolling, spewing, fighting men in all stages of intoxication as a result of the illicit sale of liquor which is being carried on."

The worst offender, Spracklin claimed, was the Chappell House. Then he turned his gunsights on the Sandwich Police Department, and Chief Alois Masters in particular. He said he had even seen Chief Masters on the verandah of the hotel with a drunken girl sitting on his lap. Spracklin wanted the liquor traffic stopped and the police department investigated. Trumble, of course, denied that liquor was being sold on his premises with his knowledge, and said that he fired any waiters he caught peddling alcohol. Chief Masters said the charges against his department were nonsense.

The Council told Spracklin they would look into the matter, but then moved with the turtle-slowness typical of bureaucrats. Spracklin was back on July 5 and again on July 19, haranguing the members over their lack of action. He was threatened with arrest at one particularly stormy meeting. Even though Mayor E. H. Donnelly would not give him permission to speak, the fiery preacher called the bootlegging situation in the border region "a stench in the nostrils of Ontario." In a written statement, Spracklin demanded a thorough public investigation of the police administration. "Only such investigation, I submit, will satisfy the moral sentiment of the law-abiding citizens of the town."

While the council members argued, Mayor Donnelly told Spracklin he was out of order. A crowd of onlookers hissed the mayor. Reeve Charles McKee tried to reply to Spracklin's charges of municipal incompetence, but Spracklin said, "You can't intimidate me, McKee. I could set you down in about one minute, and you know it."

As reported in the Toronto *Globe* of July 20, no one was sure what to do next. A committee was formed to investigate the police department and Chief Powers, but as the *Globe* pointed out, that was clearly a case of the police investigating themselves. (By the end of the month, the department and the Chief had been exonerated.) Then Ontario Attorney General William Raney, a self-righteous foe of all things "immoral," from the demon drink to fishing on Sunday, had a brilliant idea. Take this fiery young man of the cloth, Spracklin, who had already demonstrated that he had a stiff backbone and plenty of sand in his craw, and make him a specially licensed liquor

Leslie Spracklin (holding cigar) and three of his deputies. Spracklin's admirers praised his tough stand against bootlegging, but others deplored his heavy-handed methods.

inspector with a squad of men at his command. Then turn him loose on the rum-runners the way you'd sic a dog on a burglar. The fact that Spracklin had absolutely no training in police work was beside the point.

Wild Bill Hickok could not have taken on the task of cleaning up a lawless town with greater enthusiasm. Spracklin strapped on a Colt .45 revolver, a small cannon more powerful than the .38s the police were allowed to carry. To help him let the bad guys know there was a new sheriff in town, he had a squad of "special" officers. It isn't certain how he recruited them, but two of his men—Vincent and William Hallam (both in their twenties)—were hoodlums cut from the same cloth as the bootleggers Spracklin was supposed to crack down on.

For his booze-busting operations on land, the government gave Spracklin a classy Paige Touring car. To stem the tide of alcohol flowing across the Detroit River he had a speedboat called the *Leopard II*. (There would be complaints that Spracklin's men used the motor launch to run down suspected rum-runners on the river, cutting their small boats in two.) Spracklin also took the extra-legal step of providing himself with a stack of blank search warrants, which he could fill out on the spot should the situation require it. "Why not have martial law and be done with it?" one exasperated member of the town council complained.

On his first day on the job, Spracklin raided four roadhouses and made five arrests for violations of the Ontario Temperance Act and obstruction of an officer. It was the beginning of what would be a five-month reign of terror, as far as the bootleggers were concerned. They found that Spracklin could not be bribed and he knew how to handle his fists. No psalm-quoting, pantywaist church deacon, he. Nor was he reluctant to use his gun to stop fleeing bootleggers, as two miscreants learned when Spracklin fired two shots at their booze-laden car after they failed to stop on his order. Some bootleggers moved their operations to the St. Clair River. Others tried to scare Spracklin with written death threats. But the cocky, preacher-lawman told the *Globe*, "...the last thing I do at night is to read over the death threat and then—go to sleep."

This kind of bravado would make Spracklin a hero to a large segment of the public and, in the following weeks, accounts of the "Fighting Parson's" exploits would fill the papers. One day early in August he posed as a bootlegger trying to buy liquor for export to the U.S., and seized 104 cases of whiskey. Two people were arrested. Then, acting on a tip, Spracklin took a trip down to Amherstburg and arrested Mayor William F. Park for violating the OTA. Liquor was found on Park's premises, but the mayor protested that he'd been framed. (There were no subsequent newspaper accounts about the charges against Park, who was loved in the community both as a mayor and a doctor, so we can assume that nothing came of them).

Later in August, Spracklin and his men intercepted a fleet of rum boats on the Detroit River. The cabin cruiser *Eugenia* and an escort of four motor launches made a run for it, the men on board frantically tossing kegs of booze overboard. When Spracklin and the officers fired warning shots, a bootlegger on the *Eugenia* returned fire with a .45-calibre rifle. Fortunately, no one on either side was hit. Spracklin arrested ten men, and seized all five vessels as well as the cargo that had not been jettisoned. The parson wasn't as lucky a few days later when he saw a man at a dock, loading his small boat with booze. Spracklin stopped his car and called to the man to surrender, but the suspect jumped into his boat and roared out onto the river. Spracklin and the officer with him drew their guns and sent a hail of lead after the fleeing bootlegger. Bullets plowed into the water all around the little boat, but the bootlegger got away. The man had left a stolen car on the dock, however, and Spracklin was able to restore it to its rightful owner. So even when things weren't one hundred percent successful, the Fighting Parson looked good.

But not everyone was an admirer of the minister who packed a .45 along with a Bible. Police Chief Masters had been cleared by an investigative committee, but he still smarted over remarks Spracklin had made about his competence and integrity. He called the minister "a dog lost in the wilderness. He just sits in one spot and howls." Moreover, there had been a flood of complaints against Spracklin's squad for "using poor judgement" while conducting investigations, and for indiscriminate use of firearms. Spracklin's men, especially the Hallam brothers, showed little regard for private property when searching for alcohol, and were just a little too anxious to show off their guns to nervous citizens. Most embarrassing was an incident in which Spracklin and the Hallams crashed a party aboard a lawyer's private yacht. They found no liquor, but did succeed in scaring the daylights out of some female guests. That escapade would cost Spracklin five hundred dollars in damages.

While most of the people in Spracklin's Methodist congregation supported his campaign against the bootleggers, others objected to having his boys search their cars for whiskey while they attended his church. A fellow liquor inspector, M.N. Mousseau, was very critical of Spracklin's methods. He was technically Spracklin's superior, but because of the special status Attorney General Raney had given the parson, Mousseau could not exert any control over him. Spracklin's response to the criticism was to point out that he had made more arrests than had Mousseau.

The Hallam brothers were proving to be a liability, though. There were reports of them being drunk in public. Worse, local bootleggers said that the Hallams were extorting money and doublecrossing them. Spracklin finally had to fire the troublesome pair. But his association with the unruly brothers would come back to haunt him.

Meanwhile, Bev Trumble and the other bootleggers did not like the attention Spracklin was giving their operations. Spracklin had raided the Chappell House a couple of times, which hurt business. In retaliation, the bootleggers took out a personal vendetta against Spracklin. They uttered threats to members of his family. They tried to vandalize the *Leopard II*. They fired shots at his house. They attempted to bribe his staff. Once, Spracklin was jumped and thrown into a canal. Spracklin took to wearing a gun everywhere, even at home. Sometimes he slept in his car. Inspector Mousseau, who never carried a gun, warned that Spracklin was in for "troubled times." Dr. Forbes Godfrey, MPP, was almost prophetic when he told Spracklin, "That gun will get you in trouble sometime."

A few days later it did. During the early hours of November 6, 1920, Spracklin was cruising the streets of Sandwich with four officers, looking for bootleggers to bust. As they passed the Chappell House they saw two men on the front lawn. One was half crouched over, with his face in his hands and blood trickling through his fingers. The other man was standing over him. Spracklin stopped the car and he and the officers got out. He recognized the man with the bloody face as Ernie Deslippe. The other man he knew well: Bev Trumble.

"Hello, Bev," he said. "What's wrong here?"

"Hello, Les," Trumble replied. "It's Ernie Deslippe. He had a little trouble and got his nose punched." Spracklin began to question Deslippe, who he thought had been drinking. Trumble quietly went up the steps into the hotel and locked the door.

Sure that there must be booze on the premises, Spracklin and his men went up to the door and tried to open it. They later said they saw faces in a window, and a gun in somebody's hand. When no one responded to Spracklin's command to open the door, he and his officers gained entry by means of an unlocked front window. What happened next would be a subject of debate for the next four months, until the whole story came out at the climax of a sensational trial.

In the hotel when Spracklin and his men entered were Bev Trumble, his wife Lulu, Bill Morton (who had punched Deslippe in the face during a drunken argument), Jack Bannon, and Edward (or Edgar) Smith. Smith was the only one, besides the other officers, who witnessed what happened between Trumble and Spracklin. The parson told Trumble he wanted to search the hotel. Trumble demanded a warrant. The two men exchanged words, then Spracklin shot Trumble. The heavy .45-calibre slug struck Trumble in the groin and tore through his body. He fell into Smith's arms and bled to death within fifteen minutes.

Immediately after the shooting, Spracklin left the hotel and went to Windsor where he turned himself in to the police, saying that he had just shot Bev Trumble. He did not yet know that Trumble was dead. After sending men to the Chappell House to investigate the shooting, the Windsor police held Spracklin in an undisclosed location. They said that if his whereabouts were known, his life would not be worth five cents. Indeed, it was said that when news of Trumble's death reached Detroit, known gangsters from across the river began showing up in Windsor and Sandwich, and a mysterious figure was seen lurking about Spracklin's home.

At the coroner's inquest held the following day, Spracklin testified, "We were met by Bev Trumble. He looked at me a second, and then his hand went to his pocket. He pulled a gun and yelled to me, 'Spracklin, this is my fight. Get out of here or I'll kill you.'" (Spracklin later enlarged on this by testifying that Trumble pressed the gun into his [Spracklin's] stomach, saying "I've got you now. I'm going to kill you.") The preacher continued, "It was then I drew my pistol and shot, to save my life." As Trumble was dying, he gasped, "Spracklin, you sucker, you've killed me."

Mrs. Trumble gave an entirely different version. She did not see the shooting, but said that when her husband went out of the bedroom to confront Spracklin, he had nothing in his hands but a hot water bottle and a cigarette. She testified that he had never owned a gun. The same claim was made by Bev's father, Hamilton Trumble, a former alderman. "My son was not armed. He never carried a weapon in his life. Spracklin murdered him, and he can't hide behind his ministry to save his life."

Police who arrived on the scene after the shooting could not find a gun. Nor could they find Ed Smith, who had fled from the hotel and was making a mad dash for Detroit. Two of Spracklin's officers said that Trumble had a gun, and had threatened them with it. Bill Morton and Jack Bannon said they had not seen a gun in Trumble's hand. But two doctors who had arrived on the scene before the police said that Ed Smith had told them that Trumble did have a gun. Smith, who had been located with some difficulty, denied this. He proved to be a reluctant, evasive witness. To everyone's surprise he produced the bullet which had killed Trumble. After passing through Trumble's body, the spent slug had grazed Smith's leg, torn his coat, and lodged in his pocket.

The coroner's jury decided that the shooting had been justifiable homicide and Spracklin was freed. That same day, Bev Trumble was buried. Spracklin's mother attended the funeral. But that wasn't the end of the controversy.

There was tremendous support for Spracklin among his congregation and the public in general. He was hailed as a "man among men," a "he

*Monro Grier, Lulu Trumble's lawyer,
convinced two thousand people to sign
a petition demanding that Spracklin be
tried for manslaughter.*

man," and a champion "for the fight
he is putting up against evil forces."
An editor for the Detroit *Times*
wrote glowingly of "Canadian justice of splendid tradition" and said
"It was necessary to put the fear of
the law into the hearts of the lawless." An editor for the *Christian
Guardian*, the official organ of the
Methodist Church of Canada, called
Spracklin, "a man of courage and devo-
tion" who had been struggling against
those who would trample the law underfoot.

Of course, not everyone agreed. More
threatening letters arrived at the parsonage. Lulu Trumble was insisting that
her unarmed husband had been shot down in cold blood. Spracklin wanted
to return to his duties as a special inspector, but that was impossible. As it
was, every visitor to his home was being frisked for weapons. Mousseau
repeated his opinion that it did not take gunplay to enforce the OTA, that it
was better to let a bootlegger get away than to shoot him. At the end of
November, Attorney General Raney dismissed Spracklin's squad. It was
replaced by a new unit of officers headed by a former police chief.

Lulu Trumble's lawyer, Monro Grier, was pushing for a new trial.
He said that some members of the jury who sat for the coroner's inquest had
not been qualified to do so. He wanted Spracklin tried for manslaughter, and
got two thousand people to sign a petition, which was submitted to the
provincial government. Spracklin himself wanted a trial, to clear his name
once and for all. Raney finally consented, and a trial was set for February
1921. Spracklin's congregation raised money for his defence, and Sunday
attendance in his church boomed. One woman expressed disappointment,
after services, that she didn't get to see the reverend's gun.

Before the trial began, an incident occurred in Toronto which would
place Spracklin's name in a rather unfavourable light. On the afternoon of

Bev Trumble's friend, Jack Bannon, dropped a bombshell at the trial when he testified that he had seen a gun in Lulu Trumble's hand.

Sunday, January 23, the Hallam brothers, Spracklin's former officers, got into a fight in their boarding house over something Stanley had said to William's wife. At the height of the brawl, William had Stanley by the throat and Stanley was trying to pistol-whip William with a loaded gun. The weapon discharged twice, and one of the bullets went through a wall and struck another boarder, 21-year-old Ruby Cross, in the back. She died the next day. The Hallams were arrested and charged with criminal negligence. In addition to Stanley's gun, the police seized a pistol belonging to William. The brothers said they had bought both guns from the Reverend Mr. Spracklin. It was not the kind of publicity the defence in the Spracklin case needed.

The trial began on February 22 before Justice Sir William Mulock and a packed courtroom. Monro Grier was the prosecutor for the Crown, and R.L. Brackin represented Spracklin. Lulu Trumble attempted to win the jury's sympathy by taking the stand with her baby in her arms, but Mulock would not permit it. She again swore that her husband was unarmed when Spracklin shot him, that Bev had never owned a gun.

Ed Smith was confronted with the testimonies of the two doctors who said that he had told them Trumble had a gun. Yet, he still insisted that Trumble had not been armed. He at first said that he had only gone to the Chappell House for his dinner, but then admitted that he had been drinking.

He said he was not drunk when the shooting occurred. Questioned about his sudden departure for Detroit, he said only that he had gone to a hotel and registered under a "consumed name." When Brackin asked him if he had dropped anything in the river or taken anything to a Detroit pawnshop, Smith replied no.

The following day Spracklin took the stand. He, too, repeated his previous testimony. He said Trumble had threatened him and the other officers with a gun. He even described it as a .38. The pastor became emotionally overwrought as he admitted to pulling the trigger of his own gun, but said he could tell by the look in Trumble's eyes that the man meant to kill him. Spracklin said that he had fired low, from the hip, hoping to disable Trumble, not kill him. Mrs. Trumble was recalled to the stand and was asked again if her husband had a gun. She said he had not, and added, "If I had a gun that night, there would have been another murder."

Back on the stand, Spracklin told of an incident in September when he had searched Trumble's car for whiskey, and Bev had called him, "a dirty, low down cur." There was little doubt that there was no love lost between the two men. There was still that crucial question though, as to whether or not Trumble had threatened anyone with a gun, or had owned a gun at all.

Evelyn Bell, Spracklin's sister, told of a confrontation she'd had with Trumble on Bob Lo Island. "He will be shot if he doesn't get off the job," Trumble allegedly told her. "They will shoot a man quicker for whiskey than they will for money." Evelyn said she told her brother about the threat.

Then came the testimony that seriously challenged everything Lulu Trumble had said. First, a Windsor tailor said that when Bev Trumble came into his shop one time to be fitted for a suit, it had been necessary to ask him to remove a gun from his pocket so proper measurements could be taken. Then a garage employee said that three months before the shooting he had repaired a revolver for Trumble. Other witnesses testified that it was common knowledge that Bev Trumble often wore a gun belt. One man said he had once heard Trumble tell Spracklin, "I don't care if you are an officer, preacher, or what... Spracklin, I'll get you yet." Asked why she was not aware her husband often carried a gun, when so many other people knew of it, Lulu Trumble had no reply.

It was Jack Bannon who dropped the biggest bombshell. He repeated his earlier testimony that he had not seen a gun in Bev Trumble's hand as he lay dying on the floor. But now he added that he *had* seen a gun in *Mrs.* Trumble's hand, before Ed Smith disappeared into the night. When a

Spracklin's case was headline news, but his days as a pistol packin' parson were over.

stunned Grier asked Bannon why he hadn't volunteered this information at an earlier time, the witness replied, "Nobody asked me."

Bannon had been a friend of Bev Trumble (though Lulu said that he had now abandoned her "in my hour of need"), so the jury took him at his word. The scenario, as they saw it, was: Bev Trumble *did* have a gun when Spracklin, whom he had threatened on several occasions, confronted him. Spracklin shot Trumble in self defence. Lulu Trumble picked up the gun and gave it to Ed Smith to dispose of. At some point Smith, in a panic or because he'd had too much to drink, blurted something about the gun to the doctors. He fled from the hotel before the police arrived, taking the weapon with him.

In his address to the jury the next day, Brackin was brilliant. He placed a large share of the blame for the tragedy at the door of the provincial government:

> I don't think it was fair. I don't think it was right, for the
> Government of Ontario to say to this minister of the

Gospel, 'You complain that conditions in your town are vile, that they have reached the unbearable point. *You*, therefore, assume the responsibility of remedying them, of cleaning up the situation you complain of.'

He went on to say that the government should have sent soldiers or police to deal with the "gigantic task," not a minister of the gospel. Of Mrs. Trumble's testimony, Brackin said, "She stood there and she lied, and lied, and lied." It took the jury less than an hour to find Spracklin "Not Guilty."

Again there was a flurry of editorials congratulating the parson on his victory in court and his no-nonsense stand against the bootleggers. A few even expressed a wish that he was back on the job. One journalist likened him to Jesus driving the money changers from the Temple. But Spracklin's days as a pistol packin' parson were over. He took the Billy Sunday approach now, and fought for Prohibition from the speaker's platform. There were still death threats. One went to a London, Ontario, church where Spracklin was scheduled to speak. It said, "Don't let the murderer come here tonight. We will get him." The letter was accompanied by a mutilated picture of Spracklin. But the reverend went ahead and spoke, and nothing happened.

The troublesome Hallam brothers escaped jail over the shooting of Ruby Cross, but eventually wound up behind bars for other crimes. The pair continued to be an unholy plague for the reverend. Every time the press reported on their misdeeds, Spracklin's name was dragged into the story.

The one-time hero of the war against the liquor traffic soon left the Windsor area under a pall of suspicion. Some women in his congregation accused him of making sexual advances, so he quietly slipped out of the country. He wandered around Michigan as an itinerant preacher. He died in obscurity at Greenbush, Michigan, in 1960, at the age of 73. By that time the Fighting Parson was as forgotten as the cause for which he had tried to take a stand.

How Uncle Sam Has Faded Out
Joyous Jennie's Smile
And Buddy and Betty Co-ed Mourn

"Six Months!" Said the Judge to the Cute Little "Speako" Queen

"HELLO, EVERYBODY!"
Gay Snapshot of Jennie Justo, 23, University of Wisconsin Co-Ed, Who Was Sentenced to Serve Six Months in the Milwaukee House of Correction for Running a Speakeasy Patronized by College Students. Now, Her Smile Has Faded.

JOYOUS JENNIE JUSTO, 23, the liveliest little lady bootician who ever blended the alky or swung a mean Side Car, has had that characteristic smile wiped off her face.

Uncle Sam was the wiper. He found that Jennie was in the speakeasy racket—shaking up Gin Daisies for University of Wisconsin sophomores—compounding delectable Jack Roses for freshwomen.

These are sad days for Buddy Campus and Betty Co-Ed, who were the backbone of Jennie's trade in what used to be quaintly referred to as hooch. For their favorite whisperlow has been padlocked; dust is collecting on the arid absinthe and Fiora d'Alpe bottles; spiders and mice are cozily nesting in empty King William cases—and Jennie is doing a little stretch in the Milwaukee house of correction.

Jennie's career was brief but brilliant. When her father died, victim of a Madison gun battle early in the last decade, she was a student at the university. How to carry on? For a college education costs money.

Jennie was personable, hospitable, good-looking and vivacious, all essential qualities of a "hostess." Urged by admiring friends, she decided to cash in on her personal attractions. She did.

Jennie was smart, alert, imaginative. She sized up the local liquor situation with a keen eye and saw at once in which direction the road to monetary success lay. "Punctual deliveries!

MOIST RENDEZVOUS
The little Bar in "Jennie's Place," Madison, Wis., Where Frat Boys and Co-Eds Used to Gather—Till Federal Agents, Posing as Pals of Her Brother, "Pep," Raided the Resort.

sizeable organization with a staff of ten young assistants—"We are open day and night"—but now was the time, she decided, to open a speako.

Promptly she installed picturesque booths and a trim bar into the Justo house. Her old clientele, kids from the college, were quick to patronize the new rendezvous. So loyal were they that some even brought their home work to "Jennie's place." They would be heard muttering algebraic formulas over steins of approximate ale. Curly heads would shake dubiously over Latin verses while the owners of the heads reached absent-mindedly for bumpers

WINNING GRIN
Animated Close-Up of Joseph ("Pep") Justo, Clever Young Boxer and Brother of Jennie.

them a round of generous drinks. It was a misguided

Here a newspaper gleefully reports that the smile has been wiped from the face of the "Speako" Queen. Jennie (top left). Her bar, piled with bottles for the camera (centre). Her brother Pep (lower right).

JENNIE JUSTO
JOYOUS JENNIE

The lure of bootleg money drew entrepreneurs of every sort: hard case criminals like Al Capone and Dion O'Banion; swashbuckling adventurers like Ben Kerr and Charlie Mills; and tough, calculating women like Bessie Starkman. At the other end of the spectrum was Jennie Justo, an attractive, intelligent, vivacious young woman whom the newspapers would call "Joyous Jennie," and whom the Wickersham Commission Report on the Enforcement of Prohibition would label "The Queen of the Bootleggers." The latter was certainly an exaggeration because Jennie Justo never operated on the grand scale of the major American and Canadian bootlegging outfits centred around the Great Lakes. She got into the business out of financial desperation, and did not consider it a crime, even though bootlegging had cost her father his life.

Vinzenza DiGilormo was born in Madison, Wisconsin, on January 13, 1908, to Joseph (Carl) and Antonina (Lena) DiGilormo, who had emigrated to the United States from Italy in 1902. Their Madison neighbourhood known as Greenbush, or simply "the Bush," was largely Italian, but was also home to black and Jewish people. Jennie was one of five children, the others being Joseph Jr., Dominick, Nicholas, and Rosalie (Rose). There are several versions of the origin of the name *Justo*, but the one accepted by the family is that young Joseph earned national fame as a professional

Jennie Justo's brother "Pep" Justo, contender for the middleweight boxing championship. Prohibition agents pretended to be friends of his in order to trap Jennie.

boxer fighting under the name of "Pep" Justo. (He rose to become a contender for the middleweight title.) The rest of the family followed his lead and adopted the surname. It was not uncommon at that time for first and second generation Americans to adopt names that sounded less foreign to Anglo-Saxon ears. According to Jennie's cousin Rosalie (Coronna) Potts and her husband Frank, all of the Justo family except Nick (and perhaps Pep) were involved in bootlegging or running speakeasies at one time or other, though to a lesser degree than Jennie and her father, Carl.

Carl was the first to get into the liquor trade, and became one of the casualties of the bootleg wars. On February 13, 1923, he was gunned down in front of his home, a shotgun blast to the back of his head. His killing might have been part of a vendetta, as it seems as many as seven men might have been slain that night—the same number who died in the St. Valentine's Day Massacre in 1929. Some said the Mafia was involved. There was also speculation that Carl was killed in revenge for one of his sons allegedly being a police informer. The family recalls that there were armed "mobster types" at the funeral, as well as armed police. Carl's murder was never solved and, in later years, Jennie refused to discuss the matter with anyone. There had been an earlier bootleg-related murder on the street where Carl was cut down, and the spot was known thereafter as "Death's Corner."

After Carl's murder, his wife Lena was put into protective custody for two years, leaving 14-year-old Jennie to look after her siblings. Options were few for a girl her age with such big responsibilities. She worked for a while for her uncle, Russell Coronna, who was a pharmacist. Pharmacies were a source of legal "medicinal" alcohol until the government caught onto them. But at some point, Jennie turned to bootlegging. She must have known the right people to have been able to secure a source of supply. She would later say that she had "lots of Italian boyfriends" who got her delivering alcohol, whiskey and gin. "What else could I do?" she said. "The family needed my support, and I was too young to get a job." She must have been a girl of considerable nerve, too, because bootlegging was a dangerous game.

Her first venture was a delivery service. Someone in the neighbourhood would call the Justo house with an order for booze, and Jennie would promptly deliver the goods. She became something of a neighbourhood legend because of her speedy deliveries, and her business flourished. But it wasn't only the residents of the Bush who made up Jennie's clientele. One of the goals of the short-sighted apostles of Prohibition was to discourage young people from drinking. That idea backfired with a resounding boom. Drinking became as much a part of the "in" scene as the Charleston and raccoon coats. "Buddy Campus" and "Betty Co-ed," as one newspaper editor called college and university students, took to drinking in record numbers. Not far away from Jennie's home was the Madison campus of the University of Wisconsin. Jennie's business grew when students learned that she was the person to see if someone needed a refill for that fashionable hip flask.

Jennie had to quit school herself in order to earn a family income, but she saw to it that the other Justo children went. She made the payments on their home and put food on the table. When her mother was able to come out of hiding, Jennie supported her. She had ten people working for her and was known throughout the Bush for her generosity. She worked hard, and it seems the only luxury she allowed herself was a raccoon coat. Things apparently went well until November 1927, when local Prohibition agents

Jennie Justo: the pretty girl with a heart of gold denied being "Queen of the Bootleggers."

QUEEN OF RUM, FORMER CO-ED, GIVEN 6 MONTHS

Jennie Justo Denied Leniency at Madison.

Madison, Wis., Jan. 16.—[U.P.]—
Jennie Justo, 23, to use the parlance
of her brother's trade, "took it on the
chin" in Federal court here today.
The basement of her home was too
popular with university students; unpopular with the deans.
Federal prohibition agents from Chi-

learned of her operation. Agent Harold Wilcox picked her up, and Jennie was fined, reprimanded and warned. However, some of Jennie's customers were city officials and she felt that she could dodge the worst penalties of the law. Not long after, in January 1928, agent Wilcox caught her again, and again she was fined and reprimanded.

Since literally running booze through the streets was becoming hazardous, Jennie decided to let the customers come to her. She opened a speakeasy in the basement of her home on Spring Street. She installed a bar and booths, and stocked the place with beer, wine, scotch, and what federal agents would later call "moonshine whiskey." Jennie's place wasn't a gangster-run Cotton Club, where patrons could sip (or guzzle) champagne while being entertained by the greatest jazz musicians of the age. Nor was it one of the sleazy blind pigs where mobsters like the Terrible Gennas of Chicago peddled rotgut hooch. It was an underground bar, where neighbours got together for a quiet, forbidden drink, and students did their homework while sipping Gin Daisies or port. Whiskey was 20 cents a shot. Beer was 25 cents a glass. There were no Purple Gang gunmen or Northside gangsters with blackjacks and brass knuckles. One could not have asked for a nicer speakeasy.

Then Dean Scott H. Goodnight of the University of Wisconsin learned where his students were doing their tippling. Being something of a party-pooper, he complained to the police. On June 2, 1931, Jennie had a phone call from Chicago. Two friends of her brother Pep, the boxer, were going north on a hunting trip and wanted to stop off in Madison for a drink. Always obliging, Jennie picked them up at the train station and drove them to her speakeasy. She treated the boys to a drink on the house. Then they flashed their badges. This time Jennie was indicted and hauled into court. Her lawyer tried to argue entrapment, but the Prohibition agents denied that they had claimed to be Pep's friends. Jennie was fined five hundred dollars and sentenced to one year in the Milwaukee House of Corrections. However, a five-year suspension was placed on the prison sentence, meaning that Jennie had to keep out of trouble for that period. Any violation of her probation, she was warned, would cost her actual jail time.

Perhaps Jennie reasoned that now that the feds believed they had thrown a scare into her, they would seek bigger game and leave her alone. She went back to bootlegging, but this time she operated out of a house on Fahrenbrook Court, one block south of Spring Street. For a little while the ruse worked.

But in January 1932 the feds struck again. Jennie must have thought she was leading a charmed life, because she managed once more to evade going to jail. But by 1933 the feds had had enough. Jennie was busted yet again, and this time she was sentenced to prison. Newspapers of the time differ on just how long her sentence was, but her family believes it was a year. Her term in the Milwaukee House of Corrections was to begin on May 16, 1933. She was also handed a $500 fine. Using the boxing parlance of her brother, she said she would "take it on the chin," though one newspaper report said she wept at the prospect of going to prison. She told reporters, "I wish people wouldn't think I'm as bad as I've been painted. I'm not a criminal, though I know that I've broken the prohibition law. I'm not the queen of the bootleggers. Why do they continue calling me that? There are lots of girls here bootlegging—beautiful girls."

Perhaps. But they didn't attract the kind of attention the smiling, big-hearted Jennie did. One newspaper editor wrote rather gloatingly of how the smile had been wiped from the face of the "cute little 'Speako' Queen."

Jail Jennie Justo

Jennie Is Off For One Year Term in Cell

(Continued from page 1)
philosophically says she prefers it to a
five year probation.

"This way I will be actually free
when I get out. Before I was

Jennie served her term. She got two months off for good behaviour, then a month put back on because she wouldn't pay the $500 fine. After all, $500 was a lot of money in the Dirty Thirties, and the family would need it. Jennie would always refer to her time in jail as "finishing school."

When 26-year-old Jennie Justo was released, a welcoming committee of university students and a band met her at the train station. They presented her with a bouquet of red roses and paraded her to her home, where a party was held in her honour.

On June 8, 1935, Jennie married star athlete and radio personality Art Bramhall. From the newspaper coverage of the event, it appears that Jennie's celebrity was equal to that of her famous husband. There was no need for Jennie to go back to bootlegging. Prohibition was deservedly dead. Jennie and Art opened Justo's Club, one of the first Italian restaurants in Madison. It was a popular eating place and watering hole for university students and athletes for forty years. Jennie died at age 83 on November 27, 1991. According to her cousin Rosalie (Coronna) Potts: "Everyone knew that Jennie was as hard a worker as anyone could possibly be and that she rarely took time for herself... Regardless of her disregard for the prohibition laws, Jennie was a fine person and believed in helping people whenever she could do so." Jennie Justo would no doubt prefer to be remembered for that, rather than as "Queen of the Bootleggers."

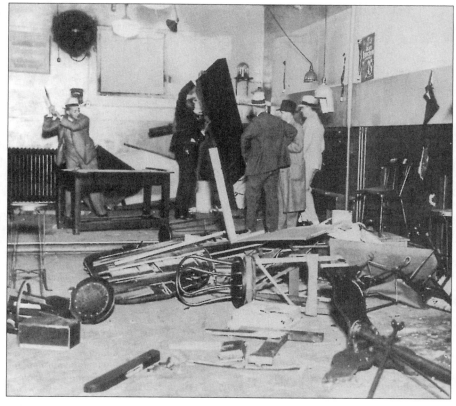

Detroit police and border patrol agents destroy a typical Prohibition Era speakeasy. In contrast, Jennie Justo's place was a small, quiet, neighbourhood bar. Jennie Justo's story captured the public imagination.

Al Capone leaving the court building during his trial for income tax evasion. Asked about his involvement in smuggling liquor from Canada, he replied, "I don't even know what street Canada is on."

PART TWO

THE GANGSTERS

Alphonse Capone. He liked to be called Big Al. It was dangerous to address him with the nickname by which he was widely known: Scarface.

Hamilton, Ontario. Situated at the western end of Lake Ontario, the city was the centre of Rocco Perri's Canadian bootleg empire. From here Perri could also direct the flow of booze to the United States.

ROCCO AND BESSIE

What Bonnie Parker and Clyde Barrow would be to bank robbery in the Dirty Thirties, Rocco Perri and Bessie Starkman were to bootlegging in the Roaring Twenties: a "couple" in what was essentially a man's criminal business. Rocco and Bessie would enjoy considerably more success than the Depression Era outlaws, but in the end they would meet similar fates.

Rocco Perri, the self-proclaimed King of the Bootleggers, "Canada's Al Capone," was born in hot, dry, desperately poor Calabria at the toe of the Italian peninsula. It was a land with strong traditions of banditry and secret societies, and general suspicion of government authority. When Rocco joined the wave of Italian emigrants heading for the Promised Land of America in 1903, he took those ingrained traits with him.

Rocco was 16 when he stepped off the ship at Boston. He went to New York City, and may well have had his initiation into crime in the squalid slums of Little Italy. In 1908 he moved to Montreal, and then on to Ontario where he drifted around—Trenton, Parry Sound, Toronto—working as a labourer. In 1912 he found room and board at a house in Toronto's Ward, an overcrowded slum which was home to thousands of immigrants from Italy, Ireland, Eastern Europe and Britain. His landlord was Harry Tobin, a Russian immigrant who drove a bakery wagon. Tobin's wife was Besha (née Starkman), a Polish Jew. By the time Rocco moved into their house, Harry

Johnny Torrio. While gangsters like were taking control of the bootleg trade in the United States, Rocco Perri was eliminating the competition in Ontario.

and Bessie had two daughters, Lilly and Gertrude, who were not much more than babies.

Rocco was just a year older than Bessie. He wasn't tall—just five foot four—but he was handsome, strong, and there was something *exciting* about him. One day Tobin came home to find Bessie and Rocco gone and the two little girls crying on the floor. He would never forgive Bessie for this desertion.

With hardly a dollar to their names, Rocco and Bessie went to St. Catharines. Rocco got a pick and shovel job on the Welland Canal, barely earning enough to keep a roof over their heads and put food on the table. Bessie had a baby which died soon after birth, some said under mysterious circumstances. Rocco loved children, but Bessie allegedly was not thrilled at the prospect of caring for another infant. There wasn't going to be time for that.

Sometime after the outbreak of the First World War, the Perris (Bessie was now claiming to be Rocco's wife) moved to Hamilton and Rocco went to work as a travelling salesman for a macaroni company. It seems he also had connections with loosely knit Calabrian and Sicilian crooks known collectively as the Black Hand, who were involved in labour rackets and extortion. Both the job and the criminal links were to prove invaluable to Rocco and Bessie.

On September 16, 1916, the golden opportunity the couple had been waiting for came along. The Ontario Temperance Act went into force and the province became officially dry. Bars closed. Nobody could legally sell alcoholic beverages. Like thousands of other entrepreneurs, Rocco and Bessie went into the bootlegging business. They were given an additional boost 15 months later when the federal government declared nationwide Prohibition as part of the War Measures Act.

The Perris started by purchasing a grocery store and selling whiskey over the counter. There may have been a little more than imbibing going on there, as Bessie soon faced charges of keeping a common bawdy house. When a man was shot and killed right outside the Perris' establishment on New Year's Day, 1919, the police decided they would have to keep an eye on the couple. On January 4 they raided the store and found large quantities of liquor, as well as whiskey labels from a Canadian distillery. Rocco's lawyer argued that the booze was Perri's legal "cellar stock." But it was evident that Rocco and Bessie had been cutting good whiskey with moonshine and then re-bottling the hooch. The liquor was confiscated and Rocco was fined $1,000. It wasn't much of a setback.

Using his cover of macaroni salesman, Rocco could travel all over Ontario and into Quebec and the United States, setting up his bootlegging network. He met with underworld dons, small time hoodlums, and legitimate, respectable members of society who happened to be the owners and managers of breweries and distilleries. Rocco did the legwork and Bessie took telephone orders and managed the money. She had a natural flair for business. She placed the orders with distillers like Gooderham & Worts and Seagrams, and with breweries like Kuntz. She also handled the bank accounts, of which the Perris had several. Thanks to Rocco's connections and Bessie's shrewd management, the Perris were soon able to move into a 19-room mansion at 166 Bay Street South in an exclusive Hamilton neighbourhood. The house was lavishly furnished and had a secret vault for storing loads of whiskey and beer under the basement floor.

The Perris handled every kind of booze: good Canadian whiskey, rotgut moonshine, and real scotch and champagne, which were smuggled into Canada through the French islands of St. Pierre and Miquelon off the coast of Newfoundland. They dealt with big-time American mobsters like Al Capone, Johnny Torrio, Arnold Rothstein, and Stefano "The Undertaker" Magaddino. Their booze went into the United States via the Windsor-Detroit Funnel, across Lake Ontario and across the Niagara River. A favourite crossing point for Rocco was Bridgeburg on the Niagara River. This little community upriver from the Falls was sheltered from the prying eyes of police on the American side by Bird Island. The Canadian rum-runners would slip

Every gangster had a legitimate "cover." Rocco Perri passed himself off as a macaroni salesman.

away from the Ontario shore at dusk, and make the New York side under cover of darkness.

Much of Rocco and Bessie's product was not destined for American consumption, but was "re-imported" into Ontario to slake domestic thirsts. Their own gang included: Rocco's cousins, Mike Serge and Rosario Carboni; Tony Papalia (father of Johnny "Pops" Papalia); and Charlie Bordonaro (destined to become a gangster boss in Hamilton). Rocco never transported the booze personally. If a shipment should be intercepted by the police, someone else would take the rap. But when a load was in transit, Rocco was always nearby.

Rocco and Bessie dealt with crime families throughout Ontario, in Windsor, St. Catharines, Niagara Falls, Toronto and Guelph. The Scaroni brothers of Guelph were, in fact, among Rocco's staunchest allies in the early days. They were to learn, however, that when huge amounts of money are involved, honour among thieves is a myth.

Joe and Domenic Scaroni were Calabrian, like Rocco. They had lived in Buffalo and probably Toronto before Domenic moved to Guelph and Joe to Brantford. They quickly took control of the bootlegging traffic in those communities. Joe, in addition, was known as a hitman, sometimes travelling to the United States on "assignments." In 1918 a gang war began involving the Scaronis, Sicilian Mafiosi in New York State, a gang of Sicilian murderers-for-hire known as the "Good Killers" (because they did their work so well), and somewhere in the background, Rocco Perri.

The first victim was a hoodlum named Joe Celoni, who was shot to death in front of his Hamilton candy store on April 16, 1918. This sparked a rash of killings that left bodies on city streets and in the countryside all across Southern Ontario. The plague of murders swept through Hamilton,

Bessie Starkman was tough and calculating. She abandoned her own children to be with Perri. Many believed she was the real brains behind the Perri empire.

Niagara Falls, Welland, Guelph and Stoney Creek. It reached across the border to strike down mobsters in Buffalo and New Jersey. Most of the killings were done with pistols and shotguns, but some, in true Mafia style, were committed with the stiletto. Over a four-year period, dozens were slain as the mobsters fought over the bootleg trade.

On May 10, 1922, the Guelph mob boss Domenic Scaroni attended a banquet in Niagara Falls, New York. That night his bullet-riddled body was found by a country road on the Niagara Escarpment. His Guelph funeral was a typical gangland send-off. Hoodlums came from far and wide to pay their respects. Rocco Perri was among the mourners. Once Domenic was decently buried, his brother Joe vowed revenge.

The killings continued, with mobsters in Hamilton and Toronto being knocked off by unknown gunmen. Little headway was made in investigations because there wasn't much cooperation amongst the various police forces, and law enforcement agencies chose not to believe that there was such a thing as organized crime in Ontario. Moreover, the press and the public paid little attention to the gang war because most of the victims were Italian "foreigners."

On September 3, 1922, Joe Scaroni had a meeting in Hamilton with Rocco and Bessie. Then Scaroni, the Perris and some other men drove to Guelph where they paid their respects to Domenic's widow. The following day Joe told his sister-in-law that he was going to get Domenic's killers. He took the train to Hamilton and met some underworld associates there and in St. Catharines. The next day, September 5, his body was found in the Welland Canal, bound and weighted down with rocks.

The Hattie C., *one of Perri's rum boats, was shot full of holes by Toronto police. One man was killed and several others were arrested. Perri, as usual, went free.*

There was circumstantial evidence linking Rocco Perri with the murders of the Scaroni brothers and some of the other killings, but nothing that would stand up in court. Did Perri turn on his Calabrian countrymen? That question was never answered. One thing *was* certain: with the elimination of the Scaronis, Perri was in firm control of all the bootlegging in Hamilton, Guelph and Brantford, and had solid ties with Sicilian mob bosses in New York State.

While Rocco was consolidating his liquid empire—and apparently liquidating the competition—he was active on another front. Rocco had taken a mistress, Olive Routledge, a native-born Ontario girl. Rocco met her while travelling as "macaroni salesman" Rocco Ross, and swept the naive farm girl off her feet. Olive knew nothing of Bessie—at first—and was sure that "Rocco Ross" intended to marry her. She had two baby girls by him, Autumn and Catharine. But he would not marry her. Instead, he promised her money for the children's support. Eventually Bessie found out about the affair, and while she could forgive Rocco for his philandering, she would not pay out money for another woman's children. (Bessie did keep in contact with her own daughters, though her legal husband would have nothing to do with her.) In February 1922, a thoroughly distraught Olive committed suicide by jumping out of the seventh-floor window of a Hamilton bank.

Olive's father took custody of the two little girls. Rocco did visit them regularly over the years and help with their support, but clearly it was not only the blood of other criminals that stained his hands.

Olive's story may have worked its way, in a sidelong fashion, into the urban lore of the city of Guelph. Legend has it that Guelph's historic Albion Hotel was a part of Al Capone's booze pipeline in Canada, and that the Chicago gangster often visited there—so often, in fact, that he kept a mistress in the hotel. When Big Al supposedly dumped the woman, she became depressed and killed herself... and, so the story goes, her ghost haunts the old hotel to this day. There is no documented proof that Capone visited Guelph (though it's entirely possible that he did), or that he kept a mistress at the Albion Hotel. It is well known, however, that Rocco Perri was often in Guelph and that the city became part of his territory after the demise of the Scaroni brothers. Perri was called "The Canadian Al Capone," and he had a mistress who killed herself. Could it be that the Albion Hotel ghost story stems from the tragedy of Rocco and Olive?

Rocco and Bessie's "boys" made hundreds of successful deliveries of contraband alcohol to destinations in Canada and the United States, but one attempt to "re-import" a boatload of booze to Toronto went terribly wrong. Late in September of 1923, Sidney Gogo and his son John, of St. Catharines, and Sidney's brother James, of Toronto, along with Fred Van Winkle, sailed Sidney's 33-foot cabin boat, the *Hattie C.* to Belleville to pick up a load of Corby's whiskey. It was a sizeable cargo: over 2,500 quart bottles of Canadian whiskey. As the *Hattie C.* chugged along in a westerly direction on Lake Ontario, the men transferred the bottles from crates to straw-stuffed burlap sacks. Sacks were preferred by most bootleggers over wooden crates because they took up less space and were easier to handle. Another advantage was that if a police boat approached, they could be dumped over the side and would sink, while wooden crates floated. The sunken sacks might be retrieved later.

On October 2, the boat reached Newcastle where Sidney went ashore and took the train to Toronto to make arrangements for delivery of the booze. Late on the night of October 5, the *Hattie C.* nosed into a little inlet of the Toronto shoreline at the foot of Leslie Street. Waiting there with two trucks and two cars were Sidney Gogo, Rocco Perri and three other men. Working quickly and quietly, the bootleggers began to transfer the sacks of whiskey from the boat to the vehicles.

Not quite a mile away, in the Pape Avenue Police Station, Sergeant George Hoag received an anonymous telephone tip (probably from a rival bootlegger) at 12:30 a.m. Something suspicious was going on at the lakeshore at the foot of Leslie Street. The sergeant sent four officers to investigate: Sergeant William Kerr and another constable in uniform, and Constables George Fraser and Bill Mitchell in plainclothes.

The police arrived at the scene and quickly arrested five men who were trying to hide in the bushes. One of them was Rocco Perri. Then, seeing that the *Hattie C.* was attempting to back down the inlet to open water, Kerr shouted, "Police! Stop your boat! Bring in your boat! We have you surrounded!"

The *Hattie C.* continued to back away. Kerr whistled and called out again, "Stop your engine, or I will sink you!" He fired a shot in the air to show he meant business. The captured men on shore began yelling in Italian for the crew of the *Hattie C.* to give up. Then Perri shouted in English, "Stop the engines, or you will be shot!"

The vessel showed no signs of stopping. Kerr ordered his men, "Fire low to sink it!" The four officers cut loose with a fusillade from their .32-calibre revolvers. The bullets, however, did not strike the boat low. Instead, they went smashing into the cabin. The engine stopped suddenly and someone cried, "Don't shoot! There are people on that boat."

Bill Mitchell ran to the other side of the inlet where the *Hattie C.* had drifted and climbed aboard. The beam of his flashlight revealed a grisly scene. James Gogo was on the floor in a pool of blood, his jaw smashed by a bullet. Sidney Gogo had only minor wounds to his hand and neck, but slumped in his arms was his son John. The 24-year-old was dying, his heart and one lung pierced by a bullet. The lure of easy money could be fatal.

This was the first time the Toronto Police had made a major bootlegging-related arrest, and the incident was the talk of the town. The bootleggers and the arresting officers gave very different versions of what had happened. According to the rum-runners, they had legally picked up a load of whiskey at Belleville for delivery to the United States, but had been forced to put in at Toronto because of engine trouble and heavy seas. They were loading their booze into the vehicles to complete the delivery to the U.S., when the police showed up and began to fire without warning. Rocco Perri said he had nothing to do with the liquor at all. He was there, he said, because a man had asked him for some directions, and he had gone with him to show him the way. He was just an innocent macaroni salesman—which didn't explain why two of the vehicles were registered in Bessie's name.

An examination showed that the boat was in perfect condition, aside from a few recently acquired bullet holes, and a navigational expert said that boating conditions on the lake that night were not such that would have forced the vessel to seek safe harbour. The police officers said that they *had* shouted warnings and had opened fire only when it appeared that the *Hattie C.* was escaping. Their judgement in using their guns came under scrutiny. The bootleggers were not armed, and .32-calibre bullets could not have sunk a boat that size. Moreover, there was no law permitting police officers to shoot at fleeing bootleggers. The officers were charged with manslaughter, but the charges were dropped after two trials resulted in hung juries.

Sidney Gogo and Frank DePietro were found guilty of violating the Ontario Temperance Act and given the choice of a $1,000 fine or thirty days in jail. DePietro paid the fine and Gogo took the thirty days. He had lost his boat, and worse than that, his son. Rocco, who had walked away with no charges laid, told him that he would pay him money to make up in some degree for his losses. But when Gogo went to the Perri house in Hamilton to collect the promised compensation, Bessie told him to go to hell.

By 1924, the names of some of America's biggest bootleggers, like Dion O'Banion and Al Capone, were household words—especially after Capone's gunmen shot and killed O'Banion in his Chicago flower shop in broad daylight. Rocco Perri craved the limelight too, and agreed to an interview with Toronto *Star* reporter David Rogers. Rogers went to Rocco and Bessie's beautiful Hamilton mansion on November 18th and scooped the story of the year. There had been rumours that Perri was responsible for the murders of two Hamilton men whose bodies had been found on Hamilton Mountain, a favourite dumping ground for hit men with corpses to dispose of. Rocco wanted to set things straight.

"Everything that happens they blame on Rocco Perri," the gangster told the journalist. "Why is it? Maybe because my name is so easy to say. I don't know. It is amusing... How came these two men to be killed? I know not."

Perri went on to say that there was no bootleg war going on, and that he did not permit his men to carry guns. "My men do not carry guns. If they do, I get rid of them. It is not necessary. I provide them with high powered cars. That is enough. If they cannot run away from the police, it is their own fault. But guns make trouble. My men do not use them."

Perri boasted of being "The King of the Bootleggers," saying "Am I a criminal because I violate a law which the people do not want?" He said that he dealt only in good quality beer and liquor, and was always a square dealer. He had never killed anyone, he said. "You may say to the people what I have told you," Rocco said at the end of the interview. "They blame everything on me now anyway. I have no good name to lose. My reputation is long since blackened. I am a bootlegger. I am not ashamed to admit it. And a bootlegger I shall remain."

The story sent shock waves that were felt across Hamilton, and in Toronto, Ottawa and the United States. Reporters for Hamilton papers, stunned that they had been scooped by a youngster from Toronto, flocked to the Perri house to get more quotes from the self-proclaimed King of the Bootleggers. Rocco and Bessie, basking in this celebrity, were happy to oblige. Religious and prohibitionist leaders in Hamilton howled that Perri should be deported back to Italy. Government officials in Toronto and Ottawa seethed in frustration because even though Perri had admitted in the press that he was a bootlegger, they could take no legal action against him without hard evidence. American officials saw the *Star* interview as proof positive that the Canadian government was doing nothing to stop the flow of booze to the United States.

Corruption was one of the main reasons Rocco and Bessie, as well as other gangsters on both sides of the border, were able to get away with their crimes. Money from the enormous profits of bootlegging found its way into the pockets of policemen, judges, politicians and civil servants from the lowest to the highest levels. Many a lawyer had a fat bank account thanks to the fees paid by bootlegging clients. Rocco and Bessie had allegedly "bought" Hamilton police chief William Whately. The chief, it was said, socialized with them and gave them advance warning of police raids. There was even a story that he'd had an affair with Bessie. Whately was on the verge of being investigated when he suddenly died of pneumonia.

Rocco was only partially correct when he said that Prohibition was a law the people didn't want. Ontario voters were divided almost equally on the matter, with the "Drys" winning by an ever decreasing margin each time a referendum was held. He was not telling the truth at all when he said that he dealt only in quality liquor. Less than a year after the *Star* interview,

Rocco would be in the papers again, but this time not as the cocky boot-legger chock full of bravado.

It was common practise for bootleggers to maximize their profits by cutting properly distilled and aged liquor with other substances. One such additive was redistilled alcohol, generally manufactured for industrial pur-poses. If the mixing was not done carefully—and it frequently wasn't—the result could be a death cocktail.

In July 1925, a concoction that was 93.9 percent wood alcohol found its way into the booze pipeline run by Perri and several other gang-sters. If anybody in the mob knew about the deadly brew that was making its way across Ontario and Western New York, they kept their mouths shut. The first deaths occurred on July 21, when three men in Allenburg, Ontario, were killed by the poisonous booze. In the weeks that followed there were similar tragedies in Toronto, Hamilton, Oakville, Parry Sound, Niagara Falls, Brantford, Sudbury, Lockport and Buffalo, until the death list reached 45. Others who drank the stuff survived but were left blind.

Police in Canada and the United States began rounding up known bootleggers. Rocco Perri was number one on the wanted list, and many of the other men arrested were known to be his associates. For a while Rocco couldn't be found. Then on July 31 he walked into the Hamilton police sta-tion with a pair of lawyers and surrendered himself. Reporters begged him for a statement, but this time Rocco didn't feel like talking. They tried call-ing Bessie, but she didn't have much to say either. After several days in the lock-up Rocco was released on bail while the police and a Pinkerton under-cover agent tried to track down the source of the poison alcohol. The inves-tigation was severely hampered by a lack of cooperation between Canadian and American authorities. The undercover agent did learn that the lethal booze had originated in the United States, and that Canadian bootleggers were furious with the Americans for endangering the business with their bad brew. He also heard the underworld scuttlebutt on Rocco Perri: that the law couldn't touch him because "he has plenty on the big fellows in this town." In the end, four men—none of them big-league bootleggers—went to jail for manslaughter. Rocco Perri walked away scot-free.

The poison liquor scare had one important consequence for Ontario. In spite of the opposition of the most fanatical of the "Drys," on June 1, 1927, Prohibition ended in Ontario. There were still no legal bars or licensed restaurants, some towns and counties voted to remain dry, and government-operated liquor stores were few and far between. In fact, regulations governing the legal sale of alcohol were such that it was easier to buy a firearm than it was to buy a bottle. Nonetheless, the bootleg market in Ontario was drying up. But there was still the good old U.S. of A.

The smuggling of alcohol and other goods was costing the Canadian government vast sums of money in lost customs taxes. In March 1927 a Royal Commission on Customs and Excise began hearings on the matter. Among the many people summoned to testify were Rocco and Bessie Perri. Bessie showed up for the hearing alone. She said that Rocco was out of town and she didn't know where to reach him. It seemed there were a lot of things Bessie didn't know. She didn't know what her husband's business was. She didn't know anything about the countless long-distance telephone calls made from her house to the Gooderham & Worts Distillery (of which the Commission had the records). She didn't know anything about the men who frequently came to her house to see Rocco. "I'm only a woman," she said. When asked about money she had in the bank, she produced a bank book which showed a balance of $98. The Commission would soon discover that she had several bank accounts holding hundreds of thousands of dollars—millions in today's terms. Throughout the two days of questioning Bessie was evasive, and Bessie lied.

The Commission still wanted to question Rocco, but nobody could find him. Then two Hamilton police officers pretended to be prowlers breaking into Perri's garage. The "out of town" Rocco came out of the house to investigate the noise, and the cops served him with a subpoena to appear before the Commission on April 4.

The Commission got right to the interview that had appeared in the Toronto *Star*. Rocco explained that the *Star* had been pestering him for an interview so he just told the reporter a big story to get rid of him. When asked directly if he was a bootlegger, he said that he had done a little mail-order bootlegging at one time, but that he had long since quit. Pressed on the matter of the interview, Rocco said that he didn't really know what was in that article because he didn't read English very well.

Like Bessie, Rocco was evasive and he lied. He also threw in some convenient memory lapses and difficulty with English. The one honest statement he made was the one that was most shocking to many of the people there. He admitted that he and Bessie had been living together for 15 years, but had never been married.

There were other people to be interviewed. By the time the Commission was finished, it was pretty clear, despite all of the Perris' denials, that they were both heavily involved in bootlegging and had lied on the stand. Warrants were issued for their arrests on charges of perjury. But Rocco and Bessie could not be found.

Meanwhile, the government was going after the distilleries and breweries whose products had not been shipped to the United States, but had been sold in Canada. There were taxes owing on that, even though the Canadian sales had been illegal. They decided to prosecute Gooderham & Worts in a test case, and who knew that company's dealings better than its best customers, Rocco and Bessie! A deal was made, and suddenly the Perris were there in Hamilton, ready to testify against their old supplier. Under the protection of the Canada Evidence Act, which made them immune from prosecution for anything they might say at the hearing, Rocco and Bessie took the stand and helped the government stick the distillery with a bill for almost half a million dollars in unpaid taxes. Success with this case enabled the Crown to move on and collect millions of dollars from the other distilleries and breweries that had been active in the bootleg business. The Perris' good deed in testifying for the Crown did not go unrewarded. When they had to face a judge themselves for perjury, the charges against Bessie were dropped and Rocco was sentenced to a mere six months in the Ontario Reformatory at Guelph. That was no problem. Like everybody else in the rackets, Rocco knew that doing a little time now and then went with the territory.

It wasn't bootleg liquor that brought disaster to Rocco and Bessie, but narcotics. The Perris had been involved in smuggling morphine, cocaine and heroin into the United States and Canada since the early 1920s. Through informants and the work of a courageous RCMP agent who went undercover to infiltrate the drug-dealing underworld, police learned that by 1929 the Perris operated the biggest drug ring in Ontario. They were part of an international criminal organization, and were responsible for a lot of the narcotics that went to American cities. Bessie, the agent reported, was the brains of the gang. As, province by province, Canada gave up on Prohibition, and it became evident that sooner or later the United States would also abandon the Noble Experiment—thus putting many bootleggers out of business—the Perris invested more and more in narcotics. But they carried out their business so carefully that the police could never get enough

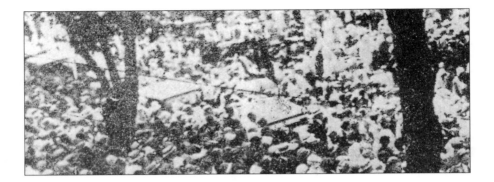

hard evidence on them. Had the RCMP been successful in bringing them to book, Bessie would have lived longer, even if it had been behind bars.

The drug trade was (and still is) even nastier than the bootlegging business, and involved the most vicious elements of the underworld—vile men who could commit the lowest sort of cold-blooded murder without batting an eye. At some point, Bessie received a shipment of narcotics from gangsters operating out of Rochester, New York, and then refused to pay for it. On the night of August 12, 1930, three men showed up at the Perris' house in Hamilton and demanded payment. Rocco advised Bessie to pay up, but she was stubborn. She had got away with chiselling people in the past; why should this time be any different? She and Rocco *owned* the rackets in Ontario. Who was going to mess with them? Bessie ordered the men out of her house.

The following night, August 13, Rocco and Bessie pulled into their garage at 11:35, not suspecting that assassins were crouched behind another car parked there. The Perris got out of their car; Rocco to go back and close the garage doors, Bessie to go and turn on the light and unlock the back door. The night suddenly exploded with three shotgun blasts. The first one missed, but the next two tore into Bessie. Rocco later claimed that he could see nothing because of the smoke. He ran. When he came back with a neighbour, they found Bessie dead on the garage floor, her head and body perforated by buckshot. There was no sign of the killers except for the guns they had carefully left behind, *sans* fingerprints. The slaying had all the earmarks of a professional hit.

That a *woman*—even a suspected criminal like Bessie Perri—could be so brutally murdered, shocked the country. There was an intense police

(Above) Rocco was inconsolable at Bessie's funeral, but when gunmen had opened fire on her, he ran. (Page left) Most of the crowd at Bessie Starkman's funeral were there out of morbid curiosity, not because they were mourners. She was gunned down after she double-crossed the wrong people.

investigation, but the killers were never found. Harry Tobin, still Bessie's legal husband, said that in his opinion she got what she deserved.

Bessie's murder devastated Rocco. He gave her an elaborate funeral and buried her in a coffin that cost more than some people's houses. He swore he would have revenge on her killers and he put a price on their heads—whoever they might be. But police suspected he knew who the killers were and that he did nothing because he feared further retribution.

Grief and mental depression clouded the next few years of Rocco's life. There were adverse external forces at work, too. The stock market crash of 1929 had ushered in the Great Depression, throwing millions of would-be customers out of work. Then the United States repealed the Volstead Act, ending American Prohibition. Ironically, this brought about a reverse in the direction of the flow of bootleg booze. American liquor was

Rocco Perri, who had rubbed out so many rivals, became a target himself. He was miraculously thrown clear when a bomb demolished his car.

cheaper than Canadian liquor, and Rocco had the apparatus to smuggle it into Canada. He could also make whiskey more readily available than the over-regulated Ontario Liquor Control Board could. But Rocco did not handle money well, and his crime empire began to crumble.

Then, in 1933, Perri had a new girlfriend and business partner, Annie Newman. Like Bessie, Annie was a Polish Jew, and though she was petite and beautiful she was hard as nails when it came to business. With Annie at the helm, Rocco's business began to flourish again. The new Perri couple made a fortune smuggling American booze as well as illegal gambling equipment into Canada. But as is always the case with criminal enterprises, Rocco's success did not please everybody.

In 1938 there were two attempts to kill Rocco with bombs. One left the front porch of his house a smoking ruin. The other blew his car to pieces. Rocco, who had been in the car when the bomb went off, was miraculously thrown clear and suffered only minor injuries. To add to their troubles, Annie was arrested for possession of an unregistered handgun.

In 1939, on the very eve of the outbreak of the Second World War, Rocco and Annie were arrested for bribing customs officers and conspiracy to breach the Customs Act. The RCMP had been investigating them for a long time, and was sure they had enough on the pair to get a conviction. However, when the case went to trial early in 1940, a jury acquitted them. It seemed that as far as the law was concerned, Rocco Perri was untouchable... until Benito Mussolini declared war on Britain in June 1940.

The Canadian federal government and the RCMP responded with a plan to intern all Italians in Canada suspected of having "Fascist" sympathies.

Annie Newman became the woman in Rocco's life after Bessie's murder. She revived Perri's deteriorating business, but could not keep him out of a wartime internment camp... or herself out of jail.

It was a good excuse to round up and lock away all the Italian gangsters (as well as a lot of innocent people) who had thus far kept out of the clutches of the law. Rocco Perri's name was again at the top of the list. He was sent to an internment camp at Petawawa, Ontario, and try as she would, Annie could not get him out. Rocco would endure three years of imprisonment not for his many crimes, but for being Italian.

While Rocco sat out the early war years in Petawawa, Annie became involved in a new kind of racket. During Prohibition, booze had been called "liquid gold." Now Annie was dealing with the real thing. The war had driven up the value of gold, so of course those whose greed outweighed patriotism looked for a way to cash in. Annie became a key link in an international ring smuggling high-graded gold from Northern Ontario mines into the United States. It was an extremely lucrative business. The problem was that American police and the RCMP were onto it, and had the gang under surveillance for a long time. When the cops moved in, Annie was caught in the net. She was sentenced to five years in Kingston, of which she would serve over two.

On October 10, 1943, with Italy all but knocked out of the war and people of Italian background no longer considered a threat to national security, Rocco Perri was released from Petawawa. He was, in effect, on parole, and one of the conditions was that he find legitimate employment. Before being sent off to jail herself (she was still incarcerated at the time of Rocco's release) Annie had bought the Metro Theatre in Toronto. Rocco got a "job" there as doorman and janitor. But like his old position of "macaroni salesman," it was only a cover. Rocco intended to pick up where he had left off when the government and the RCMP had so rudely interfered. He was going to get back into the rackets. The situation was different, though, than it had been three years earlier.

Perri (right) with Hamilton's acting police chief, Joe Crocker, after the car bombing. Perri survived two attempts on his life. His luck was to run out the third time.

When the RCMP swooped down on Ontario's Italian gangsters in 1940 and packed them off to internment camps, they thought that in so doing they would break the strength of the mob in the province. Instead, they created a power vacuum, which was quickly filled by the Buffalo crime family of Stefano Magaddino. Now Rocco Perri was starting to push his way back into Hamilton's bootlegging business. The Undertaker wasn't about to let that happen.

On April 23, 1944, Rocco was staying at the Hamilton home of his cousin Joe Serge. Complaining of a headache, he said he was going to take a walk to clear his head. It was between 10:30 and 11:00 in the morning when he went out the door. Rocco Perri was never seen again. As happens with almost numbing regularity in the stories of crime bosses, Rocco was rubbed out.

Rocco and Bessie—and Annie—were not people to be admired. They lived by deceit and violence, and did not hesitate to kill—or have someone else kill—any who got in their way. They engaged in the drug trade, which places them among the lowest dregs of humanity. But they were colourful, and they were Canadian (even though Rocco never did become a naturalized Canadian citizen). As Franklin Roosevelt said of American mobsters who were being recruited to help with the American war effort during the Second World War, "They may be sons of bitches, but they're *our* sons of bitches." In Canada, Rocco Perri was one of *our* sons of bitches.

When it comes to notorious characters, as in so many other things, Canada has been overshadowed by the United States. When Canadians do come up with an interesting bad guy, they have to see how he measures up to the American model. Thus, Canadian bank robber Red Ryan is called *the Canadian Jesse James*. Rocco Perri has been called *the Canadian Al Capone*. Why not call Al Capone *the American Rocco Perri*?

The answer lies with the media. Even though Capone died a gibbering idiot, his brain wasted by syphilis, his legend took on a life of its own, helped along by novels, biographies, a long list of Hollywood films, and even a television series, *The Untouchables*. Say the words *gangster* or *bootlegger*, and the image that comes to mind is that of Al Capone.

Rocco Perri, who held sway over a criminal empire at least as large as Capone's, provided Scarface with much of his bootleg liquor, and actually outlasted Capone in the business, was soon forgotten by the public. It was not until Canadian journalists James Dubro and Robin Rowland co-wrote their excellent biography *King of the Mob*, published in 1987, that Canadians of this generation became aware of the most notorious gangster their country has ever produced.

Rocco Perri's disappearance is still an unsolved mystery. Rumours that circulated shortly after he was last seen alive suggest that his body is in a block of cement at the bottom of Hamilton Bay. It would be poetically fitting if it were surrounded down there in the mud by a few ditched bottles of Canadian whiskey.

Rocco Perri is all smiles as he sits by an RCMP constable during a court hearing. Perri beat almost every rap against him. He served more time in a wartime internment camp for being Italian than he ever did in jail for his many crimes.

The Purple Gang in a 1928 Detroit police lineup. The men, who considered the Detroit River "our river," struck terror into the hearts of rival gangsters.

THE PURPLE GANG

In the heady days of Prohibition, Chicago was the city that was grabbing headlines around the world as the capital of bootlegging violence, but that was largely because of the antics of the publicity-hungry mobster Al Capone. Detroit, the main entry point for Canadian booze flowing into the warehouses of Capone and all the other gang leaders across the U.S., was every bit as violent. More than a hundred gangsters—from the ranks of the dime-a-dozen, small-time hoodlums to the big boys at the top—were slain in gun battles over liquor and turf. Well served by railroads, highways and water transportation, Detroit was ideally located for the trafficking of illegal alcohol. It has been estimated that 75 percent of the beer and liquor that entered the United States from Canada during the Prohibition years passed through Detroit. That meant money in amounts hitherto undreamed of by criminals, and a lot of hands trying to snatch a piece of the action.

The American government, police and apostles of temperance may have looked upon the Detroit River as a moat protecting Fortress America from the evils of Canadian booze. To the bootleggers, it was but a minor challenge. Enough liquor and beer crossed the 28-mile-long waterway to fill a Great Lake, giving the border area the nickname "The Windsor-Detroit Funnel." Much of it went by train in crates with false labels. More went by car and truck, ingeniously hidden to escape detection by border guards. Some was flown across, the planes loading up with hooch at farm fields in

Purple Gang rivals, the Licavoli Gang (also called the River Gang), led by brothers Pete and Yonnie. Among other crimes, they murdered radio personality Jerry Buckley.

Ontario, and landing secretly at farm fields in Michigan. In 1929, American officers discovered a device that used a 500-foot cable to drag cases of liquor across the river bottom. Legend has it that there was actually a booze pipeline extending under the river from the Canadian side to the American side. There were even stories of liquor-laden torpedoes being fired under the water from one shore to the other.

The most common means of rum-running, however, was by boat. Motor boats, sailboats, canoes, rafts—anything that could float was loaded up at the docks of Windsor and smaller Ontario communities and sent across the river. To beat the American border patrols, rum-runners relied on speed, stealth and cunning. And even though the lawmen stopped *some* of the contraband, the volume was just too much for them. The rum-runners bought off crooked lawmen with bribes, and carried guns to discourage those who couldn't be bought. Winter, when the river froze over, was no problem. The liquor crossed the ice in cars, on sleds or packed in a sack on a strong man's back.

The rum-runners embarking from the Canadian shore went armed not only to protect their cargo from American police, but also because the men waiting to receive the shipments on the other side weren't exactly known for their honest business dealings. Competition was stiff, and many a load of contraband liquor was hijacked.

Several criminal gangs carved up the Detroit turf—and sometimes each other. The East Side had the Gianolla Gang. The West Side was the stronghold of the Calalanotte Gang. The Downriver section was controlled by Yonnie Licavoli and the River Gang. Two other gangster organizations, the Unione Siciliana and the Pascuzzi Combine also had claims on the action. But the most notorious and vicious of Detroit's mobsters was the Purple Gang.

Like other large American cities at the turn of the twentieth century, Detroit had large areas of overcrowded, reeking, poverty-wracked slums—natural breeding grounds for criminals. One such neighbourhood, populated largely by Russian-Jewish immigrants, produced the young thugs who would one day be the nucleus of the Purple Gang. No one is certain where the unusual name originated. The most accepted anecdote is that two Hastings Street merchants who had suffered at the hands of the young hoodlums were overheard in conversation. One of the men complained, "These boys are not like the other fine children their age. They're tainted; off-colour."

"Yes," agreed the other. "These boys are rotten; purple, like the colour of bad meat. They're purple."

Credit for "founding" the gang went to a hood named Sammy Cohen. Sometime during the First World War, Cohen organized the wayward youths into a gang that preyed on their own people, specializing in shop-lifting and petty extortion. They beat up other kids, and were even known to gang up on adults. At some point Cohen disappeared, and leadership went to the Bernstein brothers: Ray, Abe, Izzy, and Joe. More than fifty racketeers and gunmen would belong to the gang at various times, but among the principals, besides the Bernsteins, were George Lewis, Sam "Gorilla" Davis, Lou and Harry Fleisher, Harry and Phil Keywell, Abe Axler, Irving Milberg, Abe "The Agent" Zussman, Zigmund "Ziggie" Selbin and Eddie Fletcher.

Under the leadership of the Bernsteins, the Purple Gang moved up from petty street crime to armed robbery, large-scale extortion and bootlegging.

Purple Gang gunman Harry Fleisher (left) one of the shooters at the Collingwood Massacre. He put a couple of extra shots into one victim who was "still living a bit."

They got an early start in the latter when Michigan went dry in 1916, three years ahead of national Prohibition. Their favourite tactic was hijacking other gangs' booze shipments, or forcing rivals to pay them "protection" to leave their operations alone. The Purple Gang's threats were not idle. They did not hesitate to use clubs, brass knuckles and guns, and they quickly developed a reputation for savage violence. Phil Keywell shot and killed a 17-year-old boy he suspected of being a spy. Irving Milberg was one of the most feared gunmen in the city. Lou Fleisher's behaviour was so unpredictable, people would leave a room when he entered, fearful of what he might do.

By preying on other gangsters, the Purple Gang not only established themselves as wolves among the dogs, but they were also somewhat insulated from the law. Criminals who were robbed by other criminals did not tend to go to the police. It was a long time before Detroit authorities were fully aware of the gang's activities.

In the early 1920s, the Purple Gang gained the attention of two older mobsters, Charlie Leiter and Henry Schorr, who ran the Oakland Sugarhouse Gang. These men employed the young toughs as "muscle," sending them out to intimidate rival gangsters and victims of their extortion rackets—work the Purple boys took to with gusto. Eventually the Sugarhouse and Purple Gangs would merge into one, and Schorr would disappear (murdered, it was suspected, by Harry and Sam Davis after having a quarrel with Leiter).

The Purples grew in power and reputation, and had their hands in every racket in which an ambitious criminal could earn a dirty dollar: gambling, prostitution, narcotics, kidnapping. They were in great demand as well-paid mercenaries in labour disputes, and were the architects of the bloody mayhem that erupted in the Cleaners and Dyers War between union and non-union shops in Detroit's dry-cleaning and clothes-dying industries.

The main source of income, however, was booze. Tens of thousands of people were involved in bootlegging in one way or another, from the gang leaders down to the people who waited tables in blind pigs and speakeasies. Collectively, the bootleggers were one of Motor City's biggest employers, coming in second only to the automobile industry. Detroit was a tempting prize for many gangsters, but to move in on Purple Gang turf was to invite swift and violent death, as two hoodlums found out in August 1927 when Irving Milberg (police believed) gunned them down in a cabaret on St. Antoine Street. That same year a crooked cop named Vivian Welsh made the mistake of shaking down speakeasies that were under the "protection" of the Purple Gang. A cop on the gangsters' payroll was one thing, but a cop who was lining his pockets independently just couldn't be tolerated. Welsh was taken for a ride. His body was found with nine bullet holes in it. No one was ever officially charged with Welsh's murder, but the message was clear: lay off Purple Gang property!

Even Al Capone thought it the better part of valour to do business with the Purple Gang rather than get into a war with them. When Scarface visited Detroit, apparently with intentions of extending his control over the "Funnel" from Windsor, the Purple boys told him in no uncertain terms, "That's *our* river." So Al became their biggest customer, buying vast quantities of their Canadian whiskey for his thirsty Chicago clients. Abe Bernstein showed Big Al his appreciation by making a crucial Valentine's Day telephone call to Capone rival George "Bugs" Moran.

That isn't to say that the Purple Gang didn't have rivals in Detroit. An equally vicious outfit which battled them throughout the latter part of the Roaring Twenties was the River Gang, led by Pete and Thomas "Yonnie" Licavoli, and Frank Cammarata. Originally from St. Louis, the

Yonnie Licavoli (left) spent time in a Canadian prison because he didn't understand that, in Canada, people were not allowed to carry around .38-calibre pistols.

Licavolies and Cammarata had been bank robbers, but turned to bootlegging when they saw the immense profits to be made. They managed to grab control of some of the river traffic, and had connections on the Canadian side. Frank and Yonnie ran afoul of Canadian law in 1927 when they were arrested in a Windsor hotel on weapons charges. At their trial their lawyer argued that because the defendants were in the bootlegging business, it was not unusual for them to be armed. The judge, however, wasn't buying it. Stating that in Canada it wasn't necessary for people to carry around .38-calibre handguns, he sentenced the pair to three years in the Kingston Penitentiary. They were paroled after two-and-a-half years for good behaviour, and went right back to bootlegging.

Among the many murders the River Gang was responsible for was that of radio personality Jerry Buckley, who was gunned down in the lobby of the La Salle Hotel. It was said at first that Buckley was killed because of his crusading, anti-crime broadcasts; but evidence later showed that Buckley had swindled the Licavolies in a real-estate deal in Canada, and had been blackmailing certain gangsters who couldn't risk the kind of publicity he could give them on his radio program. Yonnie Licavoli would eventually be sentenced to life in prison for the murder of a man he suspected of having an affair with his girlfriend. For mobsters, a well-placed bullet was the solution to all problems, from the financial to the romantic kind. Such an attitude was to finally bring about the downfall of the Purple Gang.

In 1926 the Sugarhouse Gang brought three Chicago punks to Detroit as hired gunmen: Joseph "Nigger Joe" Lebovitz; Herman "Hymie" Paul; and

Radio personality Jerry Buckley. The public thought he'd been killed because of his anti-crime radio broadcasts. He had actually made the mistake of swindling gangsters.

Joseph "Izzie" Sutker. They were street soldiers, whose job it was to protect their bosses' liquor shipments and other rackets. They got greedy, though, and decided to branch out on their own.

Lebovitz, Paul, and Sutker made connections with the Third Avenue Navy, a gang so named because they landed their cargoes of whiskey from Canada at the rail yards between Third and Fourth Avenues. It must be understood that even in the cutthroat business of bootlegging, there were rules—don't doublecross your friends, don't hijack other gangs' booze, don't horn in on other gangs' territories. Unless, of course, you have the muscle to get away with it. The trio broke all the rules, and in the end they didn't have the muscle. They hijacked from everybody. They doublecrossed everybody. They trespassed on everybody's territory. They were nicknamed "The Terrors of Third Street," they had a city-wide reputation for being untrustworthy. Others in the bootlegging fraternity were soon refusing to do business with them. So the boys turned to extortion, and selected as targets some speakeasies and blind pigs under Purple Gang protection. The owners of those establishments called the Bernsteins for help. Some gentlemen from the Purple Gang confronted the trio and made them pay back the money, then ordered them out of town. The police, too, served the three amateurs notice. They were loose cannons in an already volatile situation.

The young crooks, who should have thanked their lucky stars that they were still alive, didn't heed the warnings. Instead, they got into the bookmaking racket, taking in as a partner an old Purple Gang friend named Solly Levine. They were doing okay until the spring of 1931 when members of the East Side Mob cashed in on a bet to the tune of several hundred thousand dollars. The trio didn't have the money to cover the bet, and they knew that gangsters had no patience with welchers. Probably using Levine as a go-between, they turned to the Purple Gang for help. The Purples sold them a large quantity of liquor on credit. The trio diluted the booze, and then sold it below the "market price" to turn a quick profit. Undercutting the big boys was very, very dangerous. And the trio did it *twice!* The time had come for affirmative action.

In September 1931 the American Legion Convention was going to be held in Detroit. The demand for booze was enormous, and it was all the gangsters could do to fill the flood of orders. They were going to need every man they could find to handle the liquor, the gambling and all the other "services" the Legionnaires would be seeking. On September 14, Ray Bernstein had a meeting with Solly Levine. Sutker, Paul and Lebovitz still owed the Purple Gang money for whiskey they'd bought on credit, and the upcoming convention would be a good opportunity for everybody to settle accounts.

"We've got everything straightened out, and we're going to let you boys handle the horse bets and alcohol when you straighten out that bill," Bernstein told Levine. Solly said that his friends just needed some time to raise the money, and the convention would fix everything up for them. Bernstein said that he would arrange a peace meeting, and would let Levine know the where and the when. Solly passed this message on to the others, who were delighted. It certainly didn't hurt to be "in" with the Purple Gang.

On the morning of September 16, Levine was in his partners' bookie joint when he got a phone call. He was told to get Sutker, Paul, and Lebovitz and be at 1740 Collingwood Avenue, apartment 211 at 3:00 p.m. He wanted to leave one of them behind to look after the shop, but was told no, bring all three. Levine rounded up the boys and, travelling in Sutker's car, they were at the address at the appointed time. They were unarmed, as it would not have looked good to take guns to a peace meeting. Smoking cigars, and no doubt with thoughts of good days ahead in their minds, they walked into 1740 Collingwood and went up to apartment 211.

Ray Bernstein greeted them in the second-floor hallway. He said he was glad to see them and invited them inside. Waiting there were Harry Fleisher, Irving Milberg and Harry Keywell. Fleisher's presence was a surprise because the police were looking for him and he had gone to ground sometime earlier. Everybody shook hands and the Purples had their visitors sit down on a long couch. Levine, Paul and Lebovitz sat next to each other, and Sutker sat on the arm. Music had been playing when they entered, but now someone turned off the phonograph.

For a few minutes the men talked, friendly, casual banter. It did not seem to alarm the four on the couch that they were all bunched together, with the Purple Gang standing or sitting directly across from them. Fleisher asked Bernstein, "Where's that guy with the books?"

Bernstein said something about going to check, and went downstairs, apparently to use the phone. He went out of the building to a car the gang had waiting in an alleyway. He turned on the engine, revved it loudly, and leaned on the horn.

"That was the signal," Levine said later. "All of a sudden Fleisher pulled his gun and fired at Nigger Joe and the bullet went right by my nose. He asked me if I was hit. He seemed worried about that. At the same time, Milberg and Keywell fired at the other two."

The three young hoodlums were taken completely by surprise. They tried to run even as the first shots were fired, but all of them were cut down in a barrage of bullets from Colt .38 pistols. It was all over in a matter of seconds.

Levine couldn't believe he was still alive, and expected that within moments he would be dead. The three killers conferred for a few seconds, then one of them turned to him and said, "Let's go." Levine followed Keywell and Milberg through the kitchen, where the two gangsters dropped their guns into a can of green paint. The serial numbers had already been filed off. The paint would take care of any fingerprints. They went down the back stairs to the alley where Bernstein was waiting in a black 1930 Chrysler. Only then did they realize that Fleisher wasn't with them. Then they heard more shots from the apartment building. Moments later Fleisher came out and jumped into the car. "Nigger Joe was still living a bit," he explained.

Burning rubber on the pavement, the car shot out of the alleyway onto the street, almost running over a small boy who was playing there. "We drove like the devil for a few blocks," Levine later testified, "almost hitting a truck and just missing a woman and a little child. Then we split up and Bernstein shook hands with me again and said, 'I am your pal, Solly.' He gave me three or four hundred dollars and said to go back to the book (betting office) and he'd pick me up later."

Levine may have thought that he had been spared because he was from the gang's old neighbourhood. He learned later that they had planned to murder him and plant a gun on his body so it would look as if he had been the killer.

Irving Millberg, Ray Bernstein and Harry Keywell on trail for their part in the Collingwood Massacre. The triple murder proved to be the downfall of the gang.

Police were at the murder scene quickly, and news of the slaughter shocked Detroit. The city had certainly had its share of gangland killings, but three unarmed men executed in cold blood was a bit too much, especially just two-and-a-half years after the St. Valentine's Day Massacre. The Collingwood hit was already going into gangster lore as the Collingwood Massacre.

Levine was quickly picked up by police and questioned. He tried to lie his way out, but the police knew of his involvement and he had no choice but to talk. Tips from Purple Gang enemies were coming in from all over. Cops and rival gangsters alike saw a chance to break the gang's power. Lawmen had orders to bring in Purple Gang members "dead or alive." Wayne County Prosecutor Harry S. Toy reportedly had messages from Purple Gang leaders offering to surrender if they could cut a deal. "There will be no deals," he said.

Within 48 hours, raids on apartment buildings by heavily armed police had netted Ray Bernstein, Henry Keywell, Irving Milberg and several other key gang members. The much-feared tough guys did not put up a fight, even though their places of residence were well stocked with guns and other weapons. Harry Fleisher was not captured until 1932 and never was convicted of the Collingwood murders, though he did serve time in prison for other crimes.

The trial of Milberg, Bernstein and Keywell was one of the most sensational in Detroit history. Solly Levine was the reluctant star witness for the prosecution, and after hearing his testimony the jury took only an hour and a half to reach a "guilty" verdict. The three killers were sentenced to life imprisonment.

A terrified Solly Levine left the United States, certain that other Purple Gang members would be after him. He sailed to France, but French authorities wouldn't allow him into the country. Then he tried Ireland, but couldn't get in there either. Then he vanished from the face of the earth. Whether he successfully hid himself from gangsters and police, or was a victim of Purple Gang vengeance has never been determined. Prosecutor Harry Toy was quoted as saying, "These men checked their books with bullets and marked off their accounts with blood."

Many Purple Gang members were still at large, and still vicious, but the myth of the gang's invincibility was shattered. The remnants of the gang, as well as most of the other Detroit mobs, were absorbed when Charles "Lucky" Luciano's East Coast Syndicate, with its headquarters in New York, expanded into Detroit. Those who wouldn't knuckle under to the new regime were "taken for a ride," as happened to Eddie Fletcher and Abe Axler. Harry Millman was gunned down by New York's Murder Incorporated, an organization of professional killers-for-hire. Most surviving Purple Gang members wound up in prison sooner or later. Some died there. Others were released as broken old men. Surprisingly, Ray was the only one of the Bernstein brothers to do prison time for Purple Gang crimes. In 1963, crippled by a stroke and confined to a wheelchair, he told his parole board, "I needed correction and I got it. I learned that crime certainly does not pay." He was released on a mercy parole in 1964. In 1966 he became one of the few Prohibition Era bootleggers to die of natural causes.

February 14, 1929. Bullet-riddled bodies and pools of blood on the floor of a Chicago garage—the climax of years of gang warfare that started in a flower shop. (Right) Capone began his crim-inal career as an enforcer for the Five Points Gang in New York. He was efficient with his fists, knives, brass knuckles and guns.

Booze Wars in Chicago

Perhaps no other single image has come to epitomize the violence of Prohibition America more than that of a group of bullet-riddled mobsters crumpled on the floor of a Chicago garage. The St. Valentine's Day Massacre, as it came to be called, in which seven men were gunned down in a cold-blooded execution, would stand for over four decades as the biggest incident of mass murder in modern American history. It would establish Al Capone as the archetype American gangster. But the killing did not happen because Capone made a spur-of-the-moment decision to eliminate a few bootlegging rivals in Chicago. It was the culmination of years of open gang warfare that terrorized Chicago and made the Windy City the shame of America.

The story that would climax on that bloody February morning began years earlier in the impoverished North Side slum known as Kilgubbin, also called Little Hell—home of Dion "Deanie" O'Banion. Kilgubbin got its name from an early infusion of Irish immigrants, but by the time the O'Banion family arrived, it was populated with an added mix of Jewish, Polish and Italian poor. Its mean streets were the turf of thieves, hookers,

Dion "Deanie" O'Banion, crime boss of Chicago's North Side. His deadly pranks and double-dealing led to a fatal confrontation with the Italian gangs.

thugs and con men. One intersection was called Death Corner because 38 people were killed there in less than a year.

Deanie O'Banion was a study in contrasts. Pink-cheeked and cherub-faced, he had all the air about him of an Irish imp. He was forever laughing, joking, greeting new acquaintances as "swell fellows." He loved practical jokes, a trait which would ultimately be his undoing. As a boy he had served on the altar, and when the priests heard his beautiful singing voice they put him in the church choir. His voice developed into a fine Irish tenor, which he took advantage of in his youth by working as a singing waiter. While Deanie entertained the customers with "When Irish Eyes Are Smiling," his pals would be picking their pockets in the coatroom. Deanie would also slip the patrons Mickey Finns (spiked drinks), so they could be rolled later. Deanie considered himself a good Catholic, and was generous to a fault. He distributed carloads of food and clothing to the poor, gave money to the elderly and orphans, and paid medical bills for the underprivileged.

Yet behind the Robin Hood facade lurked a killer. O'Banion was responsible for at least 25 murders—by his own hand or on his orders. As a boy he had been a hired tough in Chicago's newspaper wars, using brass knuckles and a blackjack on rivals. This thuggery earned him a couple of short stints in reform school, the only "jail" time he would ever serve. As he grew older he took to carrying three guns: two in shoulder holsters and one in a special pocket in the front of his pants. He was a crack shot with his favourite, a .38. A streetcar accident suffered when he was a boy left O'Banion with a permanent limp, but that did nothing to diminish his abilities as a street brawler.

O'Banion graduated from cracking heads for nickels and dimes to cracking safes, though it seems he wasn't very good at it. On one occasion he used too much dynamite and blew out a wall of the office building he was trying to plunder, while the safe remained intact. Deanie thought that was one hell of a laugh.

Rising with O'Banion in the criminal ranks of Chicago's North Side were his three best friends: George Moran, Earl Wojciechowsky, and Vincent Drucci. Moran, known as "Bugs" because of his volatile temper, was of Irish-Polish stock. At age 19, Moran took the rap for a heist in which all the O'Banionites had participated, and served two years in jail without betraying his friends. This was at a time when police interrogations could be more than a little bit rough. It was the kind of loyalty O'Banion both inspired and admired. "Loyalty, lads, is the sign of a good egg," Deanie said. "Moran is aces with me."

Wojciechowsky changed his name to Weiss, and became known in the Chicago underworld as Hymie Weiss. The son of Polish immigrants, Weiss, like O'Banion, considered himself a devout Catholic. He carried a rosary in his pocket as well as a gun. But where Deanie was jocular, Hymie was always dead serious. As one of O'Banion's enforcers in the newspaper wars, Weiss even shot his own brother (though not fatally).

Vinny Drucci was a firm friend of O'Banion in spite of Deanie's general dislike of Italians. Because of the complicated and often impractical plans he dreamed up for robberies, he was called "Schemer" by the rest of the gang. These four men made up the nucleus of what would be called the North Side mob. They would prove themselves to be ruthless in their pursuit of wealth and power, while displaying a loyalty to each other that has always been rare in the criminal world.

O'Banion knew that the best way for a gangster to stay out of jail was to wield some political clout. He did that by bribing policemen, judges and politicians, and by "steering" elections for the Republican Party. On election day the O'Banionites would show up at the polling stations and ensure that their favourite candidate "won." Deanie could convince a lot of people to vote the "right" way through friendly persuasion, but just in case some uncooperative souls didn't get the message, his boys would employ some last-minute political correcting. Intimidation, brass knuckles, ballot box stuffing, even murder ensured that Deanie's man always got in. He had virtual control of Chicago's 42nd and 43rd wards, which included not only Kilgubbin, but also the elite Gold Coast along Lake Michigan, home to some of Chicago's wealthiest and most influential people. A popular jingle went, "Who holds the 42nd and 43rd wards? O'Banion in his pistol pockets."

Grateful politicians repaid Deanie by putting in "the fix" whenever it appeared that O'Banion or any of his boys might be having a little trouble with the law. Probably the most flagrant example of this happened when O'Banion, Weiss and Drucci were arrested after police found their fingerprints all over a robbery scene. A few words in the right ears, and the three were allowed to walk. "It was an oversight," Deanie told a reporter. "Hymie was supposed to wipe off the prints, but he forgot."

The lovable, deadly Irishman was therefore in a perfect position when Prohibition came along in 1920. A non-drinker himself, O'Banion got into the bootlegging business early and in style. Not for him the low-grade rotgut being brewed in alky cookers all over the city. He would bring in the best Canadian beer and liquor for "his" people. O'Banion's warehouse was a garage owned by a Jewish friend, Samuel "Nails" Morton, a decorated hero of the Great War. Booze in vehicles disguised as delivery vans and milk trucks rolled into the warehouse in a steady stream. So too did liquor owned by rival gangs. In December 1921, O'Banion pulled off Chicago's first major liquor hijacking when he climbed into a truck which had stopped at an intersection, pushed the driver out, and cheerily drove the load of whiskey to Morton's garage. O'Banion's good business relationship with Morton ended when Nails, a horse lover, was killed in a freak riding accident. A grief-stricken O'Banion (or one of his men) went to the stable and shot the "guilty" horse dead.

O'Banion would not tolerate competition in his part of Chicago. To ensure that speakeasies and blind pigs sold only *his* beer, he employed Louis "Three Gun" Alterie, a mobster with a cowboy fixation. Wearing a stetson hat and armed with a brace of pistols, Three Gun would stride into a bar that had been selling a rival gangster's beer and "explain" why it would be in the proprietor's best interests to get his suds from that broth of a boy, Deanie O'Banion.

Though O'Banion roared with laughter every time he hijacked someone else's booze, he did not find it funny at all when the same trick was played on him. In July 1921, a small-timer named Steve Wisniewski hijacked an O'Banion beer truck. Hymie Weiss caught the culprit, drove him out of town, shot him in the head and dumped the body by the roadside. Hymie coined a phrase and instituted a grim gangland ritual when he said, "We took Stevie on a ride; a *one way ride!*"

New York hoodlum Johnny "Papa" Torrio went to Chicago to help out Big Jim Colosimo. When Big Jim balked at entering the bootleg racket, Torrio had him killed.

The O'Banionites were not the only Chicago gangsters cashing in on the Prohibition bonanza. In the city's South Side a powerful Italian gang led by "Papa" Johnny Torrio held sway. Born in Naples, Italy, and raised in the tough streets of New York's Little Italy, Torrio had been brought to Chicago by his mobster uncle (actually his wife's cousin) Big Jim Colosimo. Big Jim had run into problems with some freelance extortionists, and thought perhaps his tough, brainy nephew could come up with a solution. Johnny could. He recruited some gunmen, and after a few killings the extortionists left Big Jim alone. Johnny had earned a reputation for fearlessness and brutality as a youth with New York's dreaded Five Points Gang, but he claimed to abhor violence and preferred to have others do the nasty stuff.

Big Jim's empire was built mainly on gambling and prostitution. He was heavily involved in what was then called the "white slave trade," though the victims came from all racial backgrounds. This was the recruiting of girls, some as young as 13, into prostitution. The girls were tricked by promises of jobs and money and, once in the hands of the gangsters and the madams, they lived frightful existences of degradation and violence. Few escaped to tell their awful tales to the police.

When Prohibition came along, Torrio wanted to get in on the action with all the other hoodlums, but Big Jim was reluctant. He was of the older, tradition-bound generation of gangsters, what young turks like Torrio called "Moustache Petes." He believed they were making enough money off gambling, prostitution, extortion and other rackets. He said Prohibition wouldn't last, so why risk getting involved with bootlegging? "We stay with the whores, Johnny," he allegedly told Torrio.

Johnny didn't agree. But being the conscientious sort, he couldn't bring himself to kill Big Jim. He hired someone else to do it. On May 11, 1920, Big Jim was shot dead in his restaurant. The gunman was never apprehended. Two of Torrio's old pals from New York were suspected: a professional killer named Frankie Yale, and a hard case called Al Capone.

The son of a barber from Naples, Brooklyn-born Capone, like Torrio, had been an enforcer for the Five Points Gang. He was bull-strong, skilled in the use of brass knuckles, knives and guns, and was utterly ruthless. His distinctive feature was three scars on his face, administered by a knife-wielding hood whose sister Capone had insulted while he was employed as a bouncer in a New York dive. (Capone would later invent the lie that he had been wounded in France). The disfigurement earned him the nickname "Scarface," which he hated.

Capone was already under suspicion of murder in New York, so he was glad to get the invitation from his old buddy Johnny Torrio to join him in Chicago. Whether or not it was he who actually pulled the trigger on Big Jim, Capone arrived in Chicago just in time to help Papa Johnny get into the lucrative new bootleg trade. Chicago had all the promise of being a "wide open" city. William "Big Bill" Thompson, one of the most corrupt individuals ever to disgrace a public office, was mayor, and the gangsters had him in their pocket. A Republican who said that he would make Chicago "the cleanest city in the world," Big Bill was a hard drinker and not especially bright. By the end of his reign Chicago would be called, "the only completely corrupt city in America." The biggest problem Torrio and Capone faced wasn't the law—they could even get police escorts for their booze trucks if they wanted. The thorn in their sides was "the Irish mob" on the North Side.

Right from the start, Deanie O'Banion thought it a great lark to hijack trucks from "them damn greaseballs." Capone would retaliate by hijacking O'Banion's trucks, which enraged the Irishman. Once, when Deanie confronted a pair of suspected hijackers in front of a theatre, he pulled a gun and shot them both right there under the marquee. One man took a slug in the stomach (not fatally) and the other was spared when the bullet glanced off his belt buckle.

Torrio was a level-headed businessman, and he knew that unnecessary violence was bad for the trade. He had managed to bring many of the

Hymie Weiss, "inventor" of the one-way ride. Weiss took over leadership of the North Side gang after O'Banion was murdered.

competing gangs together under a "peace treaty." He even shared interests in Chicago's Sieben Brewery with O'Banion. He decided it was time to bring the North Siders into the fold, so he invited O'Banion to a meeting. Deanie accepted, but he took Hymie Weiss along because, he said, "The wops need watching." He especially distrusted Capone.

While Hymie and Scarface glared at each other, Torrio explained to O'Banion, as he had to the other gang leaders, that bootlegging was more profitable than all their other criminal activities combined, and without nearly as much risk. Why spoil it with a lot of needless fighting? There was plenty of money for everybody. Torrio suggested that each gang stay in its own territory and share sources and markets. Torrio would buy Canadian whiskey from O'Banion; Deanie could share in the Torrio-Capone gambling rackets. Everybody would respect everyone else's "turf." The O'Banionites had the North Side. Torrio and Capone ran the district called the Loop and the South Side. Among the other divisions: the Genna brothers —Little Italy; Edward "Spike" O'Donnell—the Kerry Patch; William "Klondike" O'Donnell (no relation)—the Far West Side; Joe Saltis and Frankie McErlane—the Stock Yards. Thus was America's second largest city sliced up like a pie by criminals.

All of the gangsters in this loose confederation were vicious men who could kill without batting an eye, but perhaps none had a more fearsome reputation for savagery than the Sicilian Genna brothers. Known as the Terrible Gennas, there were six of them: Sam, Jim, Pete, Bloody Angelo, Tony the Gentleman and Mike the Devil. Their section of town was referred to as The Bloody Ward. The Gennas would gun people down in the street in broad daylight with cold-blooded impunity and no concern about witnesses.

Three of the Terrible Gennas—Angelo, Peter and Tony—as family men. They took offence when O'Banion said, "Tell them Sicilians to go to hell."

Who would dare to testify against them? They disliked anyone who was not Sicilian, and that included mainland Italians. To add muscle to their gang, they brought in fellow Sicilians John Scalise and Alberto Anselmi (killers wanted for murder in their homeland). This diabolical pair rubbed the tips of their bullets with garlic, in the mistaken belief that if a bullet failed to kill the victim immediately, the garlic would give him gangrene.

The Gennas had little interest in peddling imported Canadian booze. They were in the "alky cooking" business. They owned a large distillery that turned out rivers of the worst alcohol ever brewed for human consumption, under appalling sanitary conditions. To keep up with the demand, especially from their best customers, Torrio and Capone, the Gennas had small stills in operation in storerooms and apartments throughout Little Italy. The dirt poor slum residents could earn $15 a day cooking rotgut alky for the Gennas, who generally didn't *ask* if someone wanted a still in their apartment. There were other benefits, too. Whenever a still exploded and killed someone, the Genna boys dutifully covered the funeral expenses.

O'Banion didn't like the Gennas, nor Torrio and Capone for that matter. But he agreed to Torrio's sensible compromise. Unfortunately, Deanie's greed and bent sense of humour got the better of him, and he still stole their booze whenever the opportunity arose—denying it to their faces but bragging of it to others. On one occasion he stole two thousand barrels of whiskey from a Capone warehouse, and just for laughs replaced them with barrels of water. Big Al didn't see the humour of it at all. Capone was all for killing "that mick bastard," but his boss Torrio still wanted to keep the peace. However, even Torrio came close to turning Capone loose on O'Banion when the Irish gangster pulled the most ghoulish of all his pranks.

Deanie had to get rid of a two-bit gunman named John Duffy. He arranged to have the unsuspecting Duffy meet him at the Four Deuces, a club owned by Torrio. Without being seen himself, O'Banion picked Duffy up at the club, drove him out of town, shot him dead, and left the body where it would easily be found. What brought tears of laughter to the gangster's eyes was the fact that Duffy had last been seen at the Four Deuces, which meant that the police would be paying a visit to Johnny Torrio and Al Capone. Those two were not implicated in the murder after all, but as far as Capone was concerned it was one more nail in the laughing Irishman's coffin.

Still, the "Pax Torrio" held together... at least until 1923, when things started to fall apart. Crooked Big Bill Thompson lost an election to William Dever, a reform-minded Democrat who could not be bought. Dever was no temperance fanatic, but he believed in upholding the law. He over-hauled the police force, disrupting the gangsters' payoff system. He shut down "soft drink parlours" suspected of being booze dispensers. People were being arrested for violating the Volstead Act, and finding that "the fix" was not forthcoming.

The shock waves were felt in gang headquarters all across the city. Mobsters scurried to find new outlets for their booze, which often meant muscling in on each other's territories and undercutting each other's prices. The Torrio Truce came unravelled and mobsters started shooting holes in each other.

Mayor Dever called for a crackdown on the gangsters, and there were several arrests, but there was never enough evidence to hold anyone. The Torrio-Capone and Saltis-McErlane gangs joined forces to run the Southside O'Donnells out of town. Spike O'Donnell boasted, "I can whip this bird Capone with my bare fists anytime he wants to step out in the open and fight like a man!" But that wasn't Big Al's style. He sent McErlane to take care of Spike, and Frankie certainly earned top marks for trying. O'Donnell, who seemed to live a charmed life, was shot at ten times. He complained to the press, "I've been shot at and missed so often, I've a notion to hire out as a professional target. Life with me is just one bullet after another." Spike would eventually get out of the business while his hide was still intact.

Gangster Spike O'Donnell. "I can whip this bird Capone with my bare fists." Spike quit the business after surviving ten assassination attempts.

Johnny Torrio, meanwhile, was feeling Mayor Dever's heat in Chicago. Deeming discretion the better part of valour, he decided to move his headquarters to a location outside the city. He chose the quiet little suburban town of Cicero, Illinois. (Capone said the place was named after "Cicero, the Greek.") It was close enough to Chicago for convenience, but beyond the reach of Dever. And for all its peaceful appearances, it had a corrupt administration. What more could a gangster ask? Cicero's town president Joseph Klenha *did* make an objection over some minor point to Al Capone, but Scarface settled the matter by throwing Klenha down the steps of the town hall. The head of the small police department, Joseph W. Nosek, tried to tell the gangsters to get out of town, but Capone's boys dragged him from his home and kicked and pistol whipped him into submission. Journalist Robert St. John wrote scathing (and courageous) editorials against Capone in the Cicero *Tribune*, so Big Al had his henchmen beat up the reporter and, for good measure, his brother. When the gutsy young writer continued to pen anti-Capone columns, Scarface tried to buy him off. Capone believed in the philosophy that every man had his price, so he was genuinely shocked when St. John spurned his offer. Finally, Capone bought controlling interest in the Cicero *Tribune,* making himself St. John's boss. St. John quit the paper in disgust and took a job with a newspaper in Vermont. Cicero now belonged to Torrio and Capone. To be on the safe side, Big Al established himself in a bulletproof office.

Cicero became a sin-city of gin mills and gambling halls. The gangsters' one concession to the local residents was to keep the whorehouses out—for awhile, anyway. One saloon owner, Eddie Tancl, refused to buy

Torrio and Capone's "needle beer"—legally brewed near-beer with illegal raw alcohol injected into it. He was warned that he would buy Capone's beer or he would buy no beer at all. Tancl told Capone's messenger, "That Capone guy makes bad stuff. I don't serve no needle beer in my joint." A few days later Tancl and his bartender were killed in a blazing gun battle in the saloon.

The honest citizens of Cicero demanded reform and, in the spring of 1924, there was to be a municipal election. The racketeers were not about to let the problem they had faced in Chicago repeat itself in Cicero. They were not going to be run out of town by "a bunch of hicks." On the night of March 31, the eve of the election, Capone's boys beat up the Democratic candidate for town clerk. The next day over two hundred thugs, two dozen of them generously provided by O'Banion, descended on Cicero. They cruised the streets menacingly in their long, black cars. They beat up citizens known to be opposed to their boy, Joe Klenha. At the polling stations they looked over the shoulder of every voter, uttering dire threats to anyone who hesitated to put their mark in the right place. Poll watchers and election officials were kidnapped and kept prisoner until the polls closed. A local policeman who tried to interfere was slugged with a blackjack. Other gangsters showed up to try to thwart Capone's plans, so there were shootings. Three men were shot dead and a fourth had his throat cut.

Horrified, the residents of Cicero cried to Chicago for help. Seventy patrolmen, five squads of detectives and nine squads of motorized police were sent to the embattled little town. All afternoon a deadly real-life game of cops and robbers was played out in the streets of Cicero. One victim was Frank Capone, one of several brothers who had come west from New York to lend Al a hand. As Frank drew bead on a policeman with his revolver, two other officers tore him to shreds with blasts from their double-barrelled shotguns. A grieving Al sent him off with a lavish funeral. Not surprisingly, Klenha won the election. Amazingly, it was allowed to stand. Klenha responded to criticisms and accusations in the newspapers by saying the accounts of the violence were exaggerated, and that Cicero was no worse than Chicago. One Chicago journalist quipped, "If you smell gunpowder, you're in Cicero."

In return for his help with the "elections," Deanie O'Banion demanded a share in the Cicero action. Torrio reluctantly agreed to let the North Siders sell beer in parts of Cicero, and to give them a percentage of the gambling profits. O'Banion took the offer, and then some. Without consulting Torrio, he convinced fifty Chicago speakeasy operators to relocate to Cicero. This vastly increased his profits, at Al Capone's expense. Once again "that mick bastard" had angered Big Al. But Torrio didn't want a war with the North Siders. He made O'Banion yet another offer. If Deanie would give a piece of his expanded bootleg business back to Capone, Torrio would give the North Siders a percentage of his brothel business. O'Banion's response was a sneer."Go peddle your papers!" he told Torrio. "A deal is a deal. You guinea bastards sell the flesh, but leave me out of it. Prostitution is against Our Mother the Church, and I'll have nothing to do with the stinking business."

Indeed, throughout Dion O'Banion's reign as crime boss of Chicago's North Side, there were no whorehouses in that part of the city. He often contemptuously referred to Capone and other gangsters in the prostitution racket as "pimps." It was the name Capone hated most of all, even if it was accurate.

Deanie was running into trouble with the Genna brothers, too. He discovered that they had been selling their low-grade alky rotgut in his territory. Genna booze was much inferior to the "good stuff" O'Banion insisted on selling, but it was also much cheaper, which made it attractive to the working poor. This was hurting Deanie's business. O'Banion complained to Torrio, but Papa Johnny shrugged and said, "There is nothing I can do. The Gennas are Sicilian blood. They answer only to the President of the *Unione Siciliane*." In other words, *Mafia*. But nothing scared Dion O'Banion. "Tell them Sicilians to go to hell!" he said. Then O'Banion added injury to this insult to the Gennas's tender national pride. He hijacked $30,000 worth of their whiskey. The Terrible Gennas held a family council, and voted to kill Dion O'Banion.

They *were*, however, under the authority of the *Unione Siciliane*, and the president of the Chicago branch of that organization, Mike Merlo, said no. O'Banion's assassination, he predicted, would spark a gang war that would be damaging to everybody. "Put your trigger fingers away," he told the Gennas. "Trigger fingers have no brain." But Mike Merlo was dying of cancer.

In May 1924, O'Banion learned from his informants in the police department that federal agents were planning to raid the Sieben brewery in which he shared ownership with Torrio. Its closure would cost them both a lot of money. Deanie, the inspired prankster, got an idea that would enable him to cut his losses, and top anything he had pulled thus far. Torrio had long wanted to buy out O'Banion's share of the brewery, so Deanie decided that now was as good a time as any to sell. He went to Torrio with an offer to sell out for half a million dollars. He was getting out of the business, he told Papa Johnny. He said he was worried about the Gennas. He had bought a big spread out in Colorado, and he and his wife were going there to retire.

Torrio jumped at the offer. He paid O'Banion the $500,000. As a gesture of goodwill, Deanie agreed to meet Torrio at the brewery with some of his boys on May 19 and help send out one last shipment.

That night, with two crooked cops looking on, 22 North Side and South Side gangsters and drivers loaded up 13 trucks with beer. O'Banion was there with Hymie Weiss and Three Gun Alteri. Torrio had several of his boys, but not Capone. Ten days earlier, Big Al had pumped six bullets into the head of "Ragtime" Joe Howard in broad daylight, and was in hiding. Howard was a freelance hijacker who had slapped and kicked Capone's friend "Greasy Thumb" Jake Guzik, and had called Al a "dago pimp."

Just as the beer trucks were ready to roll, the feds sprang their raid. The gangsters, including Torrio and O'Banion, were arrested. The two crooked cops had their badges ripped off on the spot. They were all hustled downtown, where Torrio paid over $1,200 in bail for himself and his men. O'Banion was left to look after his own. The Irishman pretended to have had no foreknowledge of the raid, but was actually beside himself with glee. Because he had never been arrested on a bootlegging charge before, he would get off with a first offence. Torrio, however, had been up on boot-legging charges previously, and if convicted this time would be looking at a prison sentence. Deanie found the joke just too good to keep to himself. Before going off for a few weeks vacation in Colorado, he bragged around town, "I guess I rubbed that dago pimp's nose in the mud all right." Torrio's spies told him everything, and Torrio was smart enough not to tell O'Banion he knew what had happened. Papa Johnny was a patient man.

O'Banion owned a small percentage of a Torrio-Capone gambling joint called the Ship. Every week he stopped by to collect his share of the take. On November 3, 1924, O'Banion, Hymie Weiss and Schemer Drucci dropped in for the weekly pick-up. Present were Torrio, Capone, South Side enforcer Frank Nitti and several other gunmen. Capone mentioned that Angelo Genna had lost heavily at roulette that week, and had left IOUs for $30,000. Torrio suggested that out of professional courtesy they should cancel the debt. O'Banion would have none of it. He called Bloody Angelo on the phone and told the Sicilian he had one week to pay up—*or else!*

Weiss later warned O'Banion that he had better ease up on the Gennas. Deanie scoffed. He said the Gennas, Torrio, Capone—all of them—were gutter rats and dumb bastards. "To hell with them Sicilians."

Johnny Torrio, Al Capone and the Genna brothers had a meeting. The subject of discussion was what to do about Dion O'Banion. The decision was unanimous. Then, on November 8, Mike Merlo died.

Most gang bosses had some sort of a "front"—a business they could point to as a legitimate source of income. Johnny Torrio had the Four Deuces club. (It was rumoured that in a basement room there, rival gangsters and "stool pigeons" were tortured and murdered.) Al Capone posed as a dealer in used furniture. He even had a shop with a few pieces of junk in it. The place never sold a stick of furniture. If anyone who didn't know better came around looking to buy a table or chair, they were told, "We're closed."

Dion O'Banion was half owner in a flower shop with a man named William Schofield. It was right across the street from Holy Name Cathedral. The difference between O'Banion and Capone was that Deanie actually *worked* in his flower shop. He loved flowers and enjoyed arranging them into centrepieces and wreaths. It must have been strange to see a man with so much blood on his hands cheerfully clipping roses or putting together dainty corsages. By some bizarre, unwritten agreement, most of the Chicago gangsters got their funeral flowers from O'Banion. Mob funerals tended to be lavish, with the different gangs trying to outdo each other in the size and beauty of their floral offerings, so O'Banion's flower shop was a thriving business. Torrio and Capone were regular customers, always donating expensive wreaths to the funerals of men they'd bumped off. Deanie even gave them a discount. When he heard of Frank Capone's death, he immediately called his supplier for an extra $20,000 worth of stock. When Mike Merlo died, Torrio called O'Banion and placed a $10,000 order. Capone placed one for $8,000. Deanie told them he would prepare the wreaths personally, out of respect for Merlo.

On Sunday, November 9, James Genna entered the flower shop to order a $750 wreath. A little later, Frankie Yale, the national director of the *Unione Siciliane* came in to order one for $2,000. He wanted it by mid-morning the next day. Deanie would have plenty of work to do. Both visitors quietly studied the layout of the shop.

A crowd gathers in front of the flower shop where O'Banion was killed. Crime boss Mike Merlo correctly predicted that O'Banion's murder would spark a major gang war.

The following morning at about 11:30, Deanie was busy clipping chrysanthemums in the back room, when three men entered the flower shop. The only other person present, an employee named Bill Crutchfield, had just swept up the place and was on his way to the back. He saw O'Banion come around the corner into the showroom with the clippers in his left hand. It was obvious he knew the men, because he greeted them cheerfully and extended his right hand. "Hello, boys. You want Merlo's flowers?"

One of the men took Deanie's hand and said, "Yes."

Crutchfield saw no more, because O'Banion had told him to go and close the back door. Crutchfield did not know who the three men were, but it was later established that they were Frankie Yale, Alberto Anselmi and John Scalise. The driver of their car waiting outside was identified as James Genna.

O'Banion always carried three guns, but this time he had no chance to use them. Yale shook hands with him, then tightened his grip and pulled Deanie close, pinioning his arms. Scalise and Anselmi pulled their guns and blasted O'Banion from point-blank range: two garlic-smeared bullets in the chest, two in the throat, and two in the face. When Crutchfield came running from the back the three men were gone and O'Banion was lying dead amidst some knocked over vases of carnations and lilies. His blood was spattered all over some white peonies. O'Banion was 32.

O'Banion's funeral was one of the biggest in Chicago's history. The coffin cost $10,000. "Me and Deanie was pals," Capone said.

O'Banion's funeral was one of the biggest in Chicago history. He lay in state for a week like a fallen prince rather than a murdered crime boss. His coffin cost $10,000, and the funeral procession was a mile long. Thousands of people lined the streets to watch it pass, or crowded into Mount Carmel Cemetery for the burial. The Catholic Church had refused to have him put in consecrated ground, but a priest for whom Deanie had sung as a choirboy said three Hail Marys and the Lord's Prayer while Hymie Weiss, Bugs Moran, Schemer Drucci, Three Gun Alteri—and Johnny Torrio and Al Capone—looked on. Among the forest of floral wreaths was a huge one that said, "From Al."

Beneath all the solemnity of the occasion was an undercurrent of fearful anticipation. After the funeral, Alteri issued an open invitation for those who had killed Deanie to come out in the open and shoot it out with him, and he said he didn't care how many they were. Moran thought that by such bravado Three Gun was making a fool of himself and the gang, and ordered him out of town. Al Capone, who wasn't as good as Torrio at keeping his mouth shut, told the press, "O'Banion had a swell route to make it tough for us and he did. His job had been to smooth the coppers and we gave him a lot of authority with the booze and beer business. When he broke away, for a while it wasn't so good. He knew the ropes and got running us ragged. It was his funeral."

When asked if he was responsible for O'Banion's death, Capone replied, "Me kill Deanie? What nonsense! Why, me and Deanie was pals."

The gang war which Mike Merlo had predicted would come in the wake of O'Banion's murder descended upon Chicago soon after the funeral, and bloodied the streets of the Windy City for years, claiming the lives of hundreds of mobsters and several innocent citizens. A judge would later say that killing O'Banion "was like firing on Fort Sumter in 1861."

Crime historians have said that the only man Al Capone ever truly feared was Hymie Weiss. He had believed that Weiss, rather than O'Banion, was the real brains of the North Side mob. Weiss was colder and more calculating than Deanie had been, and was not given to impetuous behavior. And now Weiss was assuming command of the North Siders.

Officially, O'Banion's murder would remain unsolved, but Weiss and company conducted their own "investigation," tapping into the underworld network of informers who would talk for a price or to save their own skins. They soon had a pretty good idea who had pulled the trigger on Deanie and who was behind it. Hymie swore an oath of vengeance.

Johnny Torrio decided now was a good time to take a holiday. He and his wife toured the United States and the Caribbean, never aware that Weiss' gunmen were trailing them. The would-be assassins never did get a chance to take a shot at Papa Johnny. Capone, left to hold down the fort in Chicago, took the brunt of the first North Sider attack. On January 12, 1925, Capone was entering a restaurant when a black limousine cruised by. In it were Weiss, Moran and Drucci, armed with automatic pistols and shotguns. Capone's driver and two bodyguards were still in his car when the O'Banionites cut loose. Their barrage practically demolished the car, but miraculously only the driver was wounded.

Capone became almost paranoid. He ordered a $30,000, bulletproof car that weighed seven tons. He never went anywhere in it without a scout car ahead and a car full of gunmen following. He insisted on travelling at night, fearful of stepping outside in the daylight. Wherever he went on foot he was surrounded by a phalanx of 15 bodyguards. In restaurants

The funeral of "Bloody" Angelo Genna, victim of North Sider vengeance. Mike "the Devil" and Tony "the Gentleman" would soon join him.

and nightclubs strangers were forbidden to occupy tables near his. His office, already a fortress, now had a chair with an armour-plated back. The windows were heavily curtained, and Al never opened a door himself. He rarely visited his suburban home, lest his family be exposed to a North Sider attack. He never kept appointments at the originally arranged times—always changing them at the last minute. When he tried to take out a life insurance policy, not an insurance company in the country would touch him. The North Siders hadn't managed to put a bullet into Scarface, but they were playing hell with his mental and physical health. Moran called him a coward. It couldn't have helped Al's nerves much when the North Siders kidnapped and murdered his replacement chauffeur.

Torrio returned to Chicago in mid-January to stand trial for the Sieben Brewery bust. He intended to plead guilty and go to jail, where the O'Banionites couldn't get at him. By the time he got out, Capone would have taken care of Hymie Weiss.

A federal judge accepted Torrio's guilty plea, and gave him five days to settle his affairs before passing sentence. The North Siders didn't waste any time. On January 24, Weiss, Moran, Drucci and a fourth man ambushed Torrio outside his apartment building. Torrio went down in a hail of buckshot and bullets. He was shot in the chest, leg and groin, and his jaws were shattered. He was still conscious as Bugs Moran leaned over him and put a pistol to his head for the *coup de grace.* "Compliments of Deanie," Moran said. Bugs squeezed the trigger... but the gun was empty!

Certain that Torrio was finished, the would-be assassins jumped into their car and sped away. The O'Banionites left Torrio at death's door, but the mob boss did not go through the portal. And in strict observance of the gangster code of *omerta*—silence—he did not give up the names of his attackers. "Sure, I know all four men," he whispered in hospital to the press, through his ruined jaws, "but I'll never tell their names."

Torrio spent three weeks in the hospital under heavy guard, and with Capone at his bedside much of the time. Upon his discharge he was sentenced to nine months in prison. When he got out he quit the rackets. Torrio handed everything over to Capone and took ship to Naples.

The North Siders weren't finished. On May 25, 1925, Weiss, Moran, Drucci and a gunman named Frank Gusenberg killed Bloody Angelo Genna. A June 13 gun battle resulted in the death of Angelo's brother, Mike the Devil. On July 8, Tony the Gentleman Genna was shot to death in a "handshake" murder similar to that of O'Banion's. Schemer Drucci was the chief suspect in that murder and in the killing of yet another Genna associate in a North Side barbershop. Police couldn't get witnesses to talk—a condition O'Banion had called "Chicago amnesia." The surviving Genna brothers got out of town.

While Capone was battling the North Siders on one front, he began to have trouble with Klondike O'Donnell on another, in Cicero. Booze joints there were buying quality beer from O'Donnell at a cheaper price than Capone was charging for his dreadful needle beer. Big Al didn't want to compete in a price war, so he decided to eliminate Klondike. This time he led the murder squad himself. He and his gunmen were in five cars in front of a Cicero restaurant at 8:30 p.m. on April 25, 1925, when Klondike O'Donnell stepped out with several of his boys and a man Capone mistakenly took to be Hymie Weiss. It was, in fact, Assistant State Attorney William McSwiggin. O'Donnell escaped unhurt from the barrage of machine gun fire that burst from the Capone ambush, but McSwiggin was killed.

McSwiggin had a reputation as an anti-mob prosecutor, and nobody was really sure just what he had been doing with the O'Donnell gang, but the fact that a public official had been gunned down in cold blood outraged the public. So far, the gangsters had just been killing each other, but the McSwiggin murder was something else altogether. Scarface slipped off to

New York and lay low for awhile. In Cicero, vigilante mobs smashed up some of his gambling halls and speakeasies, and burned down his most profitable brothel.

For a time things quieted down. A lot of press coverage was given to the McSwiggin murder investigation, and to the trial of Anselmi and Scalise who had been charged with the murder of two policemen. They were sentenced to 14 years, but they were on the Capone payroll now and Big Al said he'd take care of them.

Capone decided to take the offensive against the North Siders. On August 10, 1926, four of his gunmen opened fire on Weiss and Drucci in front of Chicago's Standard Oil Building. Hymie and Schemer fired back. Both sides were oblivious to the fact that the street was crowded with people. Fortunately, only one innocent bystander was slightly injured. The shooting continued until the combatants ran out of ammunition.

Five days later there was a repeat performance. Weiss and Drucci were in their car in front of the Standard Oil Building when another car tried to ram them, and four occupants opened fire. Hymie and Schemer dove out of their car and shot back, sending pedestrians scurrying for cover and creating chaos with traffic as frightened drivers careened into each other's vehicles. Again, unbelievably, there were no serious injuries.

Three weeks later, on September 20, the North Siders struck back in what was the most blatant display of lawlessness twentieth-century America had ever seen. Al Capone and one of his lieutenants, Frankie Rio, were having lunch in the Hawthorne Inn in Cicero. The place was packed. Suddenly there was the sound of a speeding car and the rat-tat-tat of machine gun fire out front. Then silence. Everyone, including Capone and Rio, rushed to the door to see what was going on outside. The first thing Rio noticed was that there were no bullet holes anywhere. Then he saw the procession of eight cars, each one bristling with guns, and he realized what was up. The gunner in the first car had been firing blanks—a decoy to draw Capone outside. The column bearing down on them would be throwing real lead. Rio hit the floor and dragged Capone down with him. It was a move that was lucky for Big Al, unlucky for The North Siders—and for that matter, society in general.

Each of the eight cars in turn stopped in front of the restaurant and its gunners methodically sprayed the Hawthorne with machine-gun fire. A

Capone man standing in the doorway was struck in the shoulder. One bullet skinned the leg of a little boy. A woman was struck in the eye by flying glass splinters. When the last car pulled up, a man got out, went down on one knee in the doorway of the Hawthorne, and calmly blasted the inn's interior with a 100-round ammo drum. Then he hopped back into the car and followed his confederates out of town.

The Hawthorne Inn and the stores adjacent to it looked like they had been through a battle of the Great War. Capone paid for all the damages, as well as for the surgery to repair the eye of the injured woman. He had come out of the attack unhurt, but badly shaken. He had no doubt who was behind it. He got in touch with Hymie Weiss and proposed a truce. He wanted to talk peace.

Capone was either too smart or too scared to meet Weiss personally. Instead he sent Tony Lombardo of the *Unione Siciliane* as his emissary. Lombardo told Weiss that Capone was willing to make a major concession: offer the North Siders exclusive rights to sell beer in a vast section of Capone territory. Hymie would agree to peace on one non-negotiable condition. Capone had to give the O'Banionites Scalise and Anselmi. When Capone heard that he replied, "I wouldn't do that to a yellow dog." The truce was over.

On October 11, one week after the meeting, Hymie Weiss, an attorney, a local politician and two bodyguards got out of Hymie's car in front of Holy Name Cathedral, only yards away from where Dion O'Banion had been killed. From an upstairs window across the street, two men who had been waiting in ambush opened fire with tommy guns. Ten bullets tore into Weiss, killing him on the spot. One of the men with him was killed and all of the others were badly wounded. The church itself was a casualty. Its cornerstone, which was inscribed with a quotation from St. Paul, was pockmarked by bullets. The Church left the cornerstone unrepaired for many years, as mute testimony to Chicago's violence.

Another gangster went to unconsecrated ground in Mount Carmel, and Al Capone's worst nightmare was history. But when questioned by reporters, Scarface said, "I'm sorry Hymie was killed, but I didn't have anything to do with it... There's enough business for all of us without killing each other like animals in the street. I don't want to end up in the gutter punctured by machine gun slugs, so why should I kill Weiss?"

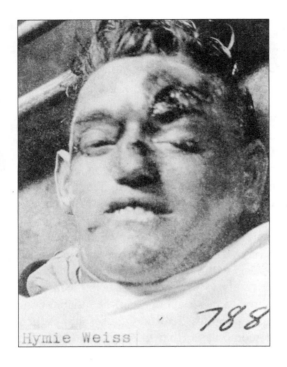

Hymie Weiss

Capone's worst nightmare is eliminated. After Weiss went down in a hail of bullets, Scarface said, "I'm sorry Hymie was killed."

By this point even the gangsters were concerned over the level to which violence had risen—mostly because they were having thoughts as to their own mortality. They called a peace meeting. It was attended by every mob boss in Chicago. Maxie Eisen, a labour racketeer who was on good terms with several of those present, including Bugs Moran, was the first to speak. "Let's give each other a break," he said. "We're a bunch of saps, killing each other this way and giving the cops a laugh."

Al Capone proposed a five-point treaty which was based on the same rules Johnny Torrio had tried to impress upon the gangs a few years earlier: each gang stay in their own territory and keep their hands off everyone else's customers and booze. "I told them we're making a shooting gallery out of a great business," Capone said later. "There's plenty of beer business for everybody—why kill each other over it?" The gangsters all agreed, and held a big party to celebrate. One Chicago paper called it "a feast of ghouls." Shortly after, Scalise and Anselmi were released from prison on bail.

There was restlessness, though, on the North Side. Moran and Drucci thought that Capone was getting too powerful, and they knew that in spite of the peace agreement, he had designs on their wealthy Gold Coast district. The nobs of that neighbourhood could still buy good Canadian liquor from the O'Banionites and weren't interested in Capone's needle beer and watered-down swill. They were worried, too, that if Capone's booze peddlers came in, they'd be followed by his blackmailers and shake-down artists. The O'Banionites wanted to find out what Capone was up to.

On January 27, 1927, Capone's friend, Theodore "The Greek" Anton, was kidnapped right from under Capone's nose in Anton's restaurant. When his body was found it was evident he had been tortured and then shot. In March Capone took a brief holiday to Hot Springs, Arkansas. Schemer Drucci followed him there and took a shot at him with a shotgun, but missed. Big Al didn't want another gang fight—yet. The mayoral election in Chicago was coming up, and the gangsters' buddy, Big Bill Thompson, was running again. Every mobster in town was working to get Big Bill back in office, and turf that damn, squeaky clean Dever out in the street.

Thompson ran one of the dirtiest campaigns in American history. He stooped to the lowest levels of mud-slinging, slander and innuendo. Most importantly for the gangsters, Thompson promised to re-open all the joints Dever had closed down, and bring back all the crooked cops Dever had fired. Capone contributed $260,000 to Thompson's campaign fund. The O'Banionites did their bit for Big Bill, too, backing him with money and muscle. Thompson won big, but it was a costly election for the North Siders.

On April 4, the day before the election, Schemer Drucci was arrested for assaulting a Dever supporter and smashing up the victim's office. In the police car, Drucci became violent and tried to grab a gun from Detective Don Healy. In the struggle for the weapon, Healy shot Drucci dead. Schemer's widow, Cecilia, lamented, "He was a wonderful husband, but a cop killed him for nothing." What surprised Chicagoans was that a top-ranking gangster had been killed, not by another gangster, but by a policeman.

Of the fearsome quartet from Kilgubbin, only Bugs Moran remained alive. Bugs beefed up the North Side gang with hired guns, and looked for an alliance. He found one with the Aiello brothers, who had moved into the old Genna territory. Joey Aiello had lost his bid for the pres-idency of the *Unione Siciliane* to Capone's man Tony Lombardo, and was now a sworn enemy of both. He put out an open contract of $50,000 on Capone's head. Four different bounty hunters from New York, St. Louis and Cleveland travelled to Chicago to try for the prize. Each was found riddled with bullets. Each had a five-cent piece clutched in his cold, dead hand: the message being that the life of anyone who tried to collect the fifty grand wasn't worth a nickel. Aiello offered the chef at Capone's favourite

"Machine Gun" Jack McGurn and his wife, Louise Rolfe. Capone promised him $10,000 if he bumped off Bugs Moran.

restaurant $35,000 to poison Big Al. The frightened chef told Capone. Scarface allegedly sighed in exasperation and said, "Geez, if I knew what I was coming to in Chicago, I never woulda left Brooklyn."

The new chief of detectives, William O'Connor, made a statement to the press in which he said he told his officers to kill gangsters on sight, "without mercy." But it was all wind. Big Bill Thompson's Chicago was more wide open than ever. The body count continued to rise.

On September 7, 1928, Capone's *Unione Siciliane* ally Tony Lombardo was shot to death, allegedly by Bugs Moran and Frank Gusenberg. On January 8, 1929, Frank Gusenberg's brother Pete and North Sider James Clark gunned down another Capone man, Patsy Larodo. Scarface told his chief hitman, "Machine Gun" Jack McGurn, "It's ten grand in your pocket, kid, if Moran shows up in the obits column." McGurn almost didn't get the chance to try for the money. The Gusenberg brothers machine gunned him as he made a call from a phone booth. But McGurn survived.

Reporters liked to talk to gangsters, and Moran never missed an opportunity to tell them what he thought of Capone, calling him "beast," "behemoth" and "pimp." Like his mentor O'Banion, Bugs would have nothing to do with prostitution. The remarks rankled Big Al, who always tried to give the boys from the press the impression that he was a regular guy.

Moran played into Capone's hand, however, when he went back to the old O'Banion trick of hijacking Capone's booze. In spite of his claim, "I don't even know what street Canada is on," Capone was getting a lot of Canadian booze through the Purple Gang in Detroit. With the assistance of the Purple Gang, Capone let Moran think he had gotten away with a hijacking, and then duped Bugs into thinking another hijacked load would be delivered to his North Side garage at 2122 North Clark St. at 11:00 a.m. on February 14, 1929. Moran would have to be there in person to receive it. Capone made sure he was at his new mansion in Florida on that St. Valentine's Day.

Waiting in the garage for the phantom liquor truck were gunmen Frank and Pete Gusenberg, James Clark, Adam Heyer, Albert Weinshank, driver-mechanic John May and Reinhart Schwimmer, an eyeglass-maker who was not a gangster at all but liked to hang out with the tough guys. Bugs Moran was late. From a window across the street from the garage, a spy had seen Weinshank, who somewhat resembled Moran, enter the building. The spy made a phone call, saying only "He's here." Then he slipped out of his observation post. Moran was actually several blocks away, walking toward the garage with his pal Ted Newberry.

The spy's phone call was a signal. A few minutes after 10:30 a.m., a 1927 Cadillac disguised as a police car pulled up in front of the garage. Three men dressed as police officers and two men in long coats got out. Under the coats were machine guns and shotguns. Of these five men, only one was later identified by a witness: Fred "Killer" Burke. Three of the others were quite possibly John Scalise, Alberto Anselmi and Machine Gun Jack McGurn, though the names of other known Capone gunmen have been suggested. McGurn almost certainly orchestrated the whole operation, whether or not he was a trigger man.

The fake policemen would have gone in first, making it appear that a raid was on. They would have lined the seven men up against the wall, their faces to the bricks, and disarmed them. The victims probably grumbled and made a few tough guy remarks about "lousy coppers," but would not have resisted. There was no booze on the premises, and if they were arrested, their boss Moran would have them out in a couple of hours. By this time the other killers would have entered and pulled out the tommy guns and shotguns. They no doubt realized now that they had missed Moran, but they didn't have time to wait, and here was the core of the North Side mob helpless against the wall.

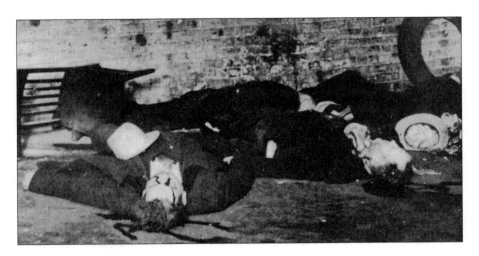

The St. Valentine's Day Massacre. Capone's gunmen slaughtered seven men but missed Moran. (Lower) Tony Lombardo, Capone's man in the Unione Siciliane, dead on a Chicago street after being gunned down by Bugs Moran's Northsiders. The war of attrition would reach its climax less than five months later.

The intended target saw the police car from down the street at the same time that he and Newberry ran into two more gang members. Thinking a raid was in progress, they ducked into a coffee shop. Bugs was telling his associates that they would get the boys out of jail that afternoon, when a noise "like a pneumatic drill," as one witness put it, echoed down the street. It was followed by two loud booms. Unseen by Moran from the coffee shop, two men in long coats emerged from the garage with their hands in the air, followed by three "policemen" covering them with pistols. To the gathering crowd it appeared that the cops had just nabbed a couple of gangsters. The five got into the "police car" and drove away. The sound of a howling dog drew one man to look in the garage. He came out gasping that the place was full of dead men.

Frank Gusenburg, North Sider gunman and St. Valentine's Day victim, along with his brother Pete. When the dying Frank was asked who had shot him, he replied, "Nobody."

Soon real police showed up and a crowd had gathered on the street outside the garage. Moran, still thinking a raid had gone down, asked one of the bystanders what was happening. He was told that the cops had just killed Bugs Moran and his whole gang.

The policemen who entered the garage had never seen anything like it. Blood spattered the walls and ran in streams along the floor. The dead men had been raked repeatedly with machine-gun fire and then blasted with shotguns. Some of the bodies had been practically cut in two. Frank Gusenberg, pierced by 14 bullets, was still alive—barely. Before he died a few hours later, police asked him who had shot him. "Nobody shot me," were his last words. The only other witness to the carnage was John May's dog, tied up and whimpering in a corner. As news of the horror flashed across the nation, an enraged Bugs Moran told reporters, "Only Capone kills like that." When Scarface heard of the remark he just shrugged and said he'd been in Florida the whole time.

The St. Valentine's Day Massacre broke the back of the North Side gang and left Capone in almost complete control of bootlegging and other rackets in Chicago. He did not enjoy it for long. Before the year was out he discovered a plot by John Scalise and Alberto Anselmi to kill him and take over his rackets. Furious that the men he had refused to hand over to Hymie Weiss would betray him, Capone pounded them to jelly with a baseball bat, then shot each one in the head. Not long after, Capone was jailed on weapons charges, and then in 1931 went to prison for income tax evasion. He was released in 1939, and died in January 1947 of a brain hemorrhage brought on by syphilis. He was 48.

Killer Burke was never indicted for the St. Valentine's Day Massacre. He was sentenced to life imprisonment in Michigan for the murder of a policeman, and died in jail in 1940. Frankie Yale, believed to be the

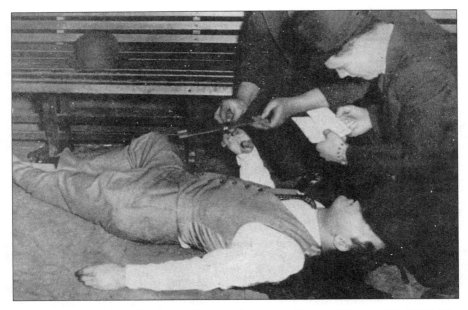

Jack McGurn, shot to death in a Chicago bowling alley on February 14, 1936. The killer, possibly Bugs Moran, left a Valentine's card in the dead gangster's hand.

"handshaker" in O'Banion's murder, was shot to death in New York City on Capone's orders in July 1927.

With his gang all but wiped out, Bugs Moran was reduced to hanging on as a small-time bootlegger. With the repeal of Prohibition in 1933, he turned to bank robbery, but never achieved the notoriety of younger desperadoes like John Dillinger and Pretty Boy Floyd. Moran was captured in 1946 and sent to prison, where he died of cancer in 1957 at the age of 64. He had, at least, outlived Capone. And he might have exacted a measure of revenge for the St. Valentine's Day Massacre. On February 14, 1936, two unknown gunmen shot Machine Gun Jack McGurn to death in a Chicago bowling alley. When police arrived, they found the hand of the slain murderer clutching a Valentine card.

Epilogue

To Prohibition's Ashes

When Uncle Sam said, "We'll go dry,"
Crooks ceased to mourn the days gone by
And tossed their hats into the sky
When Uncle Sam said, "We'll go dry."

From every source the liquor poured
As Law went splashing overboard
The conscience sank, the drink-bill soared
And what could not be drunk was stored.

Then Uncle Sam said, "We'll go wet!"
The crooks turned pale and begged, "Not yet!"
Their goose was dead; their sun had set,
When Uncle Sam said, "We'll go wet!"

—Anonymous

Books

Arnold, Bruce. The Scandal of Ulysses, *(New York: St. Martin's Press) 1991.*

Baker, Carlos (ed.). Ernest Hemingway, Selected Letters 1917 - 1961, *(New York: Charles Scribner's Sons) 1981.*

Behn, Edward. Prohibition: 13 Years That Changed America, *(New York: Arcade Publishing) 1996.*

Bergreen, Laurence, Capone: the Man and the Era, *(New York: Simon & Schuster) 1994.*

Blockson, Charles L. The Underground Railroad: First Person Narratives of Escapes to Freedom in the North, *(New York: Prentice Hall) 2000.*

Bramble, Linda. Black Fugitive Slaves in Early Upper Canada, *(St. Catharines, Ontario: Vanwell Publishing) 1988.*

Buckmaster, Henrietta. Let My People Go, *(Columbia: University of South Carolina Press) 1992.*

Burgess, Anthony. ReJoyce, *(New York: W.W. Norton & Co.) 1965.*

Butts, Ed, & Horwood, Harold. Bandits & Privateers: Canada in the Age of Gunpowder, *(Toronto: Doubleday Canada) 1987.*

Cain, Emily. Ghost Ships, *(Toronto: Musson Press) 1983.*

Cashman, Sean Dennis. Prohibition, the Lie of the Land, *(New York: MacMillan) 1981.*

Coffey, Thomas M. The Long Thirst, Prohibition in America, *(New York: W.W. Morton & Co.) 1975.*

Colombo, John Robert (ed.). Colombo's Concise Canadian Quotations, *(Edmonton: Hurtig Publishers) 1976.*

Cosner, Shaaron. The Underground Railroad, *(New York: Franklin Watts) 1991.*

Decarie, Graeme. The Prohibition Movement in Ontario 1894–1916, *(Kingston, Ontario: Queen's University Press) 1972.*

Douville, Raymond, and Casanova, Jaques-Donat. Daily Life in Early Canada, *(New York: MacMillan) 1967.*

Dubro, James, and Rowland, Robin F. King of the Mob, *(Toronto: Viking Penguin Books) 1987.*

Eccles, William J. The Canadian Frontier 1534–1760, *(Toronto: Holt, Rinehart, and Winston) 1969.*

Ellmann, Richard. James Joyce, *(Oxford: Oxford University Press) 1983.*

Erdoes, Richard. Saloons of the Old West, *(New York: Alfred A. Knopf) 1979.*

Everest, Allan Seymour. Rum Across the Border: The Prohibition Era in Northern New York, *(Syracuse, NY: Syracuse University Press) 1978.*

Farjeou, J. Jefferson. The Compleat Smuggler, *(London: George G. Harrad & Co.) 1938.*

Fradin, Dennis Brindell. Bound For the North Star, *(New York: Clarion Books), 2000.*

French, Orlando (ed.). The Rolling Hills of Northumberland, *(Belleville, Ontario: Wallbridge House Publishing) 2000.*

Gervais, C.H. The Rumrunners: A Prohibition Scrapbook, *(Toronto: Firefly Books) 1980.*

Gorman, Herbert. James Joyce, *(New York: Farrar & Rinehart) 1939.*

Gorrell, Gena K. North Star To Freedom, *(Toronto: Stoddart Publishers) 1996.*

Hallowell, Gerald A. Prohibition in Ontario, 1919 -1923, *(Ottawa: Ontario Historical Society) 1972.*

Hitsman, J. Mackay. The Incredible War of 1812, *(Toronto: University of Toronto Press) 1965.*

Howe, John. Journal Kept by Mr. John Howe While He Was Employed as a British Spy During the Revolutionary War: Also While He Was Engaged in the Smuggling Business During the Late War, *(published in Concord, New Hampshire) 1827.*

Hunt, C.W. Whiskey and Ice: The Saga of Ben Kerr, *(Toronto: Dundurn Press) 1995.*
———. Booze, Boats, and Billions, *(Toronto: McClelland & Stewart) 1988.*
———. Gentleman Charlie and the Lady Rum Runner, *(Belleville, Ontario: Billa Flint Publications) 2000.*
Kavieff, Paul. The Purple Gang, *(New York: Barricade Books) 2000.*
Kobler, John. Capone, *(New York: Da Capo Press) 1971.*
Latham, Frank B. Jacob Brown and the War of 1812, *(New York: Cowles Book Company) 1971.*
Lynn, Kenneth S. Hemingway, *(New York: Simon & Schuster) 1987.*
Mason, Philip P. Rumrunning and the Roaring Twenties: Prohibition on the Michigan-Ontario Waterway, *(Detroit: Wayne State University Press) 1995.*
McDonnell, Janet. America in the 20th Century, 1920–1929, *(New York: Marshall-Cavendish Corp.) 1995.*
McIntosh, Dave. The Collectors: A History of Canadian Customs and Excise, *(Toronto: NC Press) 1984.*
Miquelon, Dale. New France 1701–1744, *(Toronto: McClelland & Stewart) 1987.*
Nash, J. Robert. Bloodletters and Bad Men, *(New York: Warner Books) 1973.*
Parrish, Michael E. Anxious Decades, *(New York: W.W. Norton & Co.) 1992.*
Powers, Tom. Michigan Rogues, Desperados, and Cut-Throats, *(Davison MI: Friede Publications) 2002.*
Rainey, Lawrence. Institutions of Modernism, *(New Haven & London: Yale University Press) 1998.*
Rodgers, Bradley A. Guardian of the Lakes, *(Ann Arbor MI: University of Michigan Press) 1996.*
Sann, Paul. The Lawless Decade, *(New York: Bonanza Books) 1957.*
Sinclair, Andrew. Prohibition: the Era of Excess, *(Boston: Little, Brown & Co.) 1962.*

Spence, F.S. Royal Commission on the Liquor Traffic, 1896, *(Toronto: Newton & Trelour) 1896.*
Verrill, A. Hyatt. Smugglers and Smuggling, *(New York: Duffield & Co.) 1924.*
Williams, Neville. Contraband Cargoes, London: Longman's, Green & Co.) 1959.
Winks, Robin W. The Blacks in Canada: a History, *(Montreal: McGill–Queen's University Press) 1997.*
Young, David M. Chicago Maritime, *(Chicago: Northern Illinois University Press) 2001.*
The Dictionary of Canadian Biography
The Case of Leonard Wilcox, *Report to the House of Assembly of Upper Canada, Toronto, 1834.*

Newspapers and Periodicals

The Belleville Daily Intelligencer
The Chicago Tribune
The Christian Science Monitor
The Detroit Free Press
The Detroit News
The Detroit Times
The Fort William Times–Journal
The Guelph Mercury
The Hamilton Spectator
The Madison Capital Times
Michigan History Magazine
The Milwaukee Journal
The New York Times
The Syracuse Post Standard
The Toronto Globe
The Toronto Star
Watertown Daily Times

Internet

American Local History Network
Attitudes Toward Alcohol in Early American History

Internet continued...

Banned Books Online
Classen, Mikel B. Escanaba Buccaneer
Court TV's Crime Library
Crime Magazine
Decarie, Graeme. Cross Border Shopping During the War of 1812.
Early Canadiana Online
Fosburg, Kurt. Last Call for the Arbutus.
geocities
Geringer, Joseph. Dion O'Banion: Shamrocks, Gun Smoke and Beer Kegs.
_____. George "Bugs" Moran: His War With Al Capone.
Gribben, Mark. The Purple Gang: Bootlegger's Paradise.
History of Albion, Michigan
History Detroit, 1701 - 2001
History of Escabana People
History of the US Customs Service
Holland Sentinel Archives
infoplease
Lake Superior News and Mining Journal
The Legendary Guide to Prince Edward County

May, Allan. The Michigan Whiskey Rebellion.
_____. Frank McErlane and the Chicago Beer Wars.
Military.com Content
Miller, Carl H. We Got Beer.
NASA Quest > Archives
National Law Enforcement Officers–Line of Duty
Ogdensburg's Role in the War of 1812
Organised Crime Library
Palmer, Richard F. The Rum Runners.
Passic, Frank. The Purple Gang.
Pepper, Terry & Sue. Seeing the Light— Jesse James Strang.
Prohibition, The Noble Experiment
Rum_Runners.doc
Ships and Shipping News
TandemNews
The Underground Railroad
The Underground Railroad in Canada
The Underground Railroad in Rochester
Upper Canada Village
Virtual Museum of New France
The Walkerville Times
Young, David. Iron Ship Did In Timber Pirates.

ACKNOWLEDGEMENTS

Many people assisted, in ways large and small, with the research for this book. I would like to thank the following individuals and institutions:

The public libraries of Amherstburg, Hamilton, Niagara Falls, Thunder Bay, Toronto and Windsor. I would like to add a special note of thanks to the staff of the Public Library of Guelph, Ontario.

National Library of Canada
National Library of Ireland
Marine Museum of the Great Lakes, Kingston, Ontario

Escanaba, MI Public Library
Library of Michigan
Onondaga County Public Library, Syracuse NY

Paul Adamthwaite, Archives & Collections Society, Picton, Ont.; Robert E. Brennan, Sackets Harbor, NY; C.W. Hunt; Gary Jones, Onondaga County Public Library, Syracuse, NY; Tom Kowalczk, Inland Seas Archival Collection, Lakeside, OH; Karen Lago, The Roswell P. Flower Library, Watertown, NY; Sondra McGregor, Maclean's Magazine Library, Toronto; Marjorie G. McNinch, Hagley Museum & Library, Wilmington, DE; Frank and Rosalie (Coronna) Potts, Madison WI; Marjorie Strong, Vermont Historical Society; Mark Vinet, Canada Civil War Association

Archives of Ontario: 12, 208, 212

Beaver Island Historical Society: 54, 56, 57, 58, 59, 61, 62

Bettman Archives: 72 (main)

Hunt, C.W. *Whiskey and Ice: The Saga of Ben Kerr*, (Toronto: Dundurn Press) 1995: 154, 156, 158, 159, 166, 167

———. *Booze, Boats, and Billions*, (Toronto: McClelland & Stewart) 1988: 144, 146 (inset), 126, 128, 130

———. *Gentleman Charlie and the Lady Rum Runner*, (Belleville, Ontario: Billa Flint Publications) 2000: 170, 174, 175 (courtesy of Reg Powers), 177 (courtesy of Reg Powers), 178, 180

Chateaugay Record: 112 (all), 116

Cleveland Public Library: 8 (bottom), 13

Detroit Free Press: 203, 233

Detroit News: 8 (top), 10 (all), 98, 129, 226

Detroit Public Library: 20

Dossin Great Lakes Museum: 99, 110, 140

Escanaba, Michigan, Public Library: 82

Great Lakes Historical Society: 44 (top)

Hamilton Spectator: 222

Hooke, Kathy: 191

International News Photos: 152 (all), 204, 205, 232 (right), 238-240, 256, 262, 264-266

Library of Congress: 65, 67, 70

Macpherson, Duncan: 28

Metro Toronto Reference Library: 6, 14, 16-18, 22, 25, 26, 31 (bottom), 34 (main & inset), 35, 36, 40, 41, 44 (bottom), 48, 67, 69, 72 (inset), 74, 75, 80, 90(main & inset), 94-97, 100, 102, 103, 106, 109, 125, 132, 142, 143, 146 (top), 148, 151, 157, 172, 200 (lower), 202, 206, 208, 230, 236, 245, 248, 253, 260, 264

National Archives of Canada: 32, 124 (top)

National Archives, Washington: 163

National Library of Canada: 209, 220, 224

New York Public Library: 78

Philipse Manor Hall State Historic Site, NYS Office of Parks, Recreation and Historic Preservation: 31 (top)

Potts, Frank and Rosalie: 4, 198, 200 (top)

Queen's University Archives: 124 (inset)

Sophia Smith Collection, Smith College: 66

State Archives of Michigan: 42, 43, 50, 51, 137

The Border Cities Star: 194

The Marsh Papers: 145

Toledo-Lucas County Public Library: 228

Toronto Star: 221

United Press International: 242, 246, 253, 254

Windsor Star: 11, 104, 111, 120, 150, 160, 182, 184, 186, 192, (photo by Barney Gloster) 223, 225, 232 (left)

ABOUT THE AUTHOR

Edward Butts is co-author of *Pirates and Outlaws of Canada: 1610-1932*; and author of *Idioms for Aliens*, a humorous book on English grammar. Edward's articles have appeared in numerous publications in Canada and the United States. For several years he taught at the Learning Center of Sosua, a school in the Dominican Republic, and wrote humorous articles for two multilingual Dominican magazines. He now lives in Guelph, Ontario.

His newest book, *Tortured Souls: The True Stories Behind Twenty Ontario Hauntings*, will be published by Lynx Images in October 2004.

LYNX ⬯ IMAGES
BOOKS AND FILMS ON THE GREAT LAKES AND MORE...

MYSTERIOUS ISLANDS
FORGOTTEN TALES OF THE GREAT LAKES

Mysterious Islands is an adventurous historical journey to islands found within the vast basin of the five Great Lakes. Standing removed and alone, islands have been central to some of the most important, outrageous, and tragic events in Great Lakes history, from a decisive and bloody naval battle in the War of 1812, to Prohibition rumrunning, to harrowing tales of shipwreck and rescue. The waves of time have left many islands behind, but remnants of the past still mark their shores—burial grounds, grand hotels, abandoned quarries, lighthouses, strategic forts, and even a castle.

THE BOOK includes over 100 stories and over 500 rare photographs and helpful maps. **THE VIDEO** takes viewers to beautiful and intriguing places through remarkable cinematography and compelling archival footage and images. *Silver Screen Award, U.S. International Film and Video Festival*

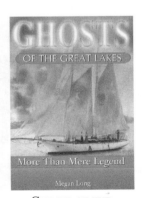

GHOSTS OF THE
GREAT LAKES
MORE THAN MERE LEGEND

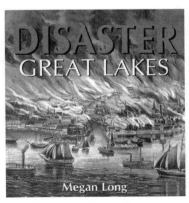

DISASTER GREAT LAKES

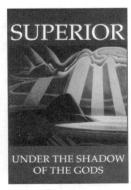

SUPERIOR:
UNDER THE SHADOW
OF THE GODS

FOR OUR CATALOGUE VISIT WWW.LYNXIMAGES.COM